From Imagination to Faërie

From Imagination to Faërie

Tolkien's Thomist Fantasy

Yannick Imbert

PICKWICK *Publications* · Eugene, Oregon

FROM IMAGINATION TO FAËRIE
Tolkien's Thomist Fantasy

Pickwick Publications
An Imprint of Wipf and Stock Publishers
199 W. 8th Ave., Suite 3
Eugene, OR 97401

www.wipfandstock.com

PAPERBACK ISBN: 978-1-6667-1045-8
HARDCOVER ISBN: 978-1-6667-1046-5
EBOOK ISBN: 978-1-6667-1047-2

Cataloguing-in-Publication data:

Names: Imbert, Yannick [author].

Title: From imagination to faërie : Tolkien's Thomist fantasy / Yannick Imbert.

Description: Eugene, OR: Pickwick Publications, 2022 | Includes bibliographical references and index.

Identifiers: ISBN 978-1-6667-1045-8 (paperback) | ISBN 978-1-6667-1046-5 (hardcover) | ISBN 978-1-6667-1047-2 (ebook)

Subjects: LCSH: Tolkien, J. R. R. (John Ronald Reuel), 1892–1973—Lord of the Rings | Tolkien, J. R. R. (John Ronald Reuel), 1892–1973—Philosophy | Tolkien, J. R. R. (John Ronald Reuel), 1892–1973—Religion | Christian fiction, English—History and criticism | Middle Earth (Imaginary place) | Theology in literature

Classification: PR6039.O32 I43 2022 (print) | PR6039.O32 (ebook)

06/16/22

Permissions

Contents

Acknowledgments | ix

Abbreviations | xi

Introduction | xiii

1   Tolkien's Catholic Background | 1

Part One: "What Is There in a Name?": Tolkien's Theory of Language | 23

2   Tolkien and the Science of Language | 25

3   The Nature of Words | 42

4   The Aesthetics of Words | 59

Conclusion: Part One | 81

Part Two: Myth, History, and Truth: Tolkien's "Mythopoeia" | 83

5   Historical Mythologists | 85

6   Mythical Language | 102

7   Tolkien's Theory of Myth | 125

Conclusion: Part Two | 145

Part Three: Tolkien's Theory of Imagination | 147

8   The Nature and Purpose of the Imagination | 149

9   Tolkien's Appropriation of the Theories of Imagination | 165

10 Literary Creation under God: Man as Sub-creator | 180

Conclusion: Part Three | 200

Part Four: The Beatitudes of Faërie | 203

11 Recovery | 205

12 Escape | 220

13 Consolation | 235

14 Faërie | 244

Conclusion | 256

Bibliography | 261

Index | 277

Acknowledgments

THERE IS PROBABLY NO proper way for me to thank Bill and Barbara Edgar for their enduring and lasting friendship, which goes beyond the few words I could write here—beyond *any* words that I could write here. I also want to thank my parents for giving me the love of books, and for offering me my first *Lord of the Rings* trilogy about thirty years ago. I did not know, then, that after several decades, I would still be fascinated by the world of J. R. R. Tolkien.

For long years of friendship and mutual exhortation, I thank Michaël de Luca and particularly Samuel Herrenschmidt. We might not have talked about this project every day, but without friendship, no project can ever be brought to fruition. Many friends have crossed my path during the multiple rewritings of this book, from its beginning during my doctoral research at Westminster Theological Seminary, until now. I want to acknowledge their friendship, even though I cannot name all of them. Because of their help and encouragements, I have written, I have graduated, and I have taught theology for more than a decade. Maybe our paths will meet again!

Countless people have also provided their help during my research, in particular the librarians at Westminster Theological Seminary. No progress would have been made, during the initial doctoral project, without the firm but gentle editing encouragement of Leslie Altena.

Finally, I want to thank my wonderful wife, Erin, who has encouraged me to publish this modest addition to the rich and often intimidating words of Tolkien studies. Without her support, these pages would never have been published!

Abbreviations

H	*The Hobbit*
HoME	*The History of Middle Earth*
L	*The Letters of J. R. R. Tolkien*
LoTR	*The Lord of the Rings*
MC	*The Monsters and the Critics, and Other Essays*
OFS	*On Fairy Stories*
PD	*Poetic Diction, a Study in Meaning*
S	*The Silmarillion*
SCG	*Summa Contra Gentiles*
ST	*Summa Theologiae: Latin Text and English Translation, Introductions, Notes, Appendices, and Glossaries.*

Introduction

Don't go getting mixed up
in the business of your betters,
or you'll land in trouble too big for you.
—J. R. R. TOLKIEN, *The Fellowship of the Ring*

ANYONE AUDACIOUS ENOUGH TO write on J. R. R. Tolkien's work enters a perilous realm. Not only does the breadth and the richness of his world invite cautious and extensive exploration, but this territory has been explored by many well-respected discoverers of lost and marvelous worlds. In this Tolkienian realm, there are some well-trodden paths; others are less familiar and much more dangerous. Some of these difficult trails will lead us over mountains and under hills; some invite us for a peaceful stroll across the fields of history; others again require us to sail upon the sea, not knowing where the winds will take us.

To us, wanderers who enter this imaginative universe, the landscape might seem very difficult to explore and might dishearten the most courageous reader. But there are, of course, helpers. We will come across, at the end of a wearisome day, or at the bottom of a cliff, other Wanderers who have been walking in Tolkien's land for decades and who know the paths better than us. They will lead us to unexplored valleys enshrined in beauty, or to the summit of a majestic peak. We might even find, on some rare occasions, magicians, who will unlock secrets long lost to us. And then also, lore-masters will, with knowledge acquired from tales and legends, open hidden doors and spell-bound pathways to ancient ruins. With these helpers, we will learn the meaning of runes and words, we will sing poems and stories, we will walk, dance, climb, and drink.

After some time spent in Tolkien's realm, we will hear of a stranger path leading to a high peak, the highest summit of Tolkien's realm. It is said that, from there, one can look over at the whole land. To some, this is an unreachable mountain, to others an unknown one, or again a legend. And unfortunately, most of our helpers will not be able to guide us on the path to this mountain. In fact, they often belong to "two distinct groups, one focused on the literary qualities of [Tolkien's] work, the other on his invented languages," their expertise, though unsurpassed in their field, is limited.[1] Despite the best of their knowledge, these two guilds will not be able to guide us to the top of the mountain. We need the guidance of others; those who have dedicated their knowledge to explore the unknown. To our helpers, these strange wizards often seem to practice the dark arts: the religious.

For these few wizards hold to the existence of this legendary summit with the strongest of faith. And they are convinced that this mountain is indeed a religious one. So we come to a crossroads. We might be tempted to simply reject the possibility of, some day, being able with one attentive look to contemplate the breadth of Tolkien's works. Of course, it would be presumptuous to pretend that the present book can succeed in doing so. In fact, it might well be that such a thing is actually impossible. The task itself might be risky, the goal unattainable. This, however, should not discourage us to go on such an adventure.

This is what I want to offer in these few chapters. An adventure. But how are we to undertake such a journey? Which map to take, which gear to put in our bags, and how many handkerchiefs not to forget? The tools are many, the road will be long, and we have to make a choice. Here my essential conviction should be made clear. I strongly believe that there is a common spell that unites all of Tolkien's works, both imaginative and academic. This unity is a religious one: Tolkien should be approached as a Christian fantasist, and more precisely, as a Thomist fantasist. Such a road, though, is treacherous. As with every mountain path, we should

---

1. Fisher, Review of *Inside Language*, 172.

beware of wandering off to the right or to the left, we should be wary of hidden traps and dangerous crossroads.

First, we must be careful not to imply that Tolkien's faith is always and necessarily explicit in his works. Because he was reserved by nature, Tolkien had no interest in the display of personal convictions and emotions of which our society has now become so enamored with. More particularly, Tolkien believed that theological discussion was the exclusive domain of trained theologians. Second, we do not imply that Tolkien, the Thomist fantasist, was quoting Thomas Aquinas directly in his works. Thomism serves as a foundation, and as such, it is often assumed rather than explained; described, rather than rationalized, hidden, rather than made visible. Third, the "Thomist Tolkien" should not be used to downplay Tolkien's others academic and personal influences. On the contrary, as we shall see, Tolkien's academic and imaginative works were informed by friends and foes, writers and scholars. Among the friends were G. K. Chesterton and Owen Barfield; among the foes were Max Müller and Andrew Lang. Thomism is not the only influence on Tolkien, even though I will argue it is the one bringing wholeness into his imaginative endeavor. On some aspects of his works, other writers, poets, and scholars, have been more than influential than Thomism. What the expression "Thomist fantasist" applied to Tolkien means is that being a Thomist was so natural to him that it informed, often quite unconsciously and ordinarily, his view of the world.

You might have noticed that already we have entered the perilous realm. Perilous, because the role and proper place of Tolkien's faith is one of the major points of contention among Tolkien scholars. On one hand, many, never denying the personal importance of his faith, argue that it was not as central as one might think, and that it definitely had no structural significance: Tolkien was merely shaped by his personal interest and academic milieu. Several reasons are often offered in explanation. To begin with, Tolkien's faith is often considered generic, a kind of "belief in Being or Beings greater than man and worthy of worship, and a belief of some sort of life after death."[2] In this case, Tolkien's faith might not be quite relevant and could easily be dispensed with. Or maybe this faith in a "Being worthy of worship" could be adapted to many different religious traditions, including the pagan world that surfaces here and there again in Tolkien's mythology. In any case, this faith would be, at best, a form of

---

2. Purtill, *Lord of the Elves and Eldils*, 105.

deism. This would have virtually no implications for the inner workings of Tolkien's fiction. Other scholars have stressed the relevance of Tolkien's natural theology, especially in the context of his Catholicism.

This is not completely mistaken. The problem is that it turns Tolkien's faith into a *formal natural religion*, defined only by the "things knowable concerning God and our Duty by the Light of Nature."[3] Often, this natural religion is embodied in basic virtues encountered throughout world religions. Love, obedience, pity, forgiveness, and all the other fundamental human values would then constitute the core "spirituality" of Tolkien's world. Such is the view, in varying degrees, of Lin Carter, Marion Zimmer Bradley, and Marjorie Evelyn Wright.[4] For other scholars, Tolkien's Christian faith is a more or less imprecise one. Catherine Madsen, for example, explains that "Tolkien borrows Christian magic, not Christian doctrine; and Christianity without doctrine is a shadow of itself."[5] Of course the implication is clear: Tolkien's faith is shallow, a mere shell. The important content is "magic." Interpreting Tolkien's lack of demonstrated faith in another direction, Dorothy K. Barber makes the role of Tolkien's faith a condition of the reader's own faith: "Tolkien has been able to let a Christian anagogical significance arise from the story, if the reader chooses to see it."[6] In other words, in and of itself, Tolkien's corpus would then be theologically *neutral*.

Of course, these observations are not made without reasons. First, Tolkien, as many other believers, had struggled with his own faith and, at times, this is evidenced in his letters.[7] This could be used by some to argue for Tolkien's precarious faith. Second, Tolkien had never felt the urge or necessity to explain his own religious beliefs, whether because he considered any religious belief to be an intimate matter or because he thought only trained theologians should make theological comments. Thus, he opposed C. S. Lewis's status as a lay theologian. In fact, Tolkien was extremely critical of Lewis's theological works, especially *Letters to Malcolm*, of which he said: "Also I personally found *Letters to Malcolm* a

---

3. Madsen, "Light from an Invisible Lamp," 39.

4. Carter, *Tolkien*; Bradley, *Men, Halflings, & Hero Worship*; Wright, "The Cosmic Kingdom of Myth."

5. Madsen, "Light from an Invisible Lamp," 37.

6. Barber, "The Meaning of *The Lord of the Rings*," 39.

7. L, 220, 413.

distressing and in parts horrifying work. I began a commentary on it, but if finished it would not be publishable."[8]

As a result, Tolkien scholars have not been too inclined to interpret Tolkien's theory of Faërie through his faith. Here again, the reasons are diverse. For some, to do so would betray Tolkien's Catholicism in turning God into an object of imagination and study. Moreover, this would be tantamount to introducing the God of the primary world into the secondary world, and thus break the necessary consistency of the secondary world. Not only would approaching Tolkien's Faërie through faith threaten the integrity of the secondary world, but it would also threaten the integrity of God's existence in the primary world. Tom Shippey, for example, concludes that "if *The Lord of the Rings* should approach too close to 'Gospel-truth', to the Christian myth in which Tolkien himself believed, it might forfeit its status as a story and become at worst a blasphemy, an 'Apocryphal gospel.'"[9] It certainly is true that we should not investigate Tolkien as if his work were a theological treatise. Even fellow Christians and contemporary reviewers of *The Lord of the Rings* did not agree on the importance of Tolkien's faith to his work. For example, C. S. Lewis never mentioned it in his review, while W. H. Auden could say: "the unstated presuppositions of the whole work are Christian."[10] Presuppositions, however, are often unseen, and appropriately so. However, the investigation of Tolkien's works through the lens of his Christian faith is not a project that has been totally abandoned. Christianity becomes a main focus of interpretation in the works of Bradley Birzer, Strafford Caldecott, Colin Duriez, Joseph Pearce, Ralph Woods, and Matthew Dickerson—to name but a few.

Of course, this begs the question of what is meant by "Christian faith." What was Tolkien's faith? This is another perilous question. The Christian tradition to which he belonged has been diversely identified. Neoplatonism (Flieger), Boethian-Manichaean (Shippey), Augustinian Catholicism (Treloar, Fisher), Christian romanticism (Reilly), secular Christianity (Dowie), Celtic Christianity (Sievers), or Roman Catholicism (Dickerson and Evan), have all been nominated. Here again, one might despair of finding any sure indication of Tolkien's true faith loyalty. Maybe we should simply doubt the relevance the question, being satisfied

---

8. L, 352.

9. Shippey, *The Road to Middle Earth*, 197.

10. Auden, "The Quest Hero," 44.

with an image of Tolkien as a "mere Christian." However, this would be a serious understatement of Tolkien's own faith. By contrast, and I believe closer to the truth, Clyde Kilby talked of Tolkien as being a "staunchly conservative Tridentine Roman Catholic."[11] Ralph Wood has made the point that, in comparison with his friend Lewis, Tolkien was in fact "no sort of Platonist at all. He espoused what might be roughly called an Aristotelian metaphysics. For him, transcendent reality is to be found in the depths of this world rather than in some putative existence beyond it."[12] This is quite to the point. Recently, the strongest and most convincing case for the "Thomist Tolkien" is Jonathan McIntosh's *The Flame Imperishable*, which brings Tolkien within the scope of Thomist metaphysics.

The point, in fact, is even more definitive. Tolkien was a Thomist, though few studies have stressed the essential Thomistic outlook of Tolkien's world. One of the first to point in that direction was the early study by Paul Kocher, *Master of Middle-earth*. In this very perceptive study of Tolkien's works, Kocher concluded that Tolkien displayed an implicit theological standpoint best understood in terms of Thomas Aquinas's natural theology. To Kocher, many ideas inherent in Tolkien's fantasy can only be understood in such a metaphysical context.[13]

It is rather remarkable, and unfortunate, that this early intuition (his study was published in 1972) has not been followed by Tolkien scholars. If the philosophical theology of Thomas Aquinas has, at times, been referred to, it has received proper and extensive attention only recently. The treatment of theological motifs by Alison Milbank in her *Tolkien and Chesterton as Theologians* (2008) readily admits the fundamental Thomist framework of Tolkien's mind. In a similar manner, Jonathan McIntosh has argued for a distinctively Thomist account of Tolkien's fantasy in his recently published book, *The Flame Imperishable: Tolkien, St. Thomas, and the Metaphysics of Faërie*. As McIntosh indicates early in his study, Thomas Aquinas is an ideal partner for understanding the metaphysics of Tolkien.[14] This observation is sustained by biographical and cultural, as well as "discernible theological and philosophical affinities between St. Thomas and Tolkien."[15]

---

11. Kilby, *Tolkien and "The Silmarillion,"* 53.
12. Wood, "Conflict and Convergence," 325.
13. Kocher, *Master of Middle-earth*, 77.
14. McIntosh, *The Flame Imperishable*, 19.
15. McIntosh, *The Flame Imperishable*, 19.

In order to show the centrality of Tolkien's Thomism on the development of his theory of Faërie, we could proceed in a variety of ways. One could be tempted to merely underline the Christian symbolism and references in his works, including in his letters. It is true that the reader would soon find some elements to support this claim. However, that would be a very simplistic approach to a very complex issue. One could also try to over-interpret Tolkien's Faërie through theological motifs, merely assuming that because Tolkien was a Roman Catholic, he should be interpreted through Thomistic theology. This conclusion, even if not mistaken, lacks arguments. In order to argue effectively for Tolkien's Thomism as the central feature of his worlds, we need a proper method of investigation. We must take the proper path, but also be prepared and not forget anything essential before setting out on our long adventure!

Our journey will take us towards the panoramic view of Tolkien's realm through three stages: language, myth, and fairy-stories. This order is not arbitrary, but reflects Tolkien's own construction of his legendarium, starting with his interest in language, giving rise to stories and myths, then finding incarnation in Faërie. Language, myth, and Faërie: such is the order of Tolkienian fantasy. Hence, such is the order of our study. Regarding each of these topics, particular attention will be paid to Tolkien's criticism of contemporary scholars. In fact, to set forth Tolkien's own theory of fantasy it is necessary to place Tolkien in his academic and social milieu. Too often Tolkien scholarship has been concerned with the potential influence of such and a such writer, thereby disconnecting Tolkien from the world in which he lived. Some may wonder, at this point, how such a historical and academic background would serve the purpose of legitimating a Thomist reading of Tolkien. However, putting Tolkien into the context of the academic debates of his times will highlight the basic answers he tried to provide—answers that have a definite Thomistic coloration.

A final word of caution should be mentioned here. By trying to present Tolkien as essentially a Thomist writer and fantasist, I do not, by any means, wish to imply that Tolkienian studies that do not recognize this fact are wholly mistaken or useless. Many studies remain extremely valuable because Tolkien's theory of Faërie is not only a theological one, and consciously not primarily a theological one, but integrates many different disciplines. Thomism, though, provides the general foundation that allows us to make sense of everything else. As such, it is a global interpretative framework.

Maybe the image of the "Pot of Soup, the Chauldron of Story," originally used by the mythologist George Webbe Dasent, an eighteenth-century mythologist, can serve to explain our goal.[16] In his essay "On Fairy Stories," Tolkien criticized the goal of certain of his contemporaries who wished to look at the "bones" from which the soup was made in order to identify all the different mythological ingredients. To Tolkien, this was mistaken. What we have are not ingredients, but a *story*, and we should be content to read it and study it as a story—or myth. We can approach Tolkienian studies in very much the same way, trying to identify his sources, his influences, the way in which the debates of his times shaped his world. I believe that such goals are legitimate, and I would not be as negative as Tolkien in evaluating such studies. But beyond the identification of all the ingredients that helped form Tolkien's theory, there is one most basic element that we can always assume to be necessary without ever being able to "see" it once the soup has been made: water. If the theories of language and mythology, Tolkien's linguistic expertise and knowledge of everything "nordic," are necessary to Tolkienian studies, I believe that the Thomistic element is like the water poured into the "Chauldron of Story." Without it, there would be no consistency to Tolkien's academic and imaginary worlds.

After leaving behind the first linguistic part of journey, we will consider his view of mythology in Part Two and dwell there for a few chapters. Turning around, we will be able to contemplate the superimposed landscape of language and myth, gaining a renewed love for Tolkien's works and genius. We could be tempted to stay there. Or walk back down the mountain. But the road still goes on and on, to the highest summit of Tolkien's realm. It reaches the top, in Part Three through an exploration of Tolkien's theory of sub-creation, that is, to the relation between the Creator God and human creativity. And then, Tolkien's realm should be seen in all its bright richness. This we will contemplate in Part Four, the Beatitudes of Faërie.

Before we undertake the long journey, there is one more thing we need. We must review our family history. Let us be hobbits for a little while and delve into family lore. We need to go back to Tolkien, our familiar author. While he is known to us, the presence of the unifying Catholic dimension must be made manifest. Thus, we will begin with a first chapter devoted to the historical and personal Roman Catholic

---

16. Dasent, *Popular Tales from the Norse*, xii.

and Thomist background in which Tolkien was born and raised. Without such a historical investigation, it is virtually impossible to argue for a "Thomist Tolkien." In fact, to only consider his works through the lens of Thomism is to forget that works have an author and that the author himself has a history that developed through place and time.

1

Tolkien's Catholic Background

TOLKIEN'S EXCEPTIONAL INFLUENCE ON twentieth-century fantasy literature, and his personal theory of "fantasy," or Faërie, cannot be seen apart from his life and times. Discerning the historical influences that have shaped Tolkien's life and works, however, proves a very arduous task. In fact, by contrast to our present-day culture, which is obsessed with biographical details, Tolkien himself was surprisingly silent on this subject. Thus, explaining the precise shaping of his worldview remains mostly a matter of conjecture. This challenge is rendered even more difficult because of the complexity of the times in which Tolkien lived.

Born during the reign of Queen Victoria, he can be called Victorian, provided that one keeps in mind the large range of meanings that can be attached to the term "Victorian."[1] Such opposite characters as Coleridge and Byron can be, in a broad sense, called "Victorians." But this label also includes late Victorians turning away from the romantic, revolutionary, heroic, Byronian virtues while falling into overt and unabashed moral cynicism. To the Victorian era also belong the Romantic Wordsworth, the Deist Carlyle, the Utilitarian and rationalist John Stuart Mill, the Christian Socialist F. D. Maurice, the Pre-Raphaelite Ruskin, the Catholic Newman, and the atheist Shelley, all very different characters promoting more or less radically different visions of society and human life. This Victorian

1. Regarding this Victorian diversity, see Altick, *Victorian People and Ideas*, 1–11.

diversity is best explained when "seen in a century's perspective"; then we realize that "the age merges at either end into epochs of very different tone, from which, retrospectively, in the one instance, by anticipation in the other, those earliest and latest years acquired their distinctive coloration."[2] While the importance of this Victorian atmosphere is crucial to understanding Tolkien, providing a complete historical background to Tolkien's life and works will not be possible. Such an investigation would take us too far back into Victorian England, and could almost be the subject of a separate study. For example, we might explore in detail the influence of Romanticism on Tolkien's view of history and nature.

Whereas all these historical facts serve to illuminate Tolkien's character, one other influence proved decisive in shaping Tolkien's worldview, and that is his belonging to the Roman Catholic Church. Indeed, Tolkien's Catholicism is one of the main interpretative frameworks through which we become conversant with the man and his works. This, of course, does not mean that Tolkien himself was a theologian or that he consciously thought as a theologian. "Tolkien was not by training a systematic theologian, nor was the primary focus of his writing exegetical or polemical; as 'sub creator,' he nevertheless brought to the texts collected in *Morgoth's Ring* some of the strategies of the speculative theologian."[3] These strategies come to full fruition in the Catholic worldview evidenced throughout his works. However, before considering how Roman Catholicism shaped Tolkien's life and work, a brief look at the condition of English Roman Catholicism during the nineteenth century is needed.

Nineteenth-Century English Roman Catholicism

The religious climate in nineteenth-century England still was one of great suspicion regarding Roman Catholicism. The general sentiment towards the Roman Catholic Church was fueled by popular clichés and by an unhealthy and almost sadistic delight in the remembrance of the past. Words like "Romish," "Popish," or "Popery" were among the gentlest ones used to refer to Roman Catholicism. In 1875, John Foxe's *Book of Martyrs*, an often very graphic depiction of Protestant martyrdom under the rule of Queen Mary I, was republished in London as a reminder to the British people of who, exactly, Roman Catholics were. Unconscious at

2. Altick, *Victorian People and Ideas*, 1.

3. Rutledge, "Justice Is Not Healing," 63.

times, anti-Catholic prejudice was as much a fruit of political and social tensions as it was the consequence of theological debates. Socially and politically, Catholics were condemned by merely being associated with Chartism—a working-class reform protest—or with the "Irish question," itself considered a "patriotic" issue. Theologically, criticisms crystallized around the denunciation of the Mass, of secular and priestly celibacy, of the church's infallibility, and of veneration of the Saints and the Virgin Mary. A few events—such as the debate over the Catholic Emancipation Act, the funding of the Catholic seminary at Maynooth, Ireland, and the reestablishment of a Roman Catholic hierarchy in England—can serve to paint a better picture of what it was, and how it *felt*, to be Roman Catholic in nineteenth-century England.

On March 24, 1829, the Catholic Emancipation Act (or Catholic Relief Act) was passed by the Parliament of the United Kingdom and received the Royal Assent on April 13. Its main purpose was to finally remove major burdens prejudicially placed upon the Roman Catholic citizens of the British Isles in the Acts of Uniformity and the Tests Acts. Among the practical consequences of the Act, Roman Catholics were now allowed to sit in Parliament. While this legal and social evolution was meant to be beneficial for the political stability of the country, it had unexpected negative outcomes. In fact, this period of intense parliamentary activity demonstrated to all careful observers of English society that the government's interests began to diverge from that of the Anglican Church. Indeed, the struggle for Catholic emancipation was vehemently opposed by Anglican bishops as well as Tories and Whig Liberals. In a period of political tension, international uncertainty, and cultural change, the dislocation of the unity between the Anglican establishment and socio-political leadership was highly controversial. The distance created between religious and political parties in turn provided an opportunity for His Majesty's Catholic subjects to finally gain a public role in their society. The fact that the "old disability laws" prohibiting them from holding office or sitting in parliament were being repealed was a sign of this changing tide.

Through such legal actions, what was clearly at stake was the social and political establishment, the core of the Elizabethan Settlement. So traumatic was the prospect of the billing of the Act that Thomas Burgess, Bishop of Salisbury, voiced Anglican discontent before the Duke of Wellington, explaining by force of argument that such an emancipation would not only be morally in contradiction to pure religion, but also a constitutional threat to parliamentary integrity and to the king's crown.[4] Despite much pressure from an already divided Anglican establishment, the Act was passed on March 24, 1829. Hence, the disintegration of the old ecclesial and political consensus seemed beneficial to the Catholic Church, even though its prohibitions remained in fact far more significant than its concessions.[5] However, even if the Act was officially a major political and social advance for influential Roman Catholic subjects of His Majesty, the daily situation barely changed for the common Roman Catholic citizen. Tensions and anti-Catholic feelings could not be stopped by official decree, be it signed by the king himself!

In 1845, another incident fueled an already strong anti-Catholic attitude. Prime Minister Sir Robert Peel proposed to increase the grant to the Royal College of St. Patrick, a Catholic seminary located in Maynooth, Ireland. In doing so, he was obviously trying to conciliate Irish sentiment towards the British Crown. However, the proposal to have its annual grant increased from £9,000 (a figure that had remained constant since 1809) to £26,000 was considered by conservatives in Parliament as somewhat excessive. It was at this time that John P. Plumptre gave, on March 10, 1845, his Anti-Maynooth Address, concluding that, if the movement towards a Catholic "conciliation" was pursued further, "our Protestant monarch would not be safe upon her throne; the liberty, the property, the lives of our Protestant fellow-countrymen would not be secure."[6] The controversy over the "Maynooth Grant" would last more than a decade and was reinforced during the Crimean War (1853–55). While the British and the French armies were attempting to capture the Russian fortifications of Sebastopol, the attention of religious feelings in England turned once again against Roman Catholics. Maynooth, seen as the intellectual center of "Irish Popery," was deemed to be the Sebastopol of the Popery, an impenetrable stronghold of "sin and idolatry."

In the last quarter of the nineteenth century, none other than W. E. Gladstone himself came to take a more critical stance regarding Roman Catholics. In response to the First Vatican Council's 1870 definition of papal infallibility, Gladstone published in 1874 a "commentary" on the Vatican Decrees entitled *The Vatican Decrees in Their Bearing on*

---

4. Wellesley, *The Dispatches*, 528–30.

5. Lewis, "Disintegration of the Tory-Anglican Alliance," 23–33.

6. Norman, *Anti-Catholicism in Victorian England*, 145.

Civil Allegiance.[7] His criticisms can be summarized under four headings, which are not far removed from sixteenth-century anti-Catholic casuistry. He argued first that Rome had substituted for the traditional *semper eadem* ("always the same") a social and political action of violence as well as an ecclesiastical policy of change in the matter of religious faith. Second, he pointed out that Rome had refurbished every old argument its opponents naively thought she had dismissed since the reign of "Bloody Mary." Third, he asserted that no one could convert to the Roman Catholic Church without thereby renouncing all moral and mental freedom. No Roman Catholic could avoid placing his civic loyalty at the mercy of another individual or institution: the pope and his church. Last, he concluded that Rome had repudiated all the development of modern thought, as well as the importance of ancient history. Under Gladstone's theological, political, and moral charges, it seemed that no Roman Catholic could be exempted from the accusation of being an enemy of the state, and a moral anarchist.

If Gladstone had realized who would take personal issue with this attitude, he might have worded his argument more carefully. Or refrain from it altogether. One of the leading lights of the day indeed took issue with this anti-Catholic prejudice: Cardinal John Henry Newman. The great educator and theologian replied with a vibrant *Letter Addressed to His Grace the Duke of Norfolk on Occasion of Mr. Gladstone's Recent Expostulation* (1875). The greatest Roman Catholic English convert had already received the same criticisms during his debate with Charles Kingsley a decade earlier. This debate became famous in its time because it saw the "victory" of a Roman Catholic in the public sphere. At first, the heart of the debate seems to have been theological, concerned with one of Newman's sermons on Wisdom and Truth. However, it soon took a very different path when Kingsley commented in his review of Froude's *History of England* that "truth for its own sake had never been a virtue with the Roman clergy," implying that no Roman Catholic could be considered trustworthy.[8]

The implications did not escape Newman: British Roman Catholics could definitely not be trusted, merely because they were Roman Catholics. Newman, of course, would certainly not let this "slip of the tongue" go unchallenged. In fact, Kingsley's *ad hominem* argument turned against

---

7. Ryan, *Newman and Gladstone.*

8. Harrold, *John Henry Newman,* 300.

him when Newman decided to write the *Apologia Pro Vita Sua*, one of the most influential pieces of Catholic polemical writing of the century. In fact, wrote Newman, "Kingsley desires to impress upon the public mind the conviction that I am a crafty, scheming man, simply untrustworthy; that in becoming a Catholic, I have just found my right place . . . to be a pure, german, genuine Catholic, a man must be either a knave or a fool."[9] This sentiment was not unique to Newman.

Whether personal impression or historical fact, Newman's evaluation of Kingsley's charges certainly reinforces an impression of great injustice. Anti-Catholic sentiments were strong enough in nineteenth-century England to create a sentiment of martyrdom. In this light, Tolkien's comment on the death of his mother becomes even more telling: "My own dear mother was a martyr indeed, and it is not to everybody that God grants so easy a way to his great gifts as he did to Hilary and myself, giving us a mother who killed herself with labour and trouble to ensure us keeping the faith."[10] Certainly then, Tolkien's devotion to the Roman Catholic Church was strengthened by the death of his mother, whom he considered to have been a martyr in the strict sense of someone who had died *because* of her faith. She had been rejected and abandoned because of her faith, the faith of the one church. The very character and person of his mother were attacked, merely because she had become a Roman Catholic. Of course the reverse could sometimes be true, and the negative attitude of Tolkien's guardian, Father Francis, towards the young Edith Bratt was certainly the result of her being older, but also of not being Catholic.[11] No matter the retaliation though, the fact remains. There is little doubt that Tolkien felt the weight of the same criticisms leveled against Newman a few decades earlier when charges were directed at his personal Christian virtue, merely because he had converted to Roman Catholicism—even though this conversion occurred after a long theological and personal agony.

Newman himself perceptively sums up the reasons behind anti-Catholic sentiments: "Not only am I now a member of a most un-English communion, whose great aim is considered to be the extinction of Protestantism and the Protestant Church, and whose means of attack are

9. Newman, *Apologia*, 71.

10. Carpenter, *Biography*, 31.

11. L, 52.

popularly supposed to be unscrupulous cunning and deceit."[12] In the social imagination of many of his contemporaries, through the emergence
of a truly public English Catholicism, it was the Elizabethan religious
settlement that was called into question. Since the settlement had guar-
anteed the social and religious peace since the 1560s, questioning the
Elizabethan settlement was nearly identical to questioning all political
and social authorities, including the parliament and the royal family.

Such, then, was the condition of Roman Catholics in England in
the century Tolkien was born, a condition that persisted well into the beginning of the twentieth century. In fact, merely two years before Mabel
Tolkien's conversion to Roman Catholicism, parliament Liberal leader
William Harcourt famously claimed on June 16, 1898, that there existed
a "conspiracy to subvert the true principles of the Church of England."[13]
The reaction of Mabel Tolkien's family can be better understood when we
remember the typical English attitude towards Roman Catholics. When
Tolkien's mother became a Roman Catholic she abandoned the purity of
the faith, and became a social and religious outcast.[14] Indeed, her family
being of Methodist tradition, and the Tolkiens mostly of Baptist confes-
sion, the opposition to her conversion could only lead to her social iso-
lation. Hostility towards Catholics was still publicly voiced even during
Tolkien's academic career.

Writing to his son Christopher in late May 1944, Tolkien would
caustically recall what had just happened at his Oxford college. The "incident" involved the Master of Pembroke College who, while sitting at
a dinner, celebrated the election of the new Rector of Lincoln College
with a loud anti-Catholic comment: "Thank heaven they did not elect a
Roman Catholic to the Rectorship anyway; disastrous, disastrous for the
college."[15] One can only imagine what Tolkien would have though, he
who believed his mother had died partly because of the rejection of her
Catholic faith by her family. This certainly, and unfortunately, was not the
harshest comment Tolkien would hear during his life as a Roman Catholic. Oxford's academia was definitely not propitious for Roman Catholics,
and indeed was becoming more and more difficult for self-confessed and
practicing Christians.

---

12. Newman, *Apologia*, 97.

13. *The Parliamentary Debates*, 142.

14. See Carpenter, *Biography*, 31–32.

15. L, 84.

Oxford and Newmanian Catholicism

While Mabel Tolkien's Catholicism was mostly the consequence of the ministering of the Birmingham Oratory, Tolkien's own would owe as much to Oxford as to Birmingham, though for similar reasons. In fact, not only would Oxford be a pivotal Catholic influence, but Oxford in itself became central to Tolkien's life, and he spent most of his academic life there. This Oxfordian life might also explain some of the oddities of Tolkien's personality.

Admittedly, being an Oxford don determined Tolkien's daily life, providing rhythm and direction, but also infinite occasions for his legendary procrastination! While socially determinant, Oxford had another influence on Tolkien, for Oxford was also religiously distinctive, nourishing a particular kind of Roman Catholicism. In fact, next to the condition of Roman Catholicism in England, the presence of Roman Catholicism in Oxford is the most important aspect to investigate in order to apprehend how Tolkien's faith was formed and nourished. For many reasons, Tolkien's Catholicism is best described historically as being an *Oxfordian* Catholicism.

If Oxford was such an important Catholic place for Tolkien, it is primarily because being a Catholic in Oxford meant living under the shadow of John Henry Newman. And for a Roman Catholic, Newman's shadow was both protective and exhortative. Under the stature of Newman, the Catholic convert, one could stand on the shoulder of a giant. In fact, the influence of the great Catholic cardinal is seen even before Tolkien set foot in Oxford. Before becoming one of the Oxfordian Catholics, Tolkien was brought up in the Catholic faith attending Newman's Birmingham Oratory while studying at King Edward's School. While the school itself had a history tied to that of English Roman Catholicism, it most likely had no impact on Tolkien's Catholicism.

It was not so with the Birmingham Oratory. On the contrary, the Oratory was exactly the sort of Oxfordian place where the renewed interest in Thomism would have affected the young Tolkien.[16] Tolkien's life at the Oratory is not well described, nor do we know what specific teachings Father Francis inculcated in the Tolkien boys. We can only assume that the Tolkien boys received a Catholic education in the Newmanian tradition and participated actively in the daily religious life, often serving

---

16. See Candler, "Tolkien or Nietzsche."

Mass for Father Francis.[17] Of course that, in itself, does not tell much about Tolkien's personal attachment to his mother's chosen faith. The emotional ties to religion should indeed not be carelessly dismissed. However, in the case of Tolkien, the scarce indications we can gather give us a picture of an intellectually proficient and religiously committed young boy who later, at sixteen, became familiar with the greatest Catholic apologist and writer of his age: Gilbert Keith Chesterton. In 1908–9, Tolkien presented to his school library two of Chesterton's great works, *Orthodoxy* and *Heretics*.

This indicates two things. First, that Tolkien had indeed become familiar with Chesterton, and contrary to common opinion did not have only a vague knowledge of him. Second, that he considered it vital that his library include the two volumes. Both imply a rather committed relationship with his Roman Catholicism, going beyond mere familial tradition. That during his three years of separation from Edith, he enclosed two devotional pamphlets—the "Seven Words on the Cross" and the "Stations of the Cross"—in the only letter written to his beloved, is quite significant.[18] To fully grasp its importance we have to identify the specific book in which these pamphlets were published, but this is a rather difficult task.

One obvious candidate is the famous Catholic devotional book, *The Garden of the Soul*, republished after the restoration of the Catholic hierarchy in England, that soon became the definite Catholic guide to sanctify every day.[19] *The Garden of the Soul* is a complete devotional guide, with a recapitulation of the days of devotion, fasting days, litanies, and prayers. It also included prayers for the Stations (likely what is referred to as "Stations of the Cross"), but also the Litany of Loreto, a prayer to the Virgin Mary, called in the *Garden of the Soul*, "Litany of the Blessed Virgin." What is fascinating here is that this is also one of the five prayers that Tolkien translated into Quenya.[20] Of his dearest Catholic prayers, including the Litany of Loreto, Tolkien wrote Christopher: "if you have these by heart you never need for words of joy."[21] There is clearly something of personal significance in Tolkien's inclusion of the "Seven Words

17. Scull and Hammond, *Companion and Guide*, 1:11.

18. Scull and Hammond, *Companion and Guide*, 1:18.

19. Challoner, *The Garden of the Soul*, 8.

20. Quenya is one of the Elvish languages invented by Tolkien, and the language into which he translated several Catholic prayers. Tolkien, "Words of Joy," 11.

21. L, 66.

of the Cross" and the "Stations of the Cross" in his letter to Edith.[22] Was this pamphlet supposed to explain to his lover the practice of his Catholic devotion? We cannot be sure, of course. However these indications suggest as much. A little more than a year after that letter, Tolkien became an undergraduate at Exeter College, Oxford, where he matriculated on October 17, 1911.[23]

The presence of Roman Catholicism in Oxford is the subject of a long and turbulent history; however, "during the time that Tolkien was an undergraduate and then a professor, the presence of the Roman Catholic Church in Oxford became more prominent."[24] Later, there even existed at Oxford a Roman Catholic Chaplaincy during the last decade leading up to the Second World War. When he was back in Oxford as a professor, Tolkien would often be active in its Catholic life. There, Roman Catholicism was part of his daily life. His children were regular attendees of the Sacred Heart Convent, especially for parties "and at Christmas, at which Tolkien was a 'famous entertainer.'"[25] Oxford Catholic friendships were also of decisive influence; for instance, Tolkien submitted the manuscript of *The Hobbit* to Allen & Unwin on October 5, 1936, through the recommendation of Susan Dagnall—a former student who worked at Allen & Unwin—and M. E. Griffiths—also a former student and a close friend of the Tolkiens.[26] Both were Roman Catholic. If life as a Roman Catholic in Oxford was easier than in other places in England, it was no doubt in great part due to the influence of the Catholic converts of the Oxford Movement.

In fact, the picture of nineteenth- and early twentieth-century English Catholicism would not be complete without a brief mention of the Oxford Movement, although, properly speaking, the Oxford Men, also known as Tractarians, did not belong to the Roman Catholic Church. Many did not even show clear signs of "Romanism" until the publication of "Tract Ninety" by Newman. Following the latter's conversion, the Oxford Movement soon lost its vitality, decayed, and eventually disappeared

---

22. The devotional practice of symbolically reenacting the path to the cross had become a distinct feature of Catholic devotion. Heimann, *Catholic Devotion in Victorian England*, 42.

23. Scull and Hammond, *Companion and Guide*, 1:28.

24. Scull and Hammond, *Companion and Guide*, 2:829.

25. Scull and Hammond, *Companion and Guide*, 2:830.

26. Scull and Hammond, *Companion and Guide*, 1:186 and 2:830. Regarding Dagnall and Griffiths, see 2:200 and 353–54, respectively.

from the religious life of Victorian England, at least as a visible movement. Even after the decay of the movement, Newman remained one of the main public figures of Victorian religious life. Apart from its theological and ecclesial distinctive, it is significant that the movement was known as the "Oxford Movement." This name was chosen by a conscious decision, even though several of the first "founders" of the movement did not have specific ties to Oxford. When the movement began, after Keble preached his sermon "National Apostasy" at St. Mary's on July 14, 1833, Newman was the first to see that the movement needed a physical location, and that this was necessary to its unity.[27] Oxford rapidly became an obvious choice to many of the Tractarians, prompting Newman to say, "Catholics did not make us Catholics. Oxford made us Catholics."[28]

To understand the importance of the Oxford Movement is first to understand the motivations leading to its birth. England, at the time, was the seat of two important philosophical and social movements, Christian Socialism and Utilitarianism. The Oxford Movement can best be seen as a challenge to both groups, as well as a tentative and prophetic answer to the socio-theological condition of the Church of England. More specifically, the Oxford Movement arose to counter the rise of its main opponent, Liberal Christianity, which Newman referred to as "muscular Christianity"—an unofficial designation that came to be accepted by none other than Charles Kingsley, Newman's nemesis. The term itself is of uncertain origin but was probably first used in a review of Kingsley's novel *Two Years Ago* in the February 21, 1857, issue of the *Saturday Review*.[29] Newman thought that this brand of Christianity was socially deviant, being motivated by a secular social engagement the church should be cautioned not to take. Thus, he saw in Kingsley "a leading example of that unbridled individualism which, 'in taking man's side and not God's,' was knocking the life out of the institutions it had inherited."[30]

Newman and the other leaders of the Oxford Movement, saw it as a spiritual and ecclesial response to the spiritual decay of the priesthood of the Church of England. However, this rather severe judgment was not directed at the Anglican priests' virtues, but at their *piety*. To the Oxford men, these priests had merely become "amiable and respectable

27. Newman, *Apologia*, 140–42.

28. Coulson, *Newman and the Common Tradition*, 161. See Ward, *The Life of John Henry*, 2:57.

29. Ladd, *Muscular Christianity*, 13–14.

30. Coulson, *Newman and the Common Tradition*, 142.

gentlemen, who were satisfied to read morning and afternoon Service on a Sunday, and to dislike Dissenters."[31] In response to this tepid Christianity, Newman always stressed the need for a spiritual renewal, and to this goal he would be dedicated until his passing.

While "muscular Christianity" was one of the Oxford Movement's main opponents, it was by no means the only target of the Tractarians' spiritual and social renewal endeavor. Before he converted to Roman Catholicism, Newman had already opposed the proponents of Utilitarianism, at the time best known by the name of Benthamists. This movement had its immediate source in the political and moral philosophy of Jeremy Bentham (February 15, 1748–June 6, 1832), even though some scholars trace its thought back to Greek Epicureans. If Utilitarianism was by no means a uniform movement, "most broadly and loosely applied [its principles] refer to the socio-economic-political ideology and set of values held by the Victorian middle class—to the entrepreneurial mentality which dominated the period and adopted these tenets to rationalize its actions and aims, habits and prejudices."[32] The key tenet of this socio-political movement was the quest for the greatest measure of happiness, for the greatest number of people—thus often leading opponents to reduce Utilitarianism to a moral arithmetic. Other critics extended that judgment to conclude that these philosophers stressed self-interest as the sole motivation behind human conduct.

Newman opposed the Benthamists in matters of education and moral life. Indeed, he saw them as one of the sources of the dismemberment of knowledge—a topic particularly sensitive and important for him. Not only was knowledge being fragmented, but it was also being rendered more abstract and economics-driven. In fact, some might have feared this utilitarian education would only be "interested in manufacturing the obedient and compliant workers the industrialists needed."[33] This fear of an economic, abstract, and artificial philosophy of education is seen in Dickens's *Hard Times* in which schoolchildren of the industrial city of Coketown are denied any expression of emotion and creativity.[34] More likely, this dissociation of knowledge and creativity was another

---

31. Harrold, *John Henry Newman*, 23.

32. Harrold, *John Henry Newman*, 115.

33. Bradley, "Victorian Lessons," 75.

34. Dickens, *Hard Times*, 3.

concern for Newman who saw education aimed at primarily not an economic goal, but wisdom.[35]

He also charged the Benthamists with being responsible for the segregation of religious knowledge into a separate and irrelevant sphere—if religious knowledge could even be considered knowledge at all. He further accused the Benthamists with significantly modifying the curriculum at Oxford, making their Utilitarian philosophy the basis of modern education. In a way, Tolkien's move from Classics to English reflects a conviction that his choice should not be based on what the majority of the Oxford students were favoring as a path to knowledge, but on a special attention to his own abilities, preference, and personal choice, disregarding its usefulness for society itself. On the other hand, the Utilitarians already charged the Classical education and curriculum with seeking fame and honor without providing anything useful to society. In Newman's opinion, Utilitarians considered education to be merely the acquisition of knowledge, forgetting that it also demanded religious and moral proficiency.

Newman's argument is, unsurprisingly, very similar to Edward Pusey's opinion that the purpose of a university was indeed "to form minds religiously, morally, and intellectually, which shall discharge aright whatever duties God, in his Providence, shall appoint to them."[36] Against the Utilitarian view, Newman advanced, among other things, the theory that all branches of knowledge were connected, and that all fell under the life-giving power of religious knowledge, noting: "I have said that all branches of knowledge are connected together, because the subject-matter of knowledge is ultimately united in itself, as being the acts and work of the Creator."[37]

None of this should suggest that the Oxford Movement was merely a defensive theological posture. On the contrary, one of the most relevant theological aspects of Newman's thought lies in the originality of his worldview. Among his positive theological affirmations, his views on the relationship between religion, education, and knowledge—best demonstrated in his *The Idea of a University*—remain influential. In fact, the Newmanian philosophy of education leads to the conclusion that "the

---

35. Newman, *The Idea of a University*, 135–37.

36. Pusey, *Collegiate and Professorial Teaching*, 215. Edward Pusey became the foremost leader of the Oxford Movement after Newman's conversion to Catholicism in 1843 and his ordination in the Roman Catholic Church two years later.

37. Newman, *The Idea of a University*, 99.

Oxford Movement was, of course, primarily religious; nevertheless it had far-reaching effects on education both in the university and the school. Nor can we ignore its influence on educational theory, for Newman, the leader of the Oxford Movement, was also to become the greatest English Catholic writer on educational theory."[38] In contrast to many of his contemporaries, Newman did not hold knowledge to be divisible; rather, all disciplines were joined and connected through religious knowledge. Moreover, Newman stood against the consensual Utilitarian definition of knowledge and promoted a more instructional and relational one, aimed at cultivating the mind.

At the very opening of his discourses, he emphatically affirmed that "the view taken of a University in these Discourses is the following: That it is a place of *teaching* universal *knowledge*."[39] In the course of all nine discourses, Newman's overall conclusion that theology *is* knowledge was repeated again and again. He even concluded further that a university without religious knowledge was un-philosophical. The briefest and most unusual conclusion for his audience would certainly have been the following one: "In a word, Religious Truth is not only a portion, but a *condition* of general knowledge."[40]

Besides, this unity of knowledge was incarnated by Newman in his stress on the value of literature. The great English Catholic convert defined, or limited, literature in terms of human nature. Thus, when devised by a Catholic believer, literature was not primarily a vehicle for faith. Rather, Newman argued for a synergistic approach to the relationship between literature and faith. In this matter, David Schwartz's comment on Dawson's attitude towards the same issue is telling: "[Dawson] shared Chesterton's and Greene's sense that a Catholic writer is one whose faith infuses his work without violating its genre's standard."[41] At this point, it is even possible to argue tentatively that Chesterton, Greene, and Dawson shared much of what appears to be a Newmanian approach to literature and faith.

Hence, literature is in essence the "Life and Remains" of the natural man, in both his innocence and guilt.[42] Therefore, human literature could

---

38. Dawson, *The Crisis of Western Education*, 53.

39. Newman, *The Idea of a University*, ix.

40. Newman, *The Idea of a University*, 70; italics mine.

41. Schwartz, *Third Spring*, 230.

42. Harrold, *John Henry Newman*, 255.

only be related to the spiritual condition of man. That, in turn, implies that a literature could not be in essence "Christian." This conclusion is a consequence of Newman's deep sense of human sin. It is impossible, he argues, to have a sinless literature written by sinful men.[43] In very much the same way, Tolkien was convinced that "there cannot be any 'story' without a fall—all stories are ultimately about the fall—at least not for human minds as we know them and have them."[44] An important conclusion for Newman is that literature itself is not Christian but can be written by Christians; indeed, "by 'Catholic Literature' is not to be understood a literature which treats exclusively or primarily of Catholic matters . . . but it includes all subjects of literature whatever, treated as a Catholic would treat them, and as he only can treat them."[45] This is probably what Tolkien tried to achieve when he set up the task of writing and developing his own "fairy stories." Certainly, his assertion that *The Lord of the Rings* is a Catholic work can be read in this light.[46]

The Catholic Literary Revival and Christopher Dawson

As the Anglican Church, and many more among the subjects of His Majesty (King Edward VII having succeeded Queen Victoria in 1901), was recovering from the turmoil of the passing of Newman and Henry Edward Manning—once a great figure of the Anglican church—to "Rome," the twentieth century was opening with a great Catholic literary revival, the influence of which can hardly be underestimated. In fact, following the conversion of Newman, the Anglican world had witnessed numerous scholarly and literary conversions to Roman Catholicism, and some of them had a profound influence, an influence as important as Newman's own in his time. G. K. Chesterton's official conversion and, before that, the publication of his already Catholic-inspired *Orthodoxy* (1908), was certainly one of these influential conversions, but certainly not the only one.

This literary renewal can be seen as an alternative answer to the climate of theological debates that had plagued the past decades. In truth, English Roman Catholics had come to the stark conclusion that if a man

43. Newman, *The Idea of a University*, 227–28, quoted in Harrold, *John Henry Newman*, 256.

44. L, 147.

45. Newman, *The Idea of a University*, 296.

46. L, 172.

of the stature of Newman could not change their fellow countrymen's attitudes through theological engagement, maybe another path was possible. Hence, the beginning of the twentieth century was marked by a move away from theological debates on the part of many Catholic intellectuals, as Allitt indicates: "After Vatican I, and especially after *Pascendi*, English and American convert intellectuals tended to stay away from strictly theological questions altogether and work in the safer realms of literature, history, and the social sciences."[47]

This move away from theological debates was certainly motivated by the context we have just described, but the mention of the papal encyclical *Pascendi Dominici gregis* ("Feeding the Lord's Flock") promulgated by Pope Pius X on September 8, 1907, was also of significance.[48] The fact that this encyclical was a broad condemnation of modernist agnostics and evolutionist positions regarding Catholic faith and dogma could only reinforce Roman Catholics' impression of being alienated from their surrounding culture. In the wake of the anti-modernist controversy and in the midst of British academic fascination with the same theses, it is no surprise that British Catholics turned towards other fields, such as literature and history, to set themselves apart from their surrounding culture.

Hence, just as the twentieth century was opening before uncertain but hopeful eyes, the English Catholic world turned towards the dawn of a new Catholic scholarship that went beyond the works of Newman and other leading theologians. In fact, Newman's famous "second spring" could be paralleled in English Catholicism's "third spring" flowering throughout the middle of the twentieth century.[49] This third Catholic momentum in the British empire has been described as a three-phases development incarnated first in the works of J. H. Newman, Coventry Patmore, and G. M. Hopkins; second, Oscar Wilde, Aubrey Beardsley, Alice Meynell, and Francis Thompson; and third, G. K. Chesterton, Maurice Baring, and Hilaire Belloc. So apparently extraordinary was the rise of Catholic novelists that George Orwell could conclude in 1953 that "a fairly large proportion of the distinguished novels of the last few decades have been written by Catholics and have been describable as Catholic novels . . . the conflict not only between this world and the next world but

---

47. Allitt, *Catholic Converts*, 11.

48. Pius X, *Pascendi Dominici gregis*.

49. See Schwartz, *Third Spring*, 13.

between sanctity and goodness is a fruitful theme of which the ordinary, unbelieving writer cannot make use."[50]

The blooming of such exceptional writers from within the Catholic church captured attention and rapidly became an appealing argument in favor of Catholicism. In fact, "it is not only non-Catholics, but Catholics too, who are not infrequently surprised when they discover many distinguished writers not only professing Catholicism but writing under the influence of the full spirit of the Church."[51] These authors became a living testimony to what looked, for many, like an appealing distinctive Catholic perspective on society, history, and humankind. This was often referred to as "Catholic Humanism."[52] What came to be the center of this new informal literary movement was the radical choice they thought had to be faced. Indeed, "thinkers drawn to the Church in the twentieth century's dawning decades were therefore almost exclusively those enticed by its own increasingly radical rebuttal of prevalent norms."[53] To many English Catholic scholars and writers associated with this "third spring," what was at stake was nothing less than a binary opposition between two competing worldview: modern or Catholic.[54]

Despite the renowned figures that "went to Rome," conversions to Roman Catholicism were far from being socially accepted, nor were they readily considered morally and intellectually legitimate. Even those who did not go all the way to "Rome," but merely to a high form of Anglo-Catholicism, were not exempt from criticism. Virginia Woolf, upon hearing of Eliot's conversion, could, for example, write her sister of the obscene nature of a "living person sitting by the fire and believing in God."[55] Ironically the obscenity observed by Woolf in one of England's most renowned contemporary poets was paralleled by the distrust that many authors now associated with this "third spring" had for the general direction taken by their society. This distrust gradually led them to hope and call for a more humane society as well as to find a ground for their own religious and spiritual agendas. In Roman Catholicism these writers discovered "a vision they voiced in the hope of revitalizing their culture

50. Orwell, "The Sanctified Sinner," 4:439, quoted in Schwartz, *Third Spring*, 11.

51. Calvert, *The Catholic Literary Revival*, 9.

52. On this topic see, Oser, *The Return of Christian Humanism*.

53. Schwartz, *Third Spring*, 8.

54. Schwartz, *Third Spring*, 8.

55. Virginia Woolf to her sister Vanessa Bell, February 11, 1928, in Nicholson and Trautmann, *The Letters of Virginia Woolf*, 457–58.

without vitiating what they deemed its subversive vitality."[56] The breadth of this "revitalizing," including a literary revival, impressed on many minds a power of persuasion that the depth of philosophical, theological, and historical enquiry could only reinforce. As such, this "third spring" created a "great network of minds energizing each other into creativity" that included well-known figures such as Hilaire Belloc, Maurice Baring, Graham Greene, Christopher Dawson, and of course J. R. R. Tolkien.

In this respect Schwartz's analysis of Chesterton's place in this Catholic literary movement can be generalized. Most, if not all, of these authors hoped for "the flowering of the Catholic Third Spring, in which traditional Christianity would again find its way out of the grave. He [Chesterton] hoped to tend that garden in which the stone had been rolled away."[57] This conclusion seems inescapably identical to the one that must be made after investigation of Christopher Dawson's works. Dawson, who has somehow fallen into oblivion, was without question one of the foremost Catholic historians of the twentieth century. Thus, Woods concludes in his review of Dawson's *Dynamics of World History* that "Dawson consistently demonstrated immense scholarship as he related the significance of religious, political, artistic, general cultural, and social happenings to the shape and flow of western civilization."[58] The breadth of his knowledge, both modern and medieval, led him to set forth an articulate picture of the development of Western culture, a vision that made him into "more like a movement than a man."[59] In fact, "in the 1930s, Christopher Dawson was considered by many to be one of England's most influential writers."[60]

Likewise, in his introduction to *Sanctifying the World*, Birzer makes a very convincing case for the crucial importance of Dawson, quoting from a wide range of highly respected Catholic theologians and scholars paying their debts to Dawson, among these, the French neo-Thomist Etienne Gilson.[61] Not only did Dawson come to be considered a major twentieth-century Catholic historian, but in 1950 a Dominican journal went as far as to compare him to the famed Newman, stating, "Mr.

---

56. Schwartz, *Third Spring*, 29.

57. Schwartz, *Third Spring*, 106.

58. Woods, "Dawson and the Christian Interpretation of History," 147.

59. Sheed, "Christopher Dawson Talks with Frank Sheed," 661.

60. Echeverria, "Christopher Dawson Revisited," 24.

61. See Birzer, *Sanctifying the World*, 4–5.

Dawson is an educator; perhaps the greatest that Heaven has sent us English Catholics since Newman."[62] This statement is all the more significant when one remembers that for Dawson, the Oxford Movement had not only been an ecclesial movement but also an educational one, and that Newman had not only been one of the greatest Victorian theologians but also "the greatest English Catholic writer on educational theory."[63]

Assuredly, the comparison between Dawson and Newman could not have left Tolkien unmoved. Adding to his credit, Dawson also reveals a major influence on his work, "one of the greatest champions of Christian culture in our time," G. K. Chesterton.[64] Spearhead of the Catholic literary renewal in the twentieth century, Dawson decidedly cannot be overlooked. The relevance of Dawson is largely due to his historical and cultural scholarship, most likely because of what he termed a metahistorical approach—what could be called a philosophy of history.[65] Further, Dawson argued that civilization and religion were strongly connected, to the point that culture was embodied religion, and a civilization was its religion.[66] While we could consider that argument *passé*, Dawson's perspective is built on a view of history as developing through periods of many different "forms" and "spirits," thus revealing a twentieth-century Aristotelian retelling. One of Dawson's often repeated concerns was about "the spiritual and intellectual cohesion which was the foundation of Western Civilization."[67] Despite his relatively restricted contemporary influence, "much of Dawson is uncannily relevant to contemporary times and historical studies."[68]

If Dawson's view of history was influential in his own time, it is not surprising that we can pinpoint several elements of his characteristic approach to history and culture in C. S. Lewis's *The Abolition of Man*. Theirs was not, however, a relationship of platitude and uncritical agreements. On the contrary, regarding fundamental aspects of Dawson's scholarship, such as the nature of history, Lewis could only disagree. Despite their

---

62. Foster, "Mr. Dawson and Christendom," 423.

63. Dawson, *Crisis of Western Education*, 53.

64. Birzer, *Sanctifying the World*, 28.

65. Dawson, *Dynamics of World History*, 287.

66. Dawson, *Enquiries into Religion and Culture*, 94.

67. This is the main thesis of such Dawson works as *The Making of Europe*; *Religion and the Rise of Western Culture*; *The Formation of Christendom*. See also Hitchcock, "Christopher Dawson," 112.

68. Woods, "Dawson and the Christian Interpretation of History," 147.

friendship, this developed into a lively debate, leading Dawson to criticize Lewis for "questioning the possibility of a Christian interpretation
of history, declaring that the supposed connection between Christianity
and historicism is largely an illusion."[69] Dawson's "spiritual" explanation
of history tended to balance the merely materialistic and deterministic
perspective of Marxists and positivists, as well as the rationalistic one of
secular humanists. Whether or not Tolkien took sides on the issue of the
philosophy of history, the fact remains: Dawson, Tolkien, and Lewis had
decidedly too much of a personal connection for this not to have played
a key role in Tolkien's own development.

Considering Dawson's influence, it is barely surprising to discover
that he also had quite an influence on Tolkien. In fact, it appears that Dawson was so familiar with Lewis, Tolkien, and the other Inklings that when
he came to be in charge of the *Dublin Review*, he listed members of the
Inklings as desirable regular contributors to the journal—including the
aforementioned authors.[70] For example, Tolkien first published his *Leaf
by Niggle* in the 1945 issue of the *Review*, at the invitation of Dawson. But
Dawson's relation to Tolkien reaches beyond mere literary recognition. In
fact, Tolkien shows decisive signs of a direct interaction with Dawson. The
first and most personal of these is the fact that Tolkien and Dawson were
co-parishioners at St. Aloysius, a church served by the Jesuits until 1981.
Even if there are no direct testimonies to their interaction at St. Aloysius, it
is almost beyond dispute that the two authors frequently met there. Moreover, like Tolkien, Dawson felt keenly the strong anti-Catholic tradition in
his family, and was affected by the knowledge that his belonging to Roman
Catholicism would be met with a deep-felt disapproval by those close to
him. Dawson knew that his mother, who was the eldest daughter of the
Archdeacon Bevan of Hay Castle, would strongly oppose his "going over
to Rome."[71] Tolkien and Dawson also shared a special interest in Newmanian Catholicism. In fact, when Dawson returned to Oxford in 1909,
after his tutored years at Bletsoe, he became rapidly interested in Newman when, "at the Newman Society he heard Wilfrid Ward speak on the
circumstances in which Newman wrote his *Apologia Pro Vita Sua*."[72] This

---

69. Dawson, *Dynamics of World History*, 233–34, here referring to C. S. Lewis,
"Historicism."

70. Birzer, *Sanctifying the World*, 8.

71. Pearce, *Literary Converts*, 41.

72. Pearce, *Literary Converts*, 41–42.

same work became a considerable influence on Dawson's own conversion, Dawson becoming "Newman's counterpart."[73]

Further, in his seminal essay, "On Fairy Stories," Tolkien evidences a familiarity with Dawson's writings, borrowing several expressions playing a key role in the developing argument. The first two, the "march of Science,"[74] and "improved means to deteriorated ends" refer to Dawson's argument in *The Judgment of Nations* that "a civilization which concentrates on means and neglects almost entirely to consider ends must inevitably become disintegrated and despiritualized."[75] A third expression used by Tolkien, the "rawness and ugliness of modern European life," is taken from Dawson's *Progress and Religion*. The original quote reads, "The rawness and ugliness of modern European life is the sign of biological inferiority, of an insufficient or false relation to environment, which produces strain, wasted effort, revolt or failure."[76]

Furthermore, Tolkien and Dawson shared a sensitivity and appreciation for myth, and Northern myths in particular, albeit for slightly different reasons. While Tolkien was moved by stories and language, Dawson's value of Northern culture was mostly an historical one. So close were they in their appreciation of Northern culture that Dawson could indeed have subscribed to Tolkien's judgment in his lecture "Beowulf: The Monsters and the Critics" that "one of the most potent elements in the fusion [of Christianity and old traditions] is the Northern courage: the theory of courage, which is the great contribution of early Northern literature."[77] Both authors emphasized the potential sacramental value of pagan legends and mythologies.

In fact, it can be argued that Dawson and Tolkien followed Newman, standing in a long tradition of emphasizing the imagination in religious and cultural life.[78] However, partly because he was less openly and directly Catholic in his outlook, and partly because he was not a trained theologian, Tolkien did not expressly present a theological defense of his work. Indeed, he did not have the sense of religious literary calling one can see

73. Birzer, *Sanctifying the World*, 26.

74. OFS, 149.

75. Dawson, *The Judgment of Nations*, 118.

76. Dawson, *Progress and Religion*, 68.

77. MC, 20. This lecture was the Sir Israel Gollancz Memorial Lecture, read at the British Academy on November 25, 1936.

78. Birzer, *Sanctifying the World*, 13. See Dawson, *Historic Reality of Christian Culture*, 93.

in Dawson's writings, nor was he a self-educated theologian, as were G. K. Chesterton and C. S. Lewis. Rather, Tolkien's Roman Catholicism—his Newmanian tradition, even—was embodied in his writing, contributing in a more subtle way to this "third spring" of Roman Catholicism.

Conclusion

The particular conditions of English Catholicism at the turn of the twentieth century and Tolkien's place within the Roman Catholic literary revival of the mid-twentieth century are both determining elements in the shaping of Tolkien's early Catholic worldview. Thus, even though Tolkien never explicitly displays his Catholic faith and piety in his works and studies, "given the importance of his Catholic faith to Tolkien, it should come as no surprise that elements of Catholicism were taken up into *The Lord of the Rings*."[79] Roman Catholicism stands as the *historical* foundation upon which most of Tolkien's positions were built. Here W. H. Auden was probably on the right track when commenting that "the unstated presuppositions of the whole work are Christian."[80] The consideration of this Roman Catholic background is crucial to the understanding of Tolkien's academic and fictional works.

We could easily be tempted to consider merely Tolkien's works and academic milieu. However, this would be a serious mistake. It would separate two inseparable realities: Tolkien was a philologist, a subcreator of words and worlds, and a pious Catholic believer. To study Tolkien by referring merely to his own works is to miss essential theological and historical connections. As an Oxford don and "Newmanian" Catholic, Tolkien was deeply influenced by these driving historical, social, and theological forces. In matters of theology, literature, and philosophy of education, the influence of Catholicism is clear. All in all, Thomism emerges as the common foundation on which Newman, Chesterton, Dawson, and Tolkien stood. This historical and theological-genealogical conclusion argues for the essential unity of Tolkien's worldview, definitely a Thomist one.

---

79. Fisher, "Working at the Crossroads," 219.
80. Auden, "The Quest Hero," 53.

Part One

"What Is There in a Name?"

—— *Tolkien's Theory of Language* ——

"When you invent a language," he said,
"you more or less catch it out of the air.
You say boo-hoo and that means something."

—J. R. R. TOLKIEN, *Letters*

NOW THAT WE HAVE become reacquainted with our author, let us pack our boxes, books and bags and set out on our journey. Our first destination is this house of language, the Cottage of Lost Play, where words, sounds, and songs dwell. The path to this first house is taken through the door of philology, Tolkien's own domain. "I am a philologist by nature and trade," thus Tolkien described himself in one of his letters.[1] Tolkien always affirmed that his primary interest and love was philology, calling it his "real professional bag of tricks."[2] Indeed, Tolkien was a philologist not only by training, but by taste and vocation, you could say by *nature*. As such, he was in love with words, with their origin, meanings, development, as well as with their internal quality, their sonority, and their beauty.

Tolkien was also a student in the Science of Language, even if a quite unorthodox and eccentric one by contemporary standards. This English

---

1. This is a paraphrase of a sentence found in L, 231.

2. L, 21.

don even spent most of his years working on the invention of his own personal languages, providing a very detailed mythical structure giving life to his creation. In his 1931 address "A Secret Vice," Tolkien humorously, and almost reluctantly, described his interest in the invention of language: "The time has come now, I suppose, when I can no longer postpone the shame-faced revelation of specimens of my own more considered effort, the best I have done in limited leisure, or by occasional theft of time, in one direction."[3] This essay, among Tolkien's most personal ones, provides a glimpse into the workings of his theory of language. It is to this overall theory of language that we turn in the three following chapters.

In order to reach our first stage, and gain a more precise understanding of Tolkien's theory of language, we will proceed in several steps. In chapter 2, we will look at Tolkien's historical context. In fact, there is little to gain from an exploration of Tolkien's theory of language if we disconnect it from his academic milieu and early twentieth-century explorations of the "Science of Language." Chapter 3 will be devoted to the different theories about the nature of words and language that constitute the background of Tolkien's own theory of language. Chapter 4 will consider how the twentieth-century debates about the origin and evolution of language also involved aesthetic considerations. This understanding of "words" for Tolkien will serve to provide a summary of his position regarding the task of translation. Thus, we hope to gain a clearer view of Tolkien's personal understanding of the nature and role of words and language.

---

3. MC, 212.

2

Tolkien and the Science of Language

To BEGIN INVESTIGATING TOLKIEN's theory of language, we first need to engage Tolkien's world and delve more deeply into the condition and challenges of his academic milieu. Since Tolkien was first and foremost a student of language, we will examine how the debates in this field affected the future of Tolkien's work—academic and fictional. The academic climate that reigned in the decades preceding Tolkien's entry into academia is of significant importance and was marked by several important debates. But before looking at these controversies, we will look briefly at the major philosophical traditions that affected the development of the Science of Language.

Among these, empiricism stands out as a major social and academic influence. By the middle of the nineteenth century, the empirical approach of Locke and Hume had deeply influenced all branches of human knowledge. The empirical tradition encouraged the rise and prevalence of the historical and comparative methods used in the sciences of language, anthropology, and religion. The coming of Darwinism would not change this initial direction of British thought towards empiricism. Rather, the Darwinian theory would prove to be of great adaptability and compatibility to the empirical tradition prevalent in England. In a way, the Darwinian evolutionary theory was the essential component the empirical tradition needed to have a lasting and overwhelming influence in philosophy and science, contributing to the shaping of a new popular mindset.

By the end of the nineteenth century, the starting point in many investigations of the science of language was the diversity *and* similarity among the world's languages. This double observation naturally led to the question of the origin and development of languages. The Darwinian theory of evolution was becoming the predominant framework for interpreting and looking at all fields of study: language did not escape this unfortunate destiny. In 1885, the English anthropologist Edward Clodd noted that Darwin had shown that "the notion of a constant relation between man and his surroundings is therefore untenable."[1] The influence of Darwin rapidly led scholars to identify either as supporters or detractors of the evolutionary theory. One scholar, however, stood in a rather ambiguous relationship to Darwinism, and that was Max Müller.

Max Müller and the Challenges of the Science of Language

Always of strong temperament and convictions, Tolkien made strong comments about the nature of myth and language, especially in his opposition to some aspects of the theory of German-born English scholar Max Müller. His comment that "Max Müller's view of mythology as a 'disease of language' can be abandoned without regret" is usually set forth as an argument in itself.[2] However, it is difficult to find Tolkien studies in which his precise argument is fleshed out. Before trying to determine the area of divergence between Tolkien and Müller regarding language, it is necessary to learn more about the latter.

Max Friedrich Müller (1823–1900) was a German scholar, born to poet Wilhelm Müller and Adelheide Müller, daughter of a Lutheran minister. Müller studied at Leipzig University and sat under Schelling, reading closely the works of Hegel. Later on he discovered the philosophy of Kant, which provided him with much of the philosophical background he used during the rest of his academic career. Of Lutheran upbringing, Müller always tried to maintain his attachment to his faith while pursuing academic excellence and launching on a quest for the truth of our ancestors' identity. In 1846, Müller moved to England in order to study the Sanskrit texts in the collection of the East India Company preserved

1. Clodd, *Myths and Dreams*, 4.
2. OFS, 41.

in a library at Oxford University. He remained in England most of his life, teaching at Oxford and militating for the involvement of his university in the Science of Language, and more specifically in the study of ancient Indian texts.[3] While in England, he came under the influence of English Romanticism and became acquainted with many significant Victorian figures, such as J. A. Froude and Matthew Arnold.

Müller was also one of the foremost German philologists, as well as one of the most significant proponents of Western academic interest in Indian studies. His work on the *Rig Veda*, even if it did not receive universal support, gave direction to the subsequent study of this collection of Vedic Sanskrit hymns and sacred texts. This involvement led him to become the editor of the massive fifty volumes of *The Sacred Books of the East*, until his death in 1910.[4] Furthermore, Müller was also the author of a new English translation of Kant's *Critique of Pure Reason*, thus demonstrating the influence Kant would come to have over his theories. The quality of this translation was such that none other than Schopenhauer qualified this translation as the most accurate expression of Kant's thought.[5] His lifetime interests also touched the Science of Religion and Mythology, and, as we will see in the next chapter, those three main fields of interest would be combined in a broader theory about the origins and development of human nature and human thought.

The overall goal of Müller's work can be best described as a metaphysical and philosophical one. Throughout his lifelong interests a main purpose emerges, that of studying mankind's history and origins, in relation to both a created universe and its Creator. If Müller was first and foremost a student and teacher of the Science of Language, he did not restrict his field of study to myth and language. Rather, he sought to attain an understanding of human nature, and its place in a created universe. To define Müller's life in such broad strokes would be very limiting, however, especially if we were to forget his starting point. In fact, he once defined the goal of the Science of Language thus: "The object and aim of philology, in its highest sense, is but one,—to learn what man is, by learning what man has been."[6] As he pointed out several times, he conducted all of his research, either in religion or language, according

3. See Müller, *Chips from a German Workshop*.

4. All except the last volume, the index, were published before Müller's death.

5. Müller refers to Schopenhauer's remarks in his *Essays on Language, Folklore, and Other Subjects*, 244.

6. Müller, *A History of Ancient Sanskrit Literature*, 8.

to an historical and comparative method. One of the starting points of Müller's academic endeavor was the similarities between all peoples and races. Müller was, properly speaking, on a quest to discover the origins of mankind. Indeed, he hoped that the Science of Language would lead to that "highest summit from whence we see into the very dawn of man's life on earth, and where the words which we have heard so often from the days of our childhood assume a meaning more natural, more intelligible, more convincing, than they ever had before."[7] Since every quest requires assumptions about what is sought, Müller came to forge assumptions regarding the direction and outcome of his quest.

The first assumption was that language is the most universal characteristic that defines being human. In this, he argued against the view of those who saw in language "nothing but a contrivance devised by human skill for the more expeditious communication of our thoughts, and who would wish to see it treated, not as a product of nature, but as a work of human art."[8] As a consequence, he was convinced that language was the door to our past, and that everything in language originally had a meaning.[9] Indeed for Müller, language was the first means for going back to this lost age, of which we remember only our fall. For him, the connection between a philosophy of religion and a philosophy of myth was founded on the Science of Language. Such an interrelation was necessary to the fullness of human consciousness and necessary to the communion between humankind and their Creator. As he affirmed, "The philosophy of religion, which must always form the true foundation of theological science, owes it to the Science of Language that the deepest germs of the consciousness of God among the different nations of the world have for the first time been laid open."[10] It was Müller's conviction that we could find within language something fundamental about our human nature. To understand Language was to understand Man.

His second assumption was that language had an origin, and that this origin could reveal something crucial about the origin and the creation of man. Müller would sometimes be criticized for the theological implications of his convictions. In fact, many feared a return of science to the tyranny of theology and charged Müller with being theological and

7. Müller, *Lectures on the Science of Language*, 398–99.

8. Müller, *Lectures on the Science of Language*, 29.

9. Müller, *Lectures on the Science of Language*, 44.

10. Müller, *Selected Essays*, 1:198.

not "scientific" in his approach to the problem of the origin of language. Müller defended his method, a truly scientific one, while not denying that his conclusions bore profound theological implications regarding the origin of mankind and the existence of a Creator.

Thirdly, Müller was convinced that the truth of the Christian faith was far from being incompatible with the "new science." As we saw in the previous chapter, the combination of a paradigm shift in the philosophical mind of the West and the discoveries of the new sciences led many Christian scholars in the late nineteenth and early twentieth centuries to submit to one of two groups. The first one relinquished altogether the "old faith," and went all the way down to argue for a more materialistic philosophy and way of life. The second group tried to harmonize the Christian faith with the conclusions of the "new sciences." As a consequence, many previously held truths of the Christian faith were being reinterpreted. In fact, Müller's view of Christian religion was close to that of his friend Charles Kingsley, a leading progressive theologian, and thus would have been at odds with the Roman Catholic teaching Tolkien had become familiar with. This theological difference might also explain the antagonism felt by Tolkien towards Müller. The latter, because of his friendship with Kingsley, could have been seen by Tolkien as antagonistic to Newman, a highly significant figure in Tolkien's theological and ecclesial development.

There seems to be no definite answer regarding the reasons for Tolkien's dislike of Müller apart from his clear academic criticisms, even though there are good reasons to think his opinion of Müller was also personal and theological. In fact, we believe that Tolkien's personal feelings are also important to take into account if we are to understand his strong opposition to Müller. We should not forget that Tolkien could react in a very emotional manner, and that might have been a factor here. This does not mean, of course, that Müller's theory of myth and language was not a main subject of contention, for it definitely was. Certainly, Tolkien expressed doubts about Müller's general theory.

Tolkien's academic criticism of Müller is all the more important because it also involves the latter's attitude towards the evolutionist theory of Charles Darwin, which was rapidly becoming the predominant framework in many disciplines. Müller entertained in the course of his career a balanced, and at times ambiguous, relationship to the theory of evolution. As a student in the comparative method most interested in language, Müller could not have missed the connections that existed between world languages. This mere observation was for Müller evidence enough of a development of language, that is, of a form of evolutionary process imbedded in language. Here again, Müller faced the fierce opposition of critics mainly concerned with his Christian faith. The radicalization of their view along such anti-Christian lines certainly led Müller to distance himself from the more extreme Darwinians. After some time had passed, the conclusion became obvious. Darwinianism was becoming a dogma, and was in danger of losing its position as a *scientific* approach to natural phenomena.

Max Müller's Theory of Language

All these assumptions regarding the Science of Language led Müller to adopt a very different view of language than the one which was predominant at the time. The origin of Müller's contemporary philosophical mindset was found in the thought of Locke and Hume. While John Locke can be considered the most significant starting point for the new philosophy that developed in eighteenth-century England, it is with David Hume that the philosophical life of England reached a new level of "consciousness": the ultimacy of sense perception. In accepting the Lockean assumption that sense perception is the prime and raw material of reality, Hume made the "senses" the only foundation of human understanding, and thus denied the reality of spiritual substances, equating the world with the crude visible and palpable reality.

By the middle of the nineteenth century, the empirical approach of Locke and Hume had deeply impacted, and to a certain extent transformed, all branches of human knowledge. The rise and prevalence of the historical and comparative methods can, in fact, be traced back to this Lockean and Humean influence. This influence later fully developed into a theory presenting language as solely the product of human development. Müller summarizes that, according to Locke, our human ancestors had communicated by pointing at things and at each other. Language appeared when they acquired other things with which to point and it was then resolved "that a number of artificial linguistic signs should be invented and assigned fixed meaning."[11] Müller personally rejected the conclusions of Locke and Hume. In fact, he considered that the empirical method was mistaken in taking the historical and comparative

---

11. Skuster, "Friedrich Max Mueller," 45.

approaches as ultimate. Thus, the view of language presented by Locke was at the same time simplistic and unrealistic as well as un-historical, in that it pretended to go back "historically" to the very origins of humankind. For Müller, the role and function ascribed to language was instrumental to man's knowledge and progress.

The empirical tradition was combined with two other philosophical trends, Darwinianism and Utilitarianism. As mentioned in chapter 1, Utilitarianism was opposed by many, not least by the Oxford Movement. In fact, even in Tolkien's early career, England lived still in the utilitarian tradition of Bentham and John Stuart Mill. The main implication of Utilitarianism, or Benthamism, was the stress on instrumental knowledge. The value of language was determined by its usefulness to society. The utilitarian reading of Locke and Hume led to the rapid demise of language both as a distinctive characteristic of humankind and as a reliable mode of cognition. Indeed, the theories of Locke and Hume carry the common implication that language, as a mere human product, is not a totally reliable mode of knowledge or mode of expressing knowledge. This, of course, is clear in Hume's radical skepticism. But Utilitarianism was not the only threat to the nature of language. By the mid nineteenth century, this "new" discovery came to have a significant impact on the Science of Language. While the utilitarian tradition answered the question of the role of language, Darwinianism answered the question of its origin.

Even if he distanced himself from the interpretations of Locke and Hume, Müller oddly still relied on the comparative and historical methods. In doing so, Müller distinguished himself in his classification of the Science of Language among the other branches of science. As he pointed out, there were two broad fields of science acknowledged in his time, the physical and the historical sciences. Müller defined physical science as that concerned with the works of God in nature, and historical science as that concerned with the works of man. The common opinion naturally held that language was an historical science, being purely a product of "human art." Müller took the opposite direction and argued that the Science of Language was actually a physical science, that which concerns the works of God. This unusual conclusion contributed to the alienation of Müller from other linguists like the American William Dwight Whitney, the most prominent American linguist of his generation.[12] This conviction was further supported by Müller's Kantian approach to the Science

12. See Whitney, *Max Müller and the Science of Language*.

of Language. Following Kant, Müller argued for a distinction between two spheres, Kant's *noumenal* and *phenomenal* realms. For Müller, the historical and comparative method was valid precisely because it investigated the only things known to us, that is, the "general" data about our world. The Science of Language was relevant precisely in that it studied general concepts formed by mankind. In turn those concepts could be "rediscovered" because man had used particular words after forming those concepts. By going back to the original words and their meanings, the "original" general concepts held by humankind were accessible again to the student of language. This had tremendous application for religion since it could be the door to the original religion held by humankind and to the ultimate sense of the Infinite, the ground for every belief and every soul.

The reason for the distance adopted by some scholars of the Science of Language toward Darwinism did not concern the modality of origination of humankind, nor did it question the possibility of an evolutionary origin of language. Müller, like many of his colleagues, did accept the evolutionary origin of language. Rather, the real issue was the multiplicity of the original geographical starting-point of language. Some radical Darwinists maintained that the beginning of humanity and of language was unique, and that there was only one "beginning." This was called *monogony*. By contrast, other scholars espoused the idea of an evolutionary process, maintaining that "evolution" does not demand monogony but allows for a multiplicity of simultaneous and parallel beginnings. This theory was called *polygony*. Müller believed that Darwin's theory itself allowed for polygony, even asserting the idea to have actually been Darwin's own. In contrast, most Darwinians argued for a monolithic beginning. Müller, following Darwin, could argue for a theory of the common origin of language, which paradoxically did not necessitate a uniform beginning. The strong opposition polygony found among Darwinians led Müller to conclude that Darwinianism was becoming a dogma rather than a scientific approach to natural phenomena. However, the question of how it was still possible to talk about *a single* common origin of language was left unresolved. Müller, after having weighed the available options and their theological implications, opted for a third direction. He found the commonality of language in the human capacity for language.[13]

---

13. Bosch, *Friedrich Max Müller*, 242.

The Break with Darwin

Here, Müller's alignment with the basic theory of evolution breaks up. It seems that Müller's distance from the Darwinians is based on the Kantian influence. According to Ludwig Noiré, what Müller learned from the *Critique of Pure Reason* is that human reason is mostly concerned with representations, not sensations, "and that these representations, arranged, co-ordinated and moulded by concepts, become objects which are the only true content of all our rational thinking, and that our thought therefore assumes an objective character throughout."[14] Skuster concurs with this statement of the Kantian influence on Müller: "As we have seen, Mueller [sic.] proposes a Kantian analysis of sensation, perception, and conception. However, he claims to make an important advance beyond Kant by asserting that a fourth component, naming, is inseparable from sensation, perception, and conception and, therefore, is an elementary component of thought."[15] Darwin, in *The Descent of Man*, had argued for the evolution of man from a lower animal-ancestor.[16] Müller strongly opposed this anthropological conclusion and constantly and consistently opposed Darwin on the question of human development.

While Darwin saw an essential continuity in the evolution from the animal-ancestor to man, Müller saw an essential discontinuity in the exclusive human capacity for language. In a letter sent to Müller, Darwin reaffirmed his conviction about the ancestry of humankind. Admitting to Müller's greater expertise in the field of language, Darwin still maintained that one who is convinced "that man is descended from some lower animal, is almost forced to believe a priori that articulate language has been developed from inarticulate cries; and he is therefore hardly a fair judge of the arguments opposed to his belief."[17] But here we also have a sense of the implications of the Darwinian theory of evolution on the Science of Language. Considering that Darwin implies that the origin of human language was in the "inarticulate cries" of lower animals, we can understand why Müller was so opposed to the Darwinian view of the origin of language. To him, the origin of language, the specificities, the development, and the diversity of human languages were one the greatest evidences for the existence of the Creator of humankind. For

14. Noiré, *The Origin and Philosophy of Language*, 55.
15. Skuster, "Friedrich Max Mueller," 90.
16. See Darwin, *The Descent of Man*.
17. Müller, *Life and Letters of Müller*, 1:478.

Müller, there is clearly a limit to the understanding that human sciences can yield. The "origin" itself is not accessible to the historical student. If language is, as Müller said, our Rubicon, then it surely is one of the most beautiful gifts of the Creator to humankind.

Müller constantly opposed a Darwinian theory but always maintained that language was the irreducible (necessary, non-negotiable) barrier between man and animal.[18] This was still a point of contention early in Tolkien's career, and both the nature and the origin of language were ongoing debates.

Tolkien and His Academic Background

The influence of Max Müller was, despite all his formidable detractors, still very strong at the turn of the twentieth century. Many of the scholars he associated with in the last decades of the nineteenth century could be identified either as Müller's friends or foes. A few came under his direct influence, an influence that would be meaningful for their careers. For example, A. H. Sayce, who was his Deputy Professor between 1876 and 1890—before becoming a famed professor of Assyriology at Oxford—dedicated his 1874 *The Principles of Comparative Philology* to him.[19]

Müller, even in his later years, could also use his influence to shape the future of Oxford's Comparative Philology. Indeed, while he held the Diebold Chair until his death in 1900, he might have been the determining force behind the election of English linguist Joseph Wright, his successor, who occupied the chair from 1901 to 1925. The relationship that developed between Müller and Wright began in 1888 when the German scholar invited Wright to Oxford, where he was appointed lecturer to the Association for the Higher Education of Women. There, among other subjects, he taught Gothic, Anglo-Saxon, and Old German, as well as becoming involved in the publication of his own massive *The English Dialect Dictionary*.

More significantly, Wright was an early influence on Tolkien.[20] Wright's influence is also evidenced in Tolkien's side comment at the end of a letter: "Philology is making a headway here. The proportion of

18. On the difference between Müller and Darwin, see also Bosch, *Friedrich Max Müller*, 77.

19. Sayce, *The Principles of Comparative Philology*.

20. Carpenter, *Biography*, 63–64.

'language' students is very high, and there is no sign of the press-gang!"[21] Of course Tolkien could rejoice with Wright not only as a fellow-philologist, but also because "Professor Jo Wright," as Tolkien once referred to him, had been influential on him.[22] The influence of Wright on Tolkien was mainly that of a philologist and of a lover of the Gothic language. Indeed, Wright's *Primer of the Gothic Language*—a major work published in 1892 that contributed to the rise of Gothic in academic studies—nourished Tolkien's fascination with the Gothic language, a language "that reached the eminence of liturgical use," noted Tolkien to a correspondent in July 1965.[23] As for Wright's 1910 *A Grammar of the Gothic Language*, it opened Tolkien's eyes to "Germanic philology," as he reminisced to his son Christopher in a letter dated early January 1969.

In fact, this publication almost coincided with Tolkien's arrival at Exeter College in 1911. Significantly, about the *Grammar of Gothic* Tolkien wrote much later to W. H. Auden, in 1955: "I discovered in it . . . for the first time the study of a language out of mere love: I mean for the acute aesthetic pleasure derived from a language for his own sake, not only free from being useful but free from even being the 'vehicle of literature.'"[24] This, as we will see in chapter 4, was highly significant for Tolkien. Love of words for words' sake, love of language for language's sake, is characteristic of Tolkien's overall outlook as a philologist and theoretician of language.

Whether or not Wright himself held to that view, what Tolkien found in *Grammar of Gothic* was a contrasting force to the prevalent opposing theories, whether of Müller or of Lang. Rather than trying to determine the use of language, or its place within a hypothetical stage of the development of human thought, Tolkien began to value language in its own right. Language was not the servant of knowledge, nor was it the mere instrument used in rising to a different stage of human consciousness. Language was not even a window into our human origins. Language did not serve any purpose but itself.

Wright's influence was facilitated by his friendship with Tolkien.[25] In a letter dated February 13, 1923, while at Leeds University, Tolkien shows

21. L, 11.

22. L, 22.

23. L, 357.

24. L, 213.

25. Anderson, *The Annotated Hobbit*, 66.

a personal familiarity with the Wrights. The mention of a "disastrous Christmas" and other more personal plights show a relative proximity to his former teacher. His remark that he has "not heard any news of him [Wright] lately" shows that he could have expected so, but only if the two had an ongoing correspondence.[26] In 1925 "old Joe"[27] wrote a letter of recommendation for Tolkien's application for the Rawlinson and Bosworth Chair of Anglo-Saxon. In later days, Tolkien noted that Wright had "proved a good friend and adviser,"[28] and it is without surprise that Tolkien was chosen as one of the executors of Wright's will.

Motivated by a deep love of words and language, Tolkien launched on a successful career as an Oxford professor, after a year teaching at the University of Leeds. His election in 1925 as Rawlinson and Bosworth Professor of Anglo-Saxon, at only thirty-three, was something of a miracle. One of the other candidates was Kenneth Sisam, who published *Fourteenth Century Verse and Prose*, for which Tolkien wrote a glossary.[29] Tolkien's letter to the Electors of the Chair provides a good view of his purpose as a professor of Anglo-Saxon. What first appears in this letter is Tolkien's understanding of the close relation between language (as *words*) and literature. This is revealed in Tolkien's presentation of the scope of his lectures including the history of English, various Old English and Middle English texts, Old and Middle English philology, introductory Germanic philology, Old Icelandic, Gothic, and Medieval Welsh.[30] Apart from the impressive range of Tolkien's learning in language, his mention of "texts" and "verses" as belonging to the same goal is significant. Tolkien argued that language and literature should not be separated. To him, separating language from literature could only contribute to the complete rejection of his field of study, philology, the love of words, from a relevant academic curriculum.

In a way, this is what Tolkien tried to argue for when he wrote to the Electors of the Chair. In his letter of June 27, 1925, he wrote in favor of not separating philology and literature.[31] To Tolkien, philology loses its coloration of dreadful endeavor only when studied along with the

---

26. L, 11.

27. L, 397.

28. L, 397.

29. Tolkien, "A Middle English Vocabulary."

30. L, 12.

31. L, 13.

texts themselves. This point is significant because of Tolkien's constant opposition to the separation of language and literature, even stating in his Valedictory Address: "I detest the segregation or separation of Language and Literature. I do not care which of them you think White."[32] However, such a separation had already begun by the time Tolkien was appointed as a professor at Oxford.

Tolkien scholar Tom Shippey well describes this gradual separation of language and literature in English universities. Shippey is well-placed to comment on this historical development, having held Tolkien's Chair of English Language at Leeds before accepting the Chair of English at the College of Arts and Science in St. Louis. He also followed somewhat the same curriculum as Tolkien, attending Edward VI School in Birmingham. Being himself a philologist, Shippey provides great insights into Tolkien's theory of language, supporting Tolkien's fears that "philology" would almost be crushed in the academy. For him, this results from a failure of philologists to maintain the relevance and connection between the words and "their" literature. Shippey further argues that this is precisely one of the reasons for Tolkien's appeal: that, even though *The Lord of the Rings* is a philological "exercise," its quality as "story" is not the least diminished. It is precisely because it is philological at core that it can be appreciated as a story. And indeed, for Tolkien, philology was inextricably connected to "dragons and goblins and giants and the rescue of princesses and the unexpected luck of widows' sons."[33] The counterpart of Shippey's demonstration is that literary critics have utterly forgotten that the structure and plot-line are not the only significance of a literary text.

As Shippey implies in another article on the Old English chronicling of Anglo-Saxon history, the texts are as much about history as they are about mere literary analysis. As Shippey reminds us, "One of the best things about the Anglo-Saxon Chronicle, as opposed to Orosius or Æthelweard or even the Frankish *Annales Regum*, is the very feeling that it is at least in contact with raw facts which have not been subjected to philosophical or literary boiling."[34] This very conclusion about the relationship between texts and history leads him to conclude in another piece that "Tolkien supplied Fairyland, or Middle-earth, with all the things which traditional fairy tales lacked: history in the form of annals

32. MC, 238.

33. Shippey, *Roots and Branches*, 149.

34. Shippey, "A Missing Army," 52.

and chronicles; geography in the form of maps; languages and linguistic relationships; a guide to non-human species."[35] In this way, Old English historical chronicles and Tolkien's own mythico-historical project are very similar: through the very stories that he wrote, Tolkien argues for the combination of language and literature to create a "new" world with its culture, its language, and its history.

In recent decades, however, a total change of direction has taken place. Shippey gives us an account of this change. Under the "pressure" of postmodern ideals the literary and historical departments of British and American universities have moved towards a more postmodern approach to literary studies. There has been a gradual push, in Shippey's opinion, towards a radical modifying of the curriculum. Anglo-Saxon is utterly forgotten, along with the History of Language and Medieval scholarly research. As a consequence of the "linguistic turn," the universities have opted for a concentration on exclusively modern, literary, and critical studies.[36] Language has become a mere pretext for the application of all sorts of individualistic philosophies to the "sciences" of language. Ironically, while trying to focus on literature, universities have forgotten the word "philology." This reflects fears Tolkien expressed more than fifty years ago. In his "Valedictory Address" to the University of Oxford, Tolkien stated the main problem of the Oxford School of English Language and Literature. The main problem is revealed in its title. "School of English *Language* and *Literature*" transforms what used to be a single unit (language *and* literature) into two sides, *Lit.* and *Lang.*[37] According to Tolkien, the danger of separation was an inevitable sclerosis of both language and literature.[38]

To Tolkien, "language" and "literature" were not two sides. Further, Tolkien argued that the title of the school reflected a wrong idea about what "language" was. Tolkien was especially against this use of language as implied in the title of the school. Such a use implies that there are two kinds of knowledge, one of which is deemed "unliterary" and therefore unnecessary. As a result Old and Middle English along with Anglo-Saxon texts, Tolkien's most cherished literary pieces, were becoming mere "language." This is what Tolkien tried to oppose in the course of his academic

---

35. Shippey, "Rewriting the Core," 272.

36. Shippey, "Rewriting the Core," 144.

37. MC, 230–31.

38. MC, 26.

career. To Tolkien, "School of English" was a sufficient title. "To choose *Literature* would be to indicate, rightly as I think, that the *central* (central if not sole) business of Philology in the Oxford School is the study of the language of *literary* texts."[39] According to Tolkien the title of the school reflects the struggle of philology to impose itself as a legitimate and relevant field of study.

However, this struggle was doomed. "Academia" won and "in the end, and in the hands of duller scholars than Tolkien, the strong verbs and the sound-shifts and the pedantic (but vital) details lost contact with the poems and the romances and the myths and the stories, to the detriment of both sides of the subject."[40] This is part of the "long defeat" suffered by Tolkien in the course of his life, the destruction of the internal working and meaning of words. In 1925, Tolkien stated his purpose in the following way:

> If elected to the Rawlison and Bosworth Chair I should endeavour to make productive use of the opportunities which it offers for research; to advance, to the best of my ability, the growing neighbourliness of linguistic and literary studies, which can never be enemies except by misunderstanding or without loss to both; and to continue in a wider and more fertile field the encouragement of philological enthusiasm among the young.[41]

In the end Tolkien was never able to fulfill such a goal. This is the conclusion of Shippey who forcefully argues that Tolkien, even though he ultimately failed in this academic project, was the one man fit for the task: "It may be said that one person perhaps had the chance, as he certainly had the talent, to reverse the trend and put Anglo-Saxondom in an imaginatively attractive setting, and that was J. R. R. Tolkien."[42] The only success he had is to be found in his own mythology and invented languages. But even Tolkien's failure serves to illuminate his place in the debates of his times. If he did not directly interact with some of his most august contemporaries, he did nonetheless interact with the main theories of his day. Most of his academic disagreements he seems to have kept to himself, though it is possible to discern some important areas of disagreement with significant figures such as Müller.

39. MC, 3.
40. Shippey, *Roots and Branches*, 144.
41. L, 13.
42. Shippey, "The Undeveloped Image," 234.

If Tolkien found himself on opposites lines than Müller, it is because of his own theories about language, but also because he rejected the
materialism prevalent in many contemporary theories of language. This
materialism was central to the evolutionary theories. Indeed, "the idea of
social and historical 'evolution', adapted metaphorically from Darwinian
biology, had made a deep impression on two generations of historical
scholars but seemed to them fatally compromised by its materialistic
premises and deterministic implications."[43] Thus, in questioning the idea
that the origin and significance of language was dependent on materialistic progress, Tolkien shared the concerns of many others, including one
with whom he shared much of his theological vision, as already indicated
in the previous chapter: Christopher Dawson. Even though he was not
working in the field of language, as Tolkien or Müller, Dawson was well
aware of the debates surrounding the origins and meanings of language
and myth as well as the theological implications that, in time, would necessarily emerge.

To Dawson the, at times incredible, optimism of the Victorians
should be no surprise "since the amazing social and material changes
that they witnessed seemed to afford a tangible proof of the theory of
progress, and to mark the beginning of a new era in the history of humanity." Despite Victorian evidences of progress, Dawson concluded by
noting that "these hopes have not been fulfilled, and the last fifty years
have seen a sharp reaction from the triumphant optimism of the earlier
period."[44] As far as language and mythology are concerned, Dawson's
anti-materialistic criticism would resonate with Tolkien's own concerns
about the nature of language, as we will see in the coming chapters. The
integrity, value, role, and development of language could not make sense
on an evolutionary basis, but only if these were an integrative part of the
human nature, of the "human mind." And, as Tolkien said in "On Fairy
Stories": "To ask what is the origin of stories (however qualified), is to ask
what is the origin of language and of the mind."

Here we can take Dawson's conclusion as also Tolkien's: "Modern
writers on anthropology and primitive thought have tended to assume
that religion is a secondary phenomenon and that man's earliest attitude
to reality was a kind of empirical materialism."[45] In an analogical man-

43. Allitt, *Catholic Converts*, 239.

44. Dawson, *Progress and Religion*, 208.

45. Dawson, *Progress and Religion*, 80.

ner, Tolkien rejected the theories that associated language to a secondary or accidental phenomenon. Language was essential to man. Here, we must resist the temptation of thinking that this conclusion was made on purely theological ground. Tolkien made this conclusion first and foremost because of his academic expertise, not because of his theological Thomist standpoint. We should well remember that Tolkien was first an academician, expert in his field, and reluctant to make explicit theological comments.

3

The Nature of Words

IF THE ACADEMIC CONTEXT of the early twentieth-century study of language is crucial to the understanding of Tolkien, it is not, however, sufficient for understanding what Tolkien had to say about the issues at hand. For a more specific description of Tolkien's distinctive theory of language, we must consider how Tolkien approached the question of the *nature* of words and language. This is probably among the two most crucial questions we have to deal with in order to come to terms with a Tolkienian theory of fantasy. In the previous chapter, we offered a brief overview of the general historical academic context that preceded Tolkien, which serves as a necessary background to our further discussions. In fact, it would be difficult to grasp the significance of Tolkien's perspective on language and words if not for this academic background. However, Tolkien made relatively few comments about his predecessors. In fact, he does not often explicitly refer to scholars such as Max Müller or Andrew Lang—except in a few key places in *On Fairy Stories*. To understand the nature of Tolkien's debate with his great academic forebears, we will have to turn to other writers with whom he shared a close proximity of thought.

Tolkien was a philologist, and as such words were his central, but not only, interest. Tolkien tackled several aspects of philology in his career, but two stand out: the nature of words and their beauty. To look into Tolkien's investigation into the nature of words is to integrate two aspects of what a word is, and one main influence on his theory. As to the former, the two aspects of words that Tolkien came to integrate were their meaning and their beauty. As to the latter, the influence is clearly that of Owen Barfield, and understanding his influence is necessary before we can move to evaluate Tolkien's view on the meaning and beauty of words.

Owen Barfield (1898–1997) was certainly the least known of the Inklings, the informal group gathered around the personality of C. S. Lewis. This is probably still true. Born in London of a family of lawyers, Barfield was educated successively at Highgate School (where T. S. Eliot would later teach) and then at Wadham College, Oxford, where in 1920 he earned a first-class degree in English language and literature, which led him to a writing career—and where he met C. S. Lewis. During their early friendship, as Barfield was already formulating his own concepts of "semantic unity" and "original participation," Lewis struggled to understand some of his friend's more obscure philosophical formulations. In a letter dated March 28, 1933, he shared his "inability" to understand some of Barfield's anthroposophical rendering of Coleridge.[1] This partly explains why Barfield's influence is difficult to describe, so marked were his views of the history of ideas, of literature, and of the "evolution of consciousness." Barfield met Lewis while the latter was still in his atheist period. Soon they became close friends, and Barfield even became Lewis's solicitor. Lewis considered him "wisest and best of my unofficial teachers,"[2] even though they engaged in a debate later known as their "Great War."[3]

Barfield was also a great influence on T. S. Eliot, and, of course, on J. R. R. Tolkien. But Barfield was not known only for his philosophical literary readings. He was also the author of the first fantasy book published by an Inkling, in 1925. In fact, in June 1936, Lewis wrote Barfield: "I lent *The Silver Trumpet* to Tolkien and hear that it is the greatest success among his children that they have ever known."[4] Tolkien's *Lord of the Rings*, however, was not quite successful with Barfield who never became an enthusiast.

Importantly, Barfield was a student of anthroposophy, a philosophy of human consciousness founded by Austrian thinker Rudolph Steiner. Early in his career, possibly while still a student, Barfield discovered the writings

1. Lewis, *Collected Letters*, 2:106.
2. Lewis's masterful *The Allegory of Love* was dedicated to Barfield.
3. Feinendegen and Smilde, "The 'Great War.'"
4. Lewis, *Collected Letters*, 2:198.

of Steiner. For him, the immediate consequence was a new literary experience, which he described as a rapid increase in the "intensity" with which he experienced poetry.[5] Moreover, a second consequence was that his attention shifted from systematic explanations to more poetic, imaginative, and creative ones. The teachings of Steiner came to have great implications for Barfield's theory of language and artistic creation. Even though displaying more clearly the influence of anthroposophy on Barfield would lead to fascinating conclusions, it is not in the purview of our study here.

In the context of his times, Barfield is answering the challenges of certain theories of the Science of Language. In fact, he opposed all theories that accepted the main materialistic premises of his day. According to him, one of the central issue was discerning the nature and function of language. In fact, in Barfield's view, many scholars of linguistics committed the same fundamental error of overlooking one important fact about language: that we use it for two different purposes. First, we use language as a mode of communication between individuals. In that capacity, language is a means to "request and supply information necessary to life." Second, we use language "as Speech in the true sense, the medium in which, as unique persons who think in the first and second person singular, we gratuitously disclose ourselves to each other and share our experiences.[6] Language is word-communication and personal revelation. Barfield maintained that language served a greater purpose than mere communication between human beings.

In his view of language Barfield directly confronted the received theories of his day. One of these, slowly reaching the status of consensus, was that the first words of man were in fact inarticulate cries, not dissimilar to that of monkeys. This was of course founded on an evolutionary approach to the origin of man and of language. These words later developed into more complex and structured languages. Barfield saw all of these theories as leading to the dissociation of meaning, word, and perception so essential to his own vision. Against this background we can turn to Barfield's philological manifesto, *Poetic Diction*.

5. Barfield, *Romanticism Comes of Age*, 9.
6. Auden, Foreword, 7.

Barfield's Anthroposophical *Poetic Diction*

In 1928, Barfield published his most influential book, *Poetic Diction*. The complete title is indicative of the whole purpose of the work. *Poetic Diction* is a "Study in Meaning." Interestingly, Barfield did not title it a study "of" but "in" meaning, pointing to the real center of the book being "meaning" itself, turning *Poetic Diction* into a defense of poetry as a means of cognition.[7] As Tolkien scholar Verlyn Flieger has said, Barfield's theory is one of *knowledge*, not merely one of poetry or of poetic diction.[8] Barfield's starting point in his construction of poetry as a means of knowledge was the Romantic tradition, and more precisely, the philosophy of Samuel Taylor Coleridge. In the foreword to *Orpheus* Barfield explains that Coleridge was right in concluding that the absence, or "funeral," of imagination was merely "superficial knowledge."[9]

This, for Barfield, justified the possibility of a theory of poetry as cognition. Barfield then commented on Coleridge's distinction between Primary and Secondary Imagination. Coleridge, he says, defined Primary Imagination as the kind performed by every man. It is the imagination that "makes things." Secondary Imagination, on the other hand, goes one step further. It represents a higher stage of "creativity," in which the imagination is at one with all the acts of perception. Only then, when the percepts and the "imagined" merge, is meaning created: the Secondary Imagination "makes meaning." In fact, in his study on Coleridge Barfield argues that the imagination unites the whole of human experience. As such, imagination—especially secondary imagination—properly becomes the means to "make" meaning.[10] Barfield does not oppose the making of "things" with the making of "meaning," but opposes the absence of meaning with the presence of meaning. Secondary Imagination does not negate the making of things (Primary Imagination) but adds "meaning" to it. It is significant that Barfield puts here the emphasis not so much on the *contrast* between Primary and Secondary Imagination, but on the *essential nature* of the latter, which is the creation of meaning. The point is not that one is a "better" or more "original" imagination. This would be too simplistic. The point is rather that one form of imagination properly brings about new meaning.

7. Lang, *Letters on Literature*, 3.

8. Flieger, *Splintered Light*, 36.

9. Barfield, *Orpheus*, 9; italics mine.

10. See Barfield, *What Coleridge Thought*, 77–78, 112–13.

While it is by no means Barfield's only significant study, *Poetic Diction* stands out as the most influential. In particular, this book announces Barfield's more articulate presentation of anthroposophy in his later works.[11] In fact, the themes of the "evolution of consciousness" and of "participation" serve to explain the philosophical significance of *Poetic Diction*. The starting point of Barfield's main philosophical concept is what he labels "participation." Barfield defined this central notion in different ways, the simplest of which is that participation is experiencing the world in *immediacy*.[12] He also said that he "occasionally used the word 'participation' to try and indicate a predominantly perceptual relation between observer and observed, between man and nature, and one which is nearer to unity than to dichotomy."[13] The essential characteristic of "participation" is its awareness of the wholeness and the interconnection of that which exists. It sees, apprehends, and gives meaning to the world *in its wholeness*. Barfield gave an example of what participation is by saying that, in contrast, non-participative consciousness is a radical "either, or." A good example, he continued, was contemporary biblical scholarship considering the Old and New Testaments as being either historical records or symbolical representations. With biblical scholarship locked up in this non-participative mindset, many theologians could only consider the pre-figuring of the New Testament in the Old Testament as "pure moonshine."[14]

By contrast, Barfield's theory of the nature and meaning of poetry and words presented in *Poetic Diction* is an early example of his integration of the concept of participation to the one of the "evolution of consciousness." The importance of poetry for Barfield, as for the other Inklings, should be a subject for another study. However, two points need to be highlighted. First, poetry, as a means of knowledge, leads to true meaning. In its turn, true meaning is the path to the last stage of the evolution of consciousness. The closing lines of Barfield's *Orpheus* are thus significant (lines 110–18):

Second Chorus.
He shall ascend Parnassus awake and find his soul:

11. See the articles by Barfield, "Philology and the Incarnation" and "Introducing Rudolf Steiner."

12. Barfield, *Saving the Appearances*, 75.

13. Barfield, *History, Guilt, and Habit*, 26.

14. Barfield, *Saving the Appearances*, 151.

Proteus shall work unsleeping for ever, and forms shall flow
As the meanings of words a poet has mastered. It shall be so
That Zeus shall abandon to Cronos the antique starry crown,
And softly out of Olympus the high gods shall come down
Shedding ambrosial fragrance in clouds that for ever abide,
And earth shall be covered with blushes and make herself sweet as a bride.
And her light shall be liquid as honey, her air taste good like bread
In the mouths of them that dwell upon earth, and all shall be fed.[15]

We see here the fulfillment of man's "evolution of consciousness" in the final parallel between the "high gods" coming down and the bliss befalling those who "dwell upon earth." It is this "coming together" which best represents the culmination of man's destiny. And this closeness, this "participation," comes through the "world-making" of the poet, the creation of, so to speak, "consciousness-meaning."

Second, to see the connection Barfield establishes between words and the concepts of participation and evolution of consciousness, it is necessary to realize that there are two kinds of participation. Barfield labels them "original" and "final" participation. In Barfield's theory, "original participation" designates the original sense man had of the whole cosmos.[16] Flieger has repeatedly argued that Tolkien's account of the awakening of the Elves is an example of this original cosmos-consciousness. Tolkien tells of the Maiar Oromë finding at last the First Children of Ilúvatar, and proclaiming the coming of those long-awaited to the cry of *I Eldar tulier*—"the Eldar have come!"[17] Of the awakening of the Elves on the shores of Lake Cuiviénen, Tolkien writes that the Elves were awakened to a world where they would give name to their perceptions, and that was to them the beginning of language.[18]

And so with language, history begins, and along with it, Tolkien's "long defeat."[19] In this beginning of language, reality and perception come together for those who "gaze in wonder at the stars."[20] *Ele!*, Behold!, is the first Elvish utterance to echo throughout Middle-earth.[21] With such an exclamation, the background is set for the close relationship between Tolkien

15. Barfield, *Orpheus*, 112.
16. Flieger, *Splintered Light*, 38.
17. HoME, I:114.
18. S, 49.
19. L, 255.
20. HoME, I:115.
21. "Appendix: Elements in Quenya and Sindarin Names," in S, 358.

and Barfield. In this one word, *Ele!*, lies the unity of reality and perception, but also of language. Tolkien's Elvish insight recalls Barfield's own example about the Greek word *pneuma* and the Latin *spiritus*. The range of meaning conveyed by these words, "wind," "breath," and also "spirit," were once perceived as one and the same phenomenon.[22] Moreover, Barfield notes that in the King James translation of the third chapter of the Gospel according to John, *pneuma* is either rendered as "spirit" or "wind," thus indicating that for John's original hearers the two were one and the same. In a very similar manner then, Elven language indeed begins with perception, as Flieger has argued, thus living out Barfield's "original participation."[23]

Flieger has rightly asserted that the Elves are the embodiment of this primordial unity of mind and nature, one in which there was absolutely no separation between "inner" and "outer" worlds. At that point in history, nature was as subjective and inward as we are. Man lived a participative life within the rest of the cosmos. Consequently, his life was holistic, and man's participation with the cosmos included an evolution of consciousness. Indeed, to Barfield, man's history is that of the evolution of consciousness from that of original participation to final participation. As Barfield comments about *Unancestral Voice*'s principal character: "In this light it seemed proper, it seemed inevitable, to Burgeon to regard human history—with all its numberless variations on the central theme—as a single process, which could properly be called the transformation of human consciousness."[24] In the same manner, Barfield characterized this original participative life as an un-figurative one, contrasting it with the Darwinian theory he considered to be deeply mistaken about the origin and nature of language. Indeed, Barfield challenges in no uncertain terms the one that has learned "half-consciously" about Darwinian man. If we revise what we have learned, we are presented "with quite a different image of the consciousness of primitive man, as it actually must have been. [We] come instead to a kind of consciousness that was figurative through and through; a kind of consciousness for which it was impossible to perceive *un*figuratively."[25] For Barfield, "primitive man" displayed this kind of consciousness.

22. Flieger, *Splintered Light*, 38.

23. Flieger, *Splintered Light*, 74.

24. Barfield, *Unancestral Voice*, 70. It is interesting to note that the name of this character is Burgeon, referring certainly to Goethe's theory of organic development.

25. Barfield, *History, Guilt, and Habit*, 46.

In this early stage, to perceive figuratively meant not perceiving man's surrounding phenomena as only material but also seeing the immaterial. The fundamental difference between the thinking of the "primitives" and ours does not lie merely in the *thinking* itself, but in the objects thought, the *phenomena*. Not only do we think differently than the "primitives," but the phenomena, or collective representations, themselves are different. As Barfield concluded, man still participates in the phenomena but needs to recover the awareness of this participation. Consequently he continued: "I myself have occasionally used the word 'participation' to try and indicate a predominantly perceptual relation between observer and observed, between man and nature, and one which is nearer to unity than to dichotomy."[26]

This shows that Barfield entertained a double attitude towards "original participation." On one hand, Barfield affirms that original participation is not meant to be absolute or eternal. Consistent with the anthroposophical view of man's evolution, he argues that original participation has been eliminated in the process of the evolution of consciousness. But on the other hand, this does not mean that participation is eliminated altogether. If Barfield does not argue for a return to original participation, he still maintains the necessity for the concept of participation. Therefore, to maintain the necessity of another form of participation, Barfield posits the coming of "final participation," defined as "a self conscious rapport with the whole phenomenal world."[27] Final participation is the consciousness of original participation raised from embryonic potentiality to full actuality.

The point is that, for Barfield, the accent is on the term *participation*, and not on the term "original." What humankind needs to regain is *participation*, and more importantly our awareness of it. Maybe we can even talk of a double evolution, that of our "participation" and of our awareness of this participation. In this case, there would be an "evolution of participation" parallel to the "evolution of consciousness." The difference between original and final participation is described in the following way: "Original participation fires the heart from a source outside itself; the images enliven the heart. But in final participation—since the death and resurrection—the heart is fired from within by the Christ; and

---

26. Barfield, *History, Guilt, and Habit*, 26.
27. Barfield, "Introducing Rudolf Steiner," 13.

it is for the heart to enliven the images."[28] The evolution of participation reflects man's participative life, which is in the process of reaching the new stage of the evolution of human consciousness.

One of the results of a participative life is the connection between word and things. In other words, a life of participation is itself the connection between the representations we all share and our collective life, what Barfield calls "collective representations." This is precisely where the importance of *Poetic Diction* lies. As noted before, this study is both a theory of cognition and a theory of man's evolution from one stage of consciousness to another. When *Poetic Diction* is read along with his anthroposophical exposition, we realize that for Barfield the importance of language lies in what it *does* for the evolution of consciousness. "Once the fact of participation is granted," he concluded once, "the connection between words and things must, we have seen, be admitted to be at any time a very much closer one than the last two or three centuries have assumed."[29] Words are a means for man's achievement of his fullest participative life. As Flieger concludes, the first Elven word carries in itself the primal unity of meaning and perception that Barfield insists words must once have had.[30]

Barfield's theory of language as mode of cognition, his concept of the poet as "world-maker," all influenced Tolkien. But the question remains, how deep was this influence? Indeed, we have seen that Barfield's theory is based on a very specific and peculiar understanding of the history of humankind. It is probably impossible to separate Barfield's theory from his adherence to anthroposophy. If the poet is the world-maker and restorer of meaning leading mankind to the final stage of evolution-consciousness, it is fitting to conclude with a piece of Barfield's poetry:

> Man's life should move, a shapely whole,
> From leaf to flower and fruit.
> Love, music, nature led my soul
> The long Romantic route. . . .
> And drives it headlong through the mind—
> Fast pouring I perceive
> Through my old nursery window-blind,
> The eyelashes of Eve.[31]

28. Barfield, "Introducing Rudolf Steiner," 172.
29. Barfield, "Introducing Rudolf Steiner," 84.
30. Flieger, *Splintered Light*, 74.
31. Barfield, "Enlightenment," 47–48.

Tolkien the Philologist

For his whole career, Tolkien was a student of words. He also lectured on Middle-English literature. But his main scholarly focus was on words, on their nature, meaning, and role in literature. Tolkien was a true philologist, interested by everything a word was. To see the relevance of the philologist Tolkien, it is best to contrast him, once again, with his "colleague" and friend, Owen Barfield. Tolkien seems to have seen the nature of philology as a double one: you could study philology in a purely formal way (studying language), but also for aesthetic reasons (the love of language). Tolkien united both. It is important to notice that Tolkien does not draw a radical line between these two philological interests and does not require philologists to choose between them.

The difference between these two aspects is not one of nature, but of emphasis. One can maintain a unity between the aesthetic and functional aspects of words, even if it is certain that some philologists were not really concerned about the "aesthetics" of words. To say that Barfield was one of those might be an overstatement, but it is undeniable that he focused his attention on one functional aspect of language, that of being a vehicle for meaning. As for Tolkien, he delighted in "ancient" words. For Barfield this would have been almost nonsensical since if there were delight in words, it would come from their meaning and the creation of new meaning. For Barfield, the significance of language lay in its importance for the history of consciousness, but for Tolkien the significance of language lay in the words themselves.

Barfield and Tolkien also considered the task of philology to be somewhat different. Regarding Tolkien's view of the task of philology, we must turn to his essay "Chaucer as a Philologist," which serves as his philological manifesto.[32] Indeed, it is more than a mere essay on Chaucer; Flieger affirms that it states Tolkien's view of philology as a discipline of study. Thus, significantly for Tolkien philology was an attempt to "recover the detail" and to "recapture an idea of what it sounded like, to make certain what it meant."[33] For Tolkien words were a means of recovering "lost riches," through the study of their meaning. Philology almost functions as a linguistic time-machine, taking us back to an original perception of the world through words. As Tolkien said in his essay, "in getting back Chaucer's original intent, we experience as fully as we can Chaucer's

32. Tolkien, "Chaucer as a Philologist," 1–70.
33. Quoted in Flieger, *Splintered Light*, 6.

meaning as understood by Chaucer's audience in Chaucer's time."[34] Here
we can discern a slight difference between Tolkien and Barfield.

For Barfield also philology was concerned with meaning, but as a
way to look forward to create meaning, while for Tolkien it was a way to
look backward to recover meaning. Without overemphasizing this difference, there is contrast between the *recovery* and the *re-creation* of meaning. The nature of these goals leads to the question of whether philology
can achieve either. Tolkien argues that the original meaning of words
always remains foreign to us. If someone had asked him if he thought
that the original meaning of words could be regained, his answer would
certainly have been that "there is always a lost part."[35] This finds an echo
in Tolkien's own invented languages. Christopher Tolkien reports that

> there were many routes by which a name might have evolved,
> and the whole etymological system was like a kaleidoscope, for
> a decision in one place was likely to set up disturbing ripples
> in etymological relations among quite distinct groups of words.
> Moreover, complexity was (as it were) built in, for the very na-
> ture of the "bases" set words on phonetic collision courses from
> their origin.[36]

This remark is surprising coming from a philologist of such a quality as
Tolkien. One might have rather expected him to argue for the possibility
of regaining original meaning. Certainly that was part of the attraction of
philology for Tolkien.

For Tolkien then, *philology* was strictly speaking the *love* of words,
a love of all that a word is: sound, spelling, beauty, rhythm, and of course
meaning. Words are beautiful and words are *historical*. Words are historical in the sense that a great part of the word-forms come to us through
history and point back at a specific historical setting. Once again we find
this also embodied in Tolkien's invented languages. Christopher Tolkien comments again that the *Etymologies*, a glossary written by Tolkien
and reproduced in *The Lost Road*, "reflects the linguistic situation in
Beleriand envisaged in the *Lhammas* (see especially the third version,
Lammasethen, p. 194), with Noldorin fully preserved as the language of
the Exiles."[37] Tolkien insists that we cannot know the meaning of words

34. Flieger, *Splintered Light*, 6.

35. L, 268.

36. HoME, V:343.

37. HoME, V:346. Christopher Tolkien also mentions that "in principle" every element in language, whether "real" or invented, is historically explicable. HoME, V:341.

without understanding their historical change.[38] Words are historically meaningful, and their change reflects the change and development in history. In *The Lord of the Rings*, it is probably Treebeard the Ent who represents most closely this Tolkienian view. When Merry and Pippin inquired about his name, Treebeard replied that giving his name would give out his own story.[39]

Some scholars have argued that in Treebeard's view—and so in Tolkien's—words *carry* magic, that is, power, and that it is the distinctive element in Tolkien's view of language. On this assumption, names should be cautiously revealed; hence Treebeard's warning to the hobbits about revealing their own names.[40] However, if we hold to Tolkien's view regarding the unity of words and meaning, there is no need for a magical explanation. The only magic we see in names is the personal story they carry. Names are both personal and historical, so to speak. In a word, in a language is found all the history of a people, of a world. In word and language we have history, meaning, and beauty all fused. For words carry more than a story, they can also carry and serve as the vehicle for feelings, as in the case of the orc-language: "There were many voices round about, and though orc-speech sounded at all times full of hate and anger, it seemed plain that something like a quarrel had begun, and was getting hotter."[41]

Further, even if meaning evolves and can become "unrecognizable" in the course of time, something of the original meaning is retained in the sound-word—as contrasted with the spelled-word. How this theory is close to Tolkien or representative of his own effort to relate meaning, words, aesthetics, and change in etymology is hard to evaluate. For Tolkien, the nature of words is closely connected to their meaning, which is internal to each individual word. In fact, we can affirm that for Tolkien they are inseparable: a word contains meaning and an aesthetic quality. As we have seen, Tolkien's love for words is his first and foremost motivation in his view of the nature of words, and that is where the difference with Barfield lies. In essence, this difference is that while Barfield's theory is one of meaning, Tolkien's is one of *words*. For Barfield, language mostly serves a purpose and he provides a defense of words and poetry for the sake of man's "participative life."

38. L, 268.
39. LoTR, II.3.iv, 454.
40. LoTR, II.3.iv, 454.
41. LoTR, II.3.iii, 435.

Thus, while Tolkien followed Barfield on main issues, he also entertained a significant disagreement. This, however, did not negate the attraction *Poetic Diction* had for Tolkien. Barfield presented a theory of poetry that was a response to the utilitarian and rationalistic philosophy of his time. Further, he defended the view that the poetic and imaginative use of words enhanced their meanings. Barfield also presented a theory of the intrinsic cognitive value of poetry, which gave poetry a renewed life and importance, as more than a literary genre. For Barfield poetry enhanced the words' meanings, thus revealing hidden aspects of reality.[42] The reality of the working of words and poetry points to the philosophical significance of Barfield's *Poetic Diction*.

Thus, while Tolkien was clearly deeply influenced by Barfield's theory of language, he nonetheless went against Barfield in providing a defense of *words as words*, not merely of words as "consciousness." More generally, Tolkien stood with Barfield in his rejection of a purely human and utilitarian theory of words. Words are more than an instrument and should be considered in themselves, according to their origin, meaning, and change. However, as Kirstin Johnson rightly argues, "there were aspects of Barfield's argument with which Tolkien and Lewis would never agree, but his 'theory of how words originally embodied an ancient, unified perception' inspired them both."[43] This had important implications for what Tolkien thought to be the origins of words and language. Considering Tolkien in relation to his fellow Inkling Lewis, Johnson concludes that "not only the abstract thoughts of man but also his imaginative inventions must originate with God, and must in consequence reflect something of original truth."[44]

The Origin of Language

Not much has been written about Tolkien's view on the origins of human language, and Tolkien himself did not spend much time commenting on this subject. However, one significant passage is contained in a letter addressed to English poet W. H. Auden, who had corresponded with Tolkien regarding the writing of *The Lord of the Rings*. Carpenter reports that Auden specifically asked Tolkien if he could "supply a few

42. See the introduction to *Romanticism Comes of Age*, by Barfield, 10.

43. Johnson, "Tolkien's Mythopoesis," 42.

44. Johnson, "Tolkien's Mythopoesis," 30.

'human touches' in the form of information about how the book came to be written."[45] Tolkien wrote, "To turn, if I may, to the 'Human Touches' and the matter of when I started. That is rather like asking of Man when language started. It was an inevitable, though conditionable, evolvement of the birth-given."[46] Significant here is his reference to "birth-given." To Tolkien, it was not only the capacity for language that was a birth-given, as Müller had argued, but also the particular sounds of words and language, what Tolkien calls the "sensibility to linguistic pattern." In his view, our artistic direction, even our emotional response to "linguistic aesthetic," is essentially birth-given. In a way, even a "created" story was originally part of us.

The notion of birth-given can seem rather strange, but his point is simple enough. Language and words are not just the fruit of a "human art," or the product of human evolution. They have another origin, which can be located in the creative act—in *God*'s creative act. Given Tolkien's Catholic faith, it is possible to assume that he believed everything that is *essentially* part of us is God-given. This also would fit well into an overall Thomist account, even though the discussion of the origin of human language is not systematic in Thomas. In many ways, such systematic treatment of the origin of language could only lead to a relative puzzlement. It was after all, at least to Müller, Barfield, and Tolkien, difficult to fit language into the purely natural causality of the world.[47] All our abilities, capacities, creative possibilities are part of what God implanted in us as part of our human nature; "that is why Aquinas thinks that to exercise our capacity for using language, our intelligence cannot be a bodily material process, but transcends materiality."[48]

Moreover, the part of Tolkien's answer that reads "inevitable, though conditionable, evolvement" can be seen as the reflection of Roman Catholic belief regarding free will. The relation between the inevitable and "conditionable" elements is parallel to the relation between the divine and human elements in the origin of language. This dilemma is resolved in and through God himself, the Divine Author of language and "Writer

45. L, 211.
46. L, 212.
47. McCabe, *On Aquinas*, 119.
48. McCabe, *On Aquinas*, 121.

of the Story."[49] God is, according to Tolkien, the "supreme Artist and the Author of Reality."[50]

This concept is not a new one and had notably been used by Max Müller indicating a possible relationship between Tolkien and Müller on the issue of the origin of language. As difficult as this relation is to establish, their common reference to Icelandic priest and scholar Tómas Sæmundsson is significant. Sæmundsson was a major figure in the Icelandic independence movement, and his importance to Iceland's renewed national identity lay in his emphasis on the necessity of nurturing Christian virtues in Iceland. Sæmundsson also argued that urbanization was a danger to Iceland's morality and to the development of Christian virtues in his country. But Sæmundsson was also interested in the value and importance of language. According to Tolkien and Müller, the Icelandic scholar argued that language is the barrier between man and beast, that words can be studied for words' sake and that they provide further understanding of a people. The first point has been regularly defended by Müller, who also refers positively to Sæmundsson's argument.

Tolkien also made a reference to Sæmundsson, in his essay "English and Welsh," but not exactly in the same way that Müller does. After quoting the original "Málin eru höfuðeinkenni þjóðanna," Tolkien explained that a people really comes into being through its language. It is the distinctive feature of any people.[51] Here, Tolkien underlines the importance of language for the formation of a people, a culture, and a history, which has implications for the difference between man and beast. If language is necessary to the formation of a particular human culture and "people," for Tolkien it is a prerequisite that language is the "distinguishing mark" between man and beast. Therefore, language cannot be merely a human creation but is part of *created* human nature itself.

To the question of the origin of language, it seemed that Müller saw only two main alternatives: that language was either of human or of divine origin. For many of his contemporaries and for many scholars devoted to Darwinism, language was of purely human origin. On the other hand, other theologians still held to the strictly divine origin of language. However, Müller found both these options simplistic. On the one hand, Müller could not subscribe to the view that presented language

49. L, 252.

50. L, 101.

51. MC, 166.

as purely the work of the human mind. On the other hand, neither could he follow other Christian scholars in maintaining the purely divine origin of human language. Müller was cautious to defend the divine element in human language, but definitely distanced himself from those theologians who held to a radical and extreme version of the divine origin of language. These theologians he humorously described as supposing the Deity "to have compiled a dictionary and grammar in order to teach them to the first man as a schoolmaster teaches the deaf and dumb."[52] Müller recounted that for some it is as if God himself taught a specific language to Adam, from which developed all human languages. This was one of the bases for the traditional theory that the Hebrew language was the oldest and original one, the source of all human languages. Müller rejected the view that the Hebrew language was the originating one, and argued instead that such an honor had to be awarded to Sanskrit.[53]

In doing so, Müller explicitly rejected the theory of the existence of a divine language and the identification of Hebrew as the original human language—thus following in the footsteps of Gottfried Leibniz, one of the first to argue scientifically against the traditional and accepted position. Another point is worth mentioning. It has already been seen that Tolkien opposed Müller's view on the relation between language and myth. One possible connection between Tolkien and Müller is the answer given to the dilemma of divine or human origin of language. No serious scholar in the Science of Language would have denied the human element in the origin of language.

As we have seen, Müller had supported this very point and had provided a theory of "double origin," emphasizing that it is the *capacity* for language that was a birth-given, and not words themselves. This point is in essence a theological one probably based on Christian natural theology so prevalent since the publications of Bishop Joseph Butler and William Paley. Of course, the influence of Butler and Paley on Müller or Tolkien is difficult to map out. There is little chance of finding hard evidence to support such an influence. However, it is important to keep in mind that Butler and Paley remained influential figures in English religious and intellectual life well into the end of the nineteenth century and that both Anglicanism and English Roman Catholicism had been influenced by these two theologians. Moreover, the relative proximity of Lutheran and

---

52. Müller, *Lectures on the Science of Language*, 351.

53. Müller, *Lectures on the Science of Language*, 144.

Catholic views on natural revelation in the nineteenth century supports such a judgment. If this point is correct, it is possible to argue that Müller's position could have been of real interest to Tolkien.

To explain the divine origin of human language, Müller relied on the notion of innate, or creaturely, capacities characteristic of humankind, among which he counted language. We could summarize Müller's conclusion by saying that there is a difference between the origins of particular languages and the origin of language *per se*. Particular languages, such as Greek, Hebrew, or French, were the product of human history and "art." Language itself, as a quasi-abstract and elusive notion, is a capacity, a God-given one. Müller's theory of the double origin of language might well have found echoes in Tolkien's own theological tradition.

In arguing so, Tolkien displays a subtle theological standpoint. From his own love and expertise in language, Tolkien was convinced that language was of the nature of man. His interaction with Barfield led him to go further in his own view of language, and Barfield indeed served as a catalyst for Tolkien's defense of words and language, not for a hypothetical evolution of consciousness, but for themselves. In doing so, Tolkien reaches the *implicit* conclusion that language reflected the divine creative act and that humankind bears within itself the mark of God the Creator.

4

The Aesthetics of Words

TOLKIEN'S VIEW ON THE nature of words was further developed through his stress on their internal beauty. Tolkien's theory of words, for words' sake, integrated several important concepts, among which was a stress on their "aesthetic" nature. In his lecture "English and Welsh," Tolkien made this very point, embodying in an academic article his theory of the sound-aesthetic. Agreeing with Icelandic scholar Sjéra Tómas Sæmundsson, Tolkien said that the Welsh was cultivated for itself, because it was the language of the people. That is because the language is loved: it is their own.[1] Tolkien pursued throughout his life the love of language. His imaginative works can actually be seen in this light. In this chapter, we will explore Tolkien's aesthetics of words under four main headings. First, if Tolkien's theory is about aesthetics it has to do essentially with the beauty of words. Through their sound and beauty words in their turn led Tolkien to invent the background stories that serve to explain the rise of the two Elven languages, Quenya and Sindarin. This linguistic invention of stories will be the second focus of this chapter. But if stories grew out of, and were nourished by, Tolkien's love of language, they also posed a serious problem for this lover of words. This problem,

---

1. MC, 166. Words for their own sake are the center of Tolkien's argument. In "A Secret Vice," Tolkien used expressions like "phonetic pleasure" or "word-music" to refer to the same point. MC, 218.

and our third topic, is translation. Finally, we will ask how we can experience or apprehend the beauty of words and language. In exploring
this question, we will go to Tolkien via the influence and theory of John
Henry Newman. Here, we will make use of the Catholic theologian's concept of the "illative sense."

The Beauty of Words

One central element in Tolkien's approach to language is the "aesthetic
of words." Tolkien refers to this element on numerous occasions in his
correspondence. In a letter to his aunt Jane Neave regarding his lecture
"English and Welsh," he said that "the only 'original' things in it, are the
autobiographical bits, and the reference to 'beauty' in language; and
the theory that one's 'native language' is not the same as one's 'cradle-
tongue.'"[2] Tolkien argued that words were beautiful and not a mere
human creation or instrument. It is often said that Tolkien invented his
"private" languages for aesthetic pleasure, for his individual taste. This
could not be more true. The centrality of his aesthetic pleasure in language is in stark contrast with Barfield's over-focus on meaning. Tolkien
forcefully maintained that meaning was not the only component of human apprehension of language and words. "Word-aesthetic" (a word's
"sound") is as much a part of what language is as "word-meaning." Both
are elements of what philo-logy is: the *love* of words. The integrity of
words, with their form, sound, and beauty, is the distinctive of Tolkien's
philosophy of words. Hence, for Tolkien philology was love of *words
proper*, not love of words for a better and greater purpose. The form
and the sound of words provide aesthetic pleasure in and of themselves.
Words as words provide such a delight, and, for example, "plenilune" or
"argent" "are beautiful words before they are understood."[3] In the same
way these words should be met, experienced in their phenomenal reality,
before being encountered in the pages of a dictionary. That is precisely
what Tolkien wrote his aunt in 1961.[4]

We can find the same aesthetic sensibility in *The Lord of the Rings*
in which the hobbit Peregrin, finds Entish aesthetically pleasant.[5] De-

2. MC, 319.

3. L, 310.

4. L, 310.

5. LoTR, II.3.iv, 469.

spite Pippin's characteristic sleepiness, the point is clear. Language and words, even if not understood by the hearer, still produce aesthetic attraction. Sometimes an unknown language can even appear to be many tongues, as the two hobbits realize from the Ent Bregalad's lament about the Ent-wives. And to the hobbits, Bregalad "seemed to lament in many tongues the fall of trees that he had loved."[6] Words are loved, words are apprehended. This does not mean they loose their beauty after being understood. It means that words do not need to have a meaning attached in order to be beautiful. For Tolkien, not only words-as-meaning but words-as-sound convey true meaning, the wholeness of what a word is.

After arguing for the beauty of words, Tolkien goes further in establishing the relation between the beauty and the meaning of words. Tolkien's initial observation is that the meaning of words cannot be made "obvious." On the contrary, they must be attached to their word-sound, their sonority and aesthetic. It is important to realize that the connection between sound and meaning was not universally accepted at the time. Rather, as Ross Smith demonstrated in his *Inside Language*, the close association between "sound and word" was embodied in a counter-tradition whose members included Otto Jespersen and Wilhelm von Humboldt.[7] This alternative contested the predominant approach that argued for a disconnection between sound and meaning, the foremost exponent of this theory being Swiss linguist Ferdinand de Saussure. In his *Cours de Linguistique Générale*, he famously affirmed that "the link between signal and signification is arbitrary. Since we are treating a sign as the combination in which a signal is associated with a signification, we can express this more simply as: *the linguistic sign is arbitrary*."[8] There is no doubt that this theory is the extreme opposite of Tolkien's own.

For Tolkien, words were aesthetic and there was no doubt in his mind that this aesthetic was connected to their meaning. Moreover, the sound of a word always reflected the nature of the language and its speakers. There is, literally speaking, a metaphysical connection between a language and the people who speak a given language. Tolkien was not only concerned about maintaining the integrity of a logical connection between word and meaning but was interested in their metaphysical

6. LoTR, II.3.iv, 88–89.

7. Smith, *Inside Language*, 56.

8. Saussure, *Course in General Linguistics*, 67. With something of an academic arrogance, Saussure writes: "No one disputes the fact that linguistic signs are arbitrary." Saussure, *Course in General Linguistics*, 68.

connection, that is, a connection that included all the elements of the formation and development of a given language.

In *The Lord of the Rings*, we find several examples of this very connection between "language" and "people," as in the Ring verse. Written in the Black Speech, the language of the Orcs and Mordor, the verse is written in Tengwar, an Elvish script. When the "Ring" words were pronounced by Gandalf during the Council of Elrond, the wizard's voice "became menacing, powerful, harsh as stone."[9] The mere sound of the Dark Speech is enough to produce these reactions. From Tolkien's description, there was no need to understand the meaning of the words to be affected by them. There was an apprehension of their harsh and evil nature.

To explain how the meaning and the aesthetics of words formed a whole, Tolkien begins by contrasting the attitude of adults and children towards words. Tolkien argued that there is a main difference between adults' apprehension of words and children's. The former have lost the habit of *hearing* the words. They hear "argent" and only think about "silver," which is extremely restrictive. [10]

For adults, the *meaning* of the word is changed because they have lost the habit of *hearing* the word's sound. For Tolkien, it is better to hear "argent" rather than to think "it only means silver," since the word-sound conveys certain responses that change depending on the word.[11] The point made by Tolkien builds on a connection between meaning and beauty.

This is illustrated in Tolkien's invented languages. Flieger demonstrates this in her argument about the origin and development of Tolkien's two Elven languages, Quenya and Sindarin. Their development is built on this unity of perception-meaning-word.[12] The genesis of Elven perception—the starry light under the skies—develops into their journey from the shadows of Arda to the Light of Valinor, as their language develops from the first utterance (*behold*) to the highly sophisticated and sonorous Quenya. In the same manner, the dimmed perception and meaning held by the Elves who did not join in the travel to Valinor, resulted in a different language, society, and history. According to Flieger this demonstrates that the unity of perception-meaning-word can provide a framework for understanding the history of Middle-earth.

9. LoTR, I.2.ii, 248.

10. L, 310.

11. L, 310.

12. See Flieger, *Splintered Light*, esp. chapters 9 ("Perception = Name = Identity") and 10 ("Ourselves as Others See Us").

Here, Flieger's philosophical interpretation of Tolkien is important to mention. Indeed, her argument on the parallel development of language and history is directed by an overarching Neoplatonic framework she considers essential to Tolkien. Flieger's argument is rooted in the metaphysics of Eru. For her, as for many Tolkien scholars, Eru is closer akin to the Platonist "One" than to the biblical God. In fact, after exploring the Neoplatonic nature of Eru, Flieger describes the creation-act along the lines of an emanationist theory that has profound implications, not only for Arda's unfolding history, but also for the creation of language. Because Eru's creative act entails such a diminution, the unfolding history can only be one of relative decay, including in the formation of languages. Indeed, with every stage of created reality, we observe a move away from the perfect One. In very much the same manner, a language moving away from Eru and the Valar will be "diluted." Even the aesthetic pleasure found in a language might suffer the same fate. That, at least, would be the implication of such an overall Neoplatonic framework.

Flieger's Barfieldean interpretation of the unity of perception-meaning-word in Tolkien has been so influential in recent scholarship that it is often thought difficult to argue for a different explanation. However, we can reinterpret much of Flieger's argument along the lines of a very different metaphysic posture. In fact we are not bound by this particular philosophical stance, quite the contrary. There is indeed a better metaphysical option in Thomism. Chapter 1 has shown the many Catholic connections Tolkien entertained throughout his life. Not only Roman Catholicism but Thomism in particular serves as a general background to Tolkien's philosophical outlook. This leads Anglican theologian John Milbank to note perceptively that Tolkien "interestingly exhibit[s] another mode of development of a Catholic and even a Thomistic aesthetic."[13] In fact, recasting the whole discussion in Thomistic terms might provide a better understanding of Tolkien. Prominent among the Tolkien scholars promoting a Thomist interpretation are Jonathan McIntosh and Alison Milbank, the former arguing strongly for such a Thomist Tolkien in his book, *The Flame Imperishable.*

Far from being a succession of "splintered light," everything in Middle-earth, as long as it has being, knows of the presence of Eru in a manner similar to Thomas's own exposition of the presence of God to his creation. Some might wonder why this modification of metaphysical structure in

13. Milbank, "Scholasticism, Modernism, and Modernity," 663.

Tolkien is so important. We have noted how an emanationist account of creation would lead towards the interpretation of Tolkien's "splintered light" as entailing a diminution of being and of aesthetics in language. A Thomist understanding of the same expression takes the "splintered light" to refer to a contrast between created and uncreated order, or between the Music of the Ainur (and the subsequent Vision) and Eru's original intent. Creation is a "splintered light" of Eru's own perfect will, to the point that "Iluvatar can even be heard speaking somewhat diminishingly of both the Music and Vision together when he says how the Music had 'been *but* the growth and flowering of thought in the Timeless Halls, and the Vision *only* a foreshowing,' whereas the task of the Valar, after the physical world has actually been created, is to 'achieve it' (S 20)."[14]

If creation is "splintered light," it is only so by contrast to the perfect divine order. There is nothing to suggest gradual decay from the original light. Rather, the many "splinters" of the divine light represent many different shades and colors. These are not related by a scale of perfection, as Tolkien himself poetically explains in "Mythopoeia":

> Man, Sub-creator, the refracted light
> through whom is splintered from a single White
> to many hues, and endlessly combined
> in living shapes that move from mind to mind.[15]

The implications for the aesthetics of language is that, while there is something specific to the language of Elves, and in particular to the Elves having stayed in Valinor, languages and their aesthetic pleasures are not diminished. Nothing of their *beauty* is lost throughout the long history of Middle-earth.[16] What can be lost, or dimmed, as Flieger here rightly argues, is the relation of the words to history and meaning. The aesthetics of words, however, remains.

This connection between aesthetics, word, and meaning is seen in Tolkien's Elven languages. For example, Shippey comments that "Elvish poetry is supposed to be able to convey meaning by its sound alone."[17]

---

14. McIntosh, *The Flame Imperishable*, 236.

15. Tolkien, "Mythopoeia," lines 63–66, in *Tree and Leaf*, 87.

16. Tolkien continues in one of his letters: "The Light of Valinor (derived from light before any fall) is the light of art undivorced from reason, that sees things both scientifically (or philosophically) and imaginatively (or subcreatively) and says that they are good—as beautiful." L, 148n.

17. Shippey, *J. R. R. Tolkien*, 147–55.

We have an example of this in the partial Sindarin poem "A Elbereth Gil-thoniel." During his first evening in Elrond's Last Homely House, Frodo listened to the song to Elbereth, and "[he] stood still enchanted, while the sweet syllables of the elvish song fell like clear jewels of blended word and melody."[18] Whether Frodo's feelings are merely due to the aesthetics of the Elvish language, or to something more at work in the poem, Tolkien does not say.[19] The beauty and meaning of the poem are closely associated, even though the hobbits are rarely, if ever, conscious of this. This supports the second step of Tolkien's argument. The sound of a word, its beauty, is meaningful and one does not need to understand the word in one's own tongue in order to know what it means. Thus, Frodo probably had no idea about the meaning and power that the name "Elbereth" could have on the Nazgûls when he shouted it during the attack on Weathertop. But, as Aragorn remarks, "all blades perish that pierce that dreadful King. More deadly to him was the name of Elbereth."[20] There is clearly a power at work in the name "Elbereth," a power that goes beyond explicit meaning, one that Frodo was not aware of. Its power lies within the name itself and thus is "a name of terror to the Nazgûl."[21] Meaning and sound are connected, but it does not necessarily imply that the person uttering the word should be aware of its meaning. But we are always aware of the aesthetics of words.

In thus uniting aesthetics and meaning, Tolkien really goes one step beyond Barfield. If he subscribed to Barfield's unity of word and meaning in the primal history of humankind, Tolkien refused Barfield's separation of beauty and meaning which tended to eliminate the aesthetic aspect of words. As a peculiar kind of philologist, Tolkien went within words to find their beauty and tried to make this beauty resurface through the proper recovery of the word's meaning. Tolkien was, more than other philologists, in love with the beauty of words, not only their meaning.

18. LoTR, I.2.i, 267.

19. Even though Sam's invocation of the same poem at Cirith Ungol might indicate that the aesthetics of the poem is not the only thing at work: "Then his tongue was loosed and his voice cried in a language which he did not know." LoTR, II.4.x, 383.

20. LoTR, I.1.xii, 223.

21. Scull and Hammond, *Companion and Guide*, 1:180.

The Linguistic Invention of Stories

In "A Secret Vice," Tolkien applied his theory of the word-aesthetic to the invention of language. In this essay he turned to the "art" of language-invention, contrasting the adult's interest in language with the child's fascination with the invention of "secret" languages. Tolkien first explained that an invented language could be more or less consistent and aesthetic, starting with the most basic invention illustrated by the "animalic" children. These children created a language based on the names of animals, a language simplistic in form and in degree of inventiveness but a language that already enabled them to converse together. Tolkien draws an important conclusion, saying that pleasure was the essential part of the children's creation of language, with no other pretext than the mere aesthetic pleasure it provided. However, he goes further to comment on the reasons behind the invention of language. Opposing a common misconception, Tolkien says that he "would not have quoted the 'animalic' children if [he] had not discovered that secrecy was no part of their object."[22] The amusement, the pleasure was in the imitation of what is essential to man: language. The children, and for that matter, any inventor of language, find pleasure in new words themselves, and as Tolkien indicates: "This idea of using the linguistic faculty for amusement is however deeply interesting to me."[23] Such is the aesthetic pleasure provided by words: it needs no other justification.

After the initial pleasure of the invention of language, once the words are producing their aesthetic *transport*, the question remains of this language's future, its life. The aesthetic transport of language can be quite independent from an understanding of its meaning. In *The Lord of the Rings*, the hobbit Merry experiences such a transport at the hearing of the tongue of the men of Rohan. While not understanding the language, his heart leapt at its intonation.[24] No comment other than the perceptive "Merry felt his heart leap" could better embody Tolkien's theory of linguistic aesthetic pleasure. The beauty of an invented language does not merely reside in its artificial word-sound and word-meaning beauty, but also in the internal workings of the language itself. The beauty of individual words is also carried in the syntax and the grammar of the invented language. The harmonious association of words into a language gives it

22. MC, 201.

23. MC, 206.

24. LoTR, III.5.iii, 775.

life, a life that needs to be sustained, nourished, and protected. Reflecting on this issue, Tolkien argued for the relative autonomy of a language's life and for the rights of the invented language upon its "originator." The creator of a language binds himself to his language, and the language thus becomes somehow *alive*:

> But, none the less, as soon as you have fixed even a vague general sense for your words, many of the less subtle but most moving and permanently important of the strokes of poetry are open to you. For you are the heir of the ages. You have not to grope after the dazzling brilliance of invention of the free adjective, to which all human language has not yet fully attained. You may say
>
> *green sun*
> or *dead life*
> and set the imagination leaping.[25]

Here we find again Tolkien's careful balance between two equally important aspects of the invention of words: their meaning and their beauty. Whenever this intrinsic combination is attained, words become truly alive and stir up the imagination. At this point, meaning and beauty are fused in mythic imagination, in *mythopoeia*. As he commented on his own invention: "Language has both strengthened imagination and been freed by it. Who shall say whether the free adjective has created images bizarre and beautiful, or the adjective been freed by strange and beautiful pictures in the mind?"[26] Significantly, Tolkien rejects the choice between the emphases on "adjective" or "pictures" as unnecessary, because both words (adjectives) and images refer to one and the same reality and both contribute to the same aesthetic and emotional response.

Tolkien's strong sense of the beauty and meaning of words leads to a stress on the integrity of words, a concern also shared by Müller in his time, even though their respective explanations are very different. But as Noiré reports, the theory of Max Müller, which we will remember, is that "a certain sound is peculiar to every being, and that the spontaneous utterance of this sound is the most immediate expression of its nature."[27] Tolkien would probably agree with the close relation established between sound, meaning, and a specific people. Lobdell, for example, makes the

25. MC, 219.

26. MC, 219.

27. Noiré, *The Origin and Philosophy of Language*, 31.

point that for Tolkien there was a close connection between the sound of a language and the nature of its speaker.[28]

The close connection he establishes between the diverse components of what a word *is* almost demands giving the word independent life. However, if words and languages are alive, we are confronted with a serious problem, that of translation. If words are not mere abstract and artificial signs but carry beauty and meaning, we must wonder if the translation endeavor is even legitimate. In fact, one of the problems that emerges is the very possibility of translation, since it seems that to preserve the integrity of a word, translation should be abandoned. To this dilemma we now turn.

Words in Translation

Already in the first years after *The Lord of the Rings* was published, Tolkien started to receive letters from foreign publishing companies informing him about projects of translating his work. In the twelve years following the initial publication of, *The Lord of the Rings* Tolkien received translation queries for publications in Dutch, Swedish, Italian, German, Spanish (in Argentina), Polish, French, Romanian, Danish, Hebrew, and even in Japanese (in November 1960). After his death in 1973, other translations would be published.

Tolkien always entertained a very cautious approach towards the task of translating, both in his own translation of Elven languages into English and also of his works into foreign languages. For Tolkien, the starting-point of any translation should be a respectful and serious approach to the text. When contacted by the Swedish translators Tolkien reacted quite angrily to the project on the ground that they did not treat the text with respect.[29] The translators did not approach their task with the expected scholarly attention. Regarding the Dutch translation, Tolkien commented that such an endeavor "will prove a formidable task, and I do not see how it can be performed satisfactorily without the assistance of the author."[30] Certainly, translation is an arduous task, but Tolkien was at times sanguine when the question of translating *The Lord of the Rings* was broached. In fact he made clear that he would be glad to be consulted

28. Lobdell, *The World of the Rings*, 33.

29. L, 304.

30. L, 248–49.

in the matter of translation, in order to avoid repetition of the unpleasing experience he had with the Swedish translation.

Tolkien's interest in the relation between words and meaning is reflected in his view of translation. It is important to realize that for him, as it was probably for Barfield, "translation" *stricto sensu* is an impossibility. Indeed, language is so bound to the perception of one's representation that a translation would most certainly fail to convey the awareness the original author had of his environment, that is, of a history and culture. A better expression to describe the impossible task of translation could be "transliteration of meaning." However, we must resist the temptation to simplify the dilemma Tolkien rightly perceived in the act of translation.

This might explain his initial reluctance to publish his prose version of *Beowulf*, even though he had already started an alliterative translation of the same poem in 1924–25 while still at Leeds.[31] However, these unfinished attempts at *Beowulf* were not the end of Tolkien's interest in the poem. Apart from his regular class on the actual text, Tolkien chose *Beowulf* as the subject for his 1936 Sir Israel Gollancz Memorial lecture, a lecture that set a "new standard in *Beowulf* criticism."[32] The significance of the lecture should not be underestimated. As Michael Drout points out, "while it does not mark the moment that *Beowulf* was studied as literature . . . it does begin the study of the poem and its workings as legitimate in their own right."[33]

Tolkien's translation has, overall, not been praised for its intrinsic quality but for his expertise in language and literature. Thus, Tolkien's translation is more literal than other modern translations, not primarily in the words he chooses but in the rhythm also. Scholars have noted that Tolkien's approach to *Beowulf* took at face value the worth of the poem as poem, as worthy of study in and of itself. In a way, then, Tolkien's translation is aimed at translating the poem as it would sound in English, but in a context close to the original. To understand his translation is to understand that he aimed at understanding the poem itself, thus Shippey's conclusion that Tolkien thought he was the only one to have understood *Beowulf!*[34]

---

31. Scull and Hammond, *Companion and Guide*, 1:124.
32. Scull and Hammond, *Companion and Guide*, 1:187.
33. Drout, *Beowulf and the Critics*, 1.
34. Shippey, *The Road to Middle-earth*, 47.

Despite all his reticence, Tolkien could recognize that translation is also a necessary act. After all, a great part of his academic and artistic life was devoted to resolving the issues of translating invented languages into English, and relating diverse forms of languages. During his academic career he also had to translate, for himself or for publication, old texts (Anglo Saxon, Welsh, etc.) into English. Tolkien was well aware of the necessity of the act of translation, and he made up his own set of rules to follow for proper translation. Again, regarding the Dutch translation of *The Lord of the Rings*, he told Rayner Unwin in a letter dated July 3, 1956 that he objected to any modification of the instruction set forth in the "nomenclature. A translator, vehemently wrote Tolkien, does not have the liberty to modify words at will.[35] While Tolkien is referring here to the "Nomenclature of *The Lord of the Rings*,"[36] there is no doubt this is applicable to his work itself and to his created languages in particular. Indeed, Tolkien's attitude towards translation remained ambiguous throughout his career as a language-creator.

In fact, his heated attitude towards the Dutch translation is telling. Tolkien's initial reaction was quite severe. He immediately wrote his publisher, Allen & Unwin, that he had been "disturbed" and "annoyed" by the initial translation he had received.[37] Tolkien's displeasure at the Dutch translation is due to the unnecessary change of names. The main mistake of the translators had been to consider that an invented language could be merely changed instead of being translated. He felt the Dutch translator, in changing the whole "Nomenclature" he had provided was remodeling the linguistic nature of the work according to his own fancies. While we can sympathize with Tolkien, he might have been overzealous in his criticisms since the Dutch translator had clearly read and studied the "Nomenclature," quoting it back to Tolkien, looking for the best linguistic options. Tolkien might have seen the value of the translation since the publication went ahead and was republished numerous times. This is further supported by Tolkien's final favorable first impressions concerning the Dutch

---

35. L, 249–50.

36. Formerly known as "Guide to the Names in The Lord of the Rings," published as "Guide to the Names in *The Lord of the Rings*," 159–75. This "Nomenclature" was written by Tolkien as a result of objections with the Dutch and Swedish translations of *The Lord of the Rings*. The "Nomenclature" has been published and republished several times in different forms—as is common with many of Tolkien's writings. We refer to the first edition of Lobdell's *A Tolkien Compass*.

37. L, 249.

edition of *The Fellowship of the Ring*.[38] The same general attitude is displayed towards Ohlmark's Swedish translation, which later was praised for its quality—and this news alleviated somewhat Tolkien's rancor.[39]

Instead, he approached the task of translation in a radical way and explained that "as a general principle for her [the Polish translator], my preference is for as little translation or alteration of any names as possible. As she perceives, this is an English book and its Englishry should not be eradicated."[40] This view seems extreme, reflecting Tolkien's love of words and language and his attempt to maintain their integrity at all costs, even at the cost of a coherent and readable narrative. However radical this might sound, it partly explains how Tolkien succeeded in uniting words, languages, and storytelling in most of his works, making *The Lord of the Rings* a masterpiece of language *and* translation. While Tolkien had a preference towards preserving names and providing an explanation for those which have a meaning in English, he could also allow diversity in the translating process. It is interesting to notice that no first names appear in the "Nomenclature," indicating that they are *not* to be translated, under any pretext, but must be kept unchanged.[41] However, some other names could be part of the translating process.

Tolkien's great sensitivity to the task of translation and to the integrity of names is visible here once again. Tolkien does not entertain any idealistic idea about the possibility of preserving all names in an invented language since this would certainly prove the downfall of the narrative. To solve the problem of maintaining the integrity of names while allowing for the possibility of translation, Tolkien relied on a study of the growth and origin of names. In Tolkien's own works we can see two sorts of names. The first sort are the invention of the author, while the second derive or are the product of older forms of languages. The first are formed with "current" elements of English, while the others are found in older forms.[42] Given such a distinction, the task of translation becomes

38. Scull and Hammond, *Companion and Guide*, 1:498. This is further confirmed in Professor P. N. U. Harting's comment that the translation was "better than expected" and "on the whole readable." Scull and Hammond, *Companion and Guide*, 1:500–501.

39. Scull and Hammond, *Companion and Guide*, 1:554–55.

40. L, 299.

41. See also LoTR, App. F, 1108.

42. Tolkien, "Guide to the Names in the Lord of the Rings," in Lobdell, *A Tolkien Compass*, 156.

easier because the words invented can be matched with equivalents in the language of translation, while the others are preserved.

Regarding the words to be translated, Tolkien navigated between a translation according to literal meaning and a translation according to phonological transliteration. As noted above, Tolkien even provided a Nomenclature to the proper translation of *The Lord of the Rings*. Consistent with this "guide to translators," Tolkien mostly left the Elven languages unchanged in the text of *The Lord of the Rings*, or provided a Common Speech translation. As such, Elven names and expressions are not directly translated into English, probably due to their reference to a specific mode of knowledge, song, and poetry. On the other hand the Common Speech is rendered into English, thus reflecting its more "popular" and ordinary usage. This reflects Tolkien's logic of translation. As far as Elvish is concerned, Tolkien tried to transliterate as best he could the "rich and elegant Fëanorian alphabet,"[43] while he translated the Common Speech "as closely as possible."[44] This difference in the mode of translation is related to Tolkien's idea that a language reflects the nature of its speakers. The prime manifestation of this connection is the orcs, whose language is described in way reminiscent of their appearance: hideous and vile, full of malice and hatred.

This passage is telling, since it links language and the creatures' nature: that only the Orcs can speak their language is a good example of their corrupted nature; no other race can speak their foul language. Tolkien goes even further in making his Orcs speak more often, and more willingly, the Common Speech than their own language. Orcs, of course, had a language of their own, at least at the time of *The Lord of the Rings*, even though in the Elder Days it was not so. Their language, moreover, was merely a perversion, a mockery of the Elvish language.[45] Soon enough though, a language for use among Sauron's own armies became necessary, and it came to be that Sauron devised his own language, the Black Speech, which he wanted to see used by all creatures that served him.[46] Orcish words and vocabulary were merely derived from other words and tongues, most likely derived from Elvish tongues. In a way then, there is

43. HoME, XII:41.
44. HoME, XII:42.
45. LoTR, "Appendix F," 457.
46. LoTR, "Appendix F," 458.

a parallel between the Orcs as a corrupted race and their language as a corrupted agglomeration of other words and tongues.

Not only that, but the Orcs also come to have a distorted perception of reality due to the profound distortion of their language. Indeed, if there is a unity of perception-word-meaning, a distortion in words can only mean a distortion of both meaning and perception. Tolkien himself seems to validate that option when he observes that their horrible language prevents them from "true thought and perception."[47] The Black Speech, then, is not a "living" language because it has no true form. A true language evolves out of a specific form and perception, but the Black Speech constantly evolves by mere agglomeration of heteroclite words. It has, then, no real history of its own. Further, the Black Speech clearly conveys the debased nature of its speakers and of its originator, Sauron. It is dark, harsh, and serves only hatred and fear. This probably explains Tolkien's reluctance to write any Orcish speech, for it was a deacying and degrading speech, something utterly intolerable. In the "Appendix to languages," Tolkien applied the same thinking to the Trolls who, brutal by nature could not have their own language. Rather, Morgoth taught them a language according to that which they could learn. There is no better example of the profound relation between a language and its speaker than the Black Speech, with the exception, of course, of the Valar's Valarin, the Eldest Speech, of which we know very little.[48]

This latter observation about the relation between a people's nature, their language, and the translation of their language points towards another theme, that of the origin of languages both invented and "real," and the nature of the aesthetic apprehension of words. If languages in any manner correspond to their speakers, there must also be an innate apprehension of language.

The Illative Apprehension of Word-Aesthetics

The observation that we have a natural and intuitive sensitivity towards the aesthetic qualities of words and language was, for Tolkien, almost obvious. This is so because the appreciation of the beauty of words is characteristic of being human. Tolkien himself was never clearly explicit about how this ability functions. Hence, in order to understand Tolkien

47. HoME, XII:21.

48. Hostetter, "Languages Invented by Tolkien," 337.

here, we must take our clues from a plausible framework that might have influenced him. Here, turning to Newman might prove useful. If Newman undoubtedly had a great influence on Tolkien's religious faith through the Birmingham Oratory and Father Francis, it is possible to discern another influence of the great Roman Catholic convert on our author: the illative sense, presented in Newman's *A Grammar of Assent*.

This work ranks as one of Newman's greatest works, in which he investigates the processes that explain and support the natural assent of faith. In this work Newman establishes several categories and distinctions that serve as a necessary foundation for the universal a-rational assent of faith. A good place to start is a basic definition of the "illative sense." This, for Newman, is a human function that explains how man can accept religious statements without consciously or explicitly using his rational faculties. The use of this illative sense is due to the apprehension of faith or, in other words, the assent that man can give to faith. In analyzing the illative sense Newman hoped to provide a foundation for both rationality and assent of faith, without the latter becoming dependent on radical rationalism. In fact, Newman considered that "it is the mind that reasons, which controls its own reasoning, not any technical apparatus of words and propositions. . . . The power to judge truth and error in the concrete things, I call illative sense."[49] The illative sense is thus the way to bridge the distance between "propositions" and "assent" to these propositions.

However, it would be a mistake to conclude that the illative sense, which functions as a practical faculty, is arbitrary and unfounded. In fact, practical judgment demonstrates that man's knowledge can be based on something other than a purely rational process: it can be the practical result of a faculty of judgment inherent to human nature.[50] As some Newman scholars remind us, the "illative sense" is parallel to a certain exercise of aesthetic faculties which do not rely on an explicit rational conscious judgment. As such, this faculty becomes the "power of judging truth and error in concrete things."[51] Its nature is well described by Newman who argues that "in any kind of concrete reasoning, whether in experimental science, research or historical theology, there is no test for absolute truth and error in our inferences besides the reliability of illative sense."[52] This

---

49. Newman, *Grammar of Assent*, 341.

50. An approximate synonym to the Aristotelian *phronèsis*. See Viau, *Le Dieu du Verbe*, 153.

51. Newman, *Grammar of Assent*, 341.

52. Newman, *Grammar of Assent*, 21.

concrete human faculty gives the opportunity to capture the presence and truth of things in our environment.

But Newman's relevance goes further. One of his brilliant intuitions was to understand that, in everyday human experience, in the experience that man *has* of things, there are two epistemological processes at work—processes that he will respectively label *real* apprehension and *notional* apprehension. We are only interested in the first kind and will therefore leave the other aside—although for the overall understanding of Newman, separating the two should be avoided. However, to clarify the possible influence on Tolkien, it is necessary to restrict our subject study.

First then, real apprehension is to Newman "first experience or information about concrete things."[53] This apprehension of things is made available through a simple consideration of the images and things that come to man. This fundamental observation that "apprehension suggests some real objects in mind through image" is crucial to Newman's epistemology.[54] Thus, the actual apprehension of things we see, hear, experience, is essentially a perception of images. This introduces another dimension in which Newman could have influenced Tolkien. We can in fact establish a direct link between this apprehension of things, including language, and imagination. In truth, Newman himself leads us in this direction when he qualifies this real apprehension as "imaginative apprehension."[55] Indeed, even if Newman's illative sense is first concerned with decision-making and assent, it is nevertheless possible to connect it to the imagination. In fact, we can go so far as to say that "the illative sense is, in reality, nothing less than the effect which the imagination has on our choices and evaluations once reality has been really and personally grasped."[56]

Thus, in the exercise of the illative sense, it is imagination in its holistic nature that is active. In its action, imagination demonstrates that it *binds together* the entire human epistemological faculties, and that it is not merely one among many epistemological processes. As Gerald Bednar indicated: "Epistemologically, imagination for Newman is necessary for real apprehension, which grasps a proposition as an image, and

---

53. Newman, *Grammar of Assent*, 346.
54. Godfrey, "Imagination," 92.
55. Newman, *Theological Papers*, 135.
56. Worgul, "The Imagination, Epistemology, and Values," 131–32.

for notional apprehension, in which the imagination abstracts from the whole to allow a person to focus on one aspect of the whole."[57]

Consequently, imagination for Newman is not an abstraction of reality but rather a *mode of reasoning* that supports true judgments concerning those things which we daily experience.[58] Imagination is therefore a human ability to make ever-present this apprehension of concrete things, even when those things have actually disappeared. Indeed, it would be easy to believe, when we have no more direct experience of things, that they are nothing more than abstract concepts. This is not the case for Newman who protests: "Nor need such an image be in any sense an abstraction; though I may have eaten a hundred peaches in times past, the impression, which remains on my memory of the flavour [is] not a general notion."[59] By the power of imagination, we are able to recall to our minds the things we have had the experience of, without these things becoming abstract. Hence, Aragorn, at the top of Cerin Amroth, picks a small elanor flower, whispering to himself *Arwen vanimelda, namarië*, remembering the time when, with Arwen, they had plighted their love. But this was not for Aragorn a mere abstract memory. In fact, as Frodo realizes, Aragorn "beheld things as they once had been in this same place."[60]

For John Coulson, the link between imagination and the exercise of the illative sense is clearly spelled out by Newman: "[His] emphasis falls upon the positive aspect of imagination which, by its intensifying and unifying power, enables us to make a whole-hearted, 'energetic,' and real assent—'as if we saw.' In other words, we become convinced."[61] It is this personal conviction to which imagination gives us access. When the latter exercises its powers on the process of human knowledge, all of what man knows becomes included in a single movement of thought. To summarize, we can say that "imaginative apprehension" enables man to keep alive things previously experienced, and on the basis of this understanding be led to aesthetic preferences. This is of particular importance for what makes the richness of Tolkien sub-creation: the invention of new languages.

57. Bednar, *Faith as Imagination*, 17.

58. Godfrey, "Imagination," 277.

59. Newman, *Grammar of Assent*, 23.

60. LoTR, I.2.vi, 395.

61. Coulson, *Religion and Imagination*, 53.

An example may serve to illustrate the importance of Newman's illative sense for a theory of imagination. As previously mentioned, the starting point for Newman was the observation of this almost intuitive apprehension of concrete things. This finds an echo in Tolkien, when he comments on the phenomenon, the desire we should even say, of creating a language. Here, it seems that his question regarding aesthetic intuition is parallel to Newman's own regarding verbal propositions. While Newman asked in effect how man, without education, may grant his assent to propositions without verbal analysis, Tolkien, for his part, asked how man gives his aesthetic assent to language and sounds without analyzing them by force of linguistic *analysis*. To Tolkien remarks, the aesthetic attraction is deeply personal and so, difficult to explain in words.[62] And so, when Newman said that this agreement is the result of a direct apprehension of concrete things, Tolkien translates this conclusion into a direct apprehension of the sound and beauty of language. The example given by Tolkien is that of a simple soldier engaged in the secret pleasure of the creation of language and suddenly exclaiming, "I express the accusative with a prefix!" is striking. Tolkien concluded thus: "Just consider the splendour of the words! '*I* shall express the accusative case.' Magnificent! Not 'it is expressed', nor even the more shambling 'it is sometimes expressed', nor the grim 'you must learn how it is expressed' . . . only a question of taste, a satisfaction of a personal pleasure, a private sense of fitness."[63] That is exactly what Tolkien tries to explain: how man can grasp the structure and beauty of an invented language, at one and the same time.

Many songs and poems in *The Lord of the Rings* testify to such an intuitive grasp of the beauty of language. As Aragorn, Gimli, and Legolas pass into Rohan, Aragorn chants one of the poems of Rohan, "Where now the horse and the rider? Where is the horn that was blowing?"[64] By the mere sound of the language, Legolas makes the connection between the words, their sound, and the country of Rohan, "for it is like to this land itself; rich and rolling in part, else hard and stern as the mountains. But I cannot guess what it means, save that it is laden with the sadness of Mortal Men."[65] While Legolas could not understand its meaning, he

62. L, 264.
63. MC, 199.
64. LoTR, II.3.vi, 497.
65. LoTR, II.3.vi, 496–97.

could easily grasp its melancholic beauty. Legolas's aesthetic appreciation and *comprehension* are difficult to explain and lead us to ask the same question about language that Newman asked about the assent of faith. On which criteria, asks Tolkien, is man to build a new language? In any case, Tolkien concludes, it is not based on rational or scientific methods or predetermined linguistic codes.[66]

It is therefore the pleasure of invention and imagination that is essential to the Tolkienian construction of language, even though the aesthetic of linguistic invention was also crucial. The lack of aesthetics was one of the criticisms Tolkien leveled against Otto Jespersen's invented language, "Novial." It was, flatly concludes Quenya's creator, "ingenious, and easier than Esperanto, but hideous."[67] Linguistic pleasure and beauty for their own sake are characteristic of Tolkien's creativity. It is even possible to conclude that "phonetic aesthetics" is based on a real understanding of the beauty and sonority of any given new language. Without imagination reality cannot be known; without imagination the pleasure of language is impossible. Coulson aptly concludes that "the real assent made to primary forms of religious belief (expressed in metaphor, symbol and story) is of the same kind as the imaginative assent we make to the primary forms of literature."[68]

Another example comes from Tolkien's fictional "The Notion Club Papers," clearly a fictionalized description of an Inklings meeting, though we should refrain from seeing in this imaginary account a an exact portrait of the Inklings.[69] During one of these reunions, one of the characters, Alwin Arundel Lowdham, shares with the other members of this informal group his dream about "Atlantis," a dream through which he (re) discovers the languages of the "Elder Days"—among which are, not surprisingly, Quenya, Sindarin, and Adûnaic, Tolkien's invented languages. This story, mostly concerned with the Atlantis/Númenor cycle, still bears significance for our discussion when Lowdham comes across the "Hail Earendel, brightest of angels" in the dictionary.

Lowdham, who comes closest to reflecting Tolkien's own voice, recalls his first impressions in the following terms: "When I came across that citation in the dictionary I felt a curious thrill, as if something had

66. MC, 255.

67. MC, 182.

68. Coulson, *Religion and Imagination*, 145.

69. HoME, IX:151.

stirred in me, half wakened from sleep. There was something very remote and strange and beautiful behind those words, if I could grasp it,
far beyond ancient English. . . . I don't think it is any irreverence to say
that it may derive its curiously moving quality from some older world."[70]
Clearly, the aesthetic of these words is not a function of their understanding. It is the result of the workings of something deeper, a sort of common
aesthetic sense that enables the reader to experience the aesthetic depth
of such language almost intuitively. There is, in the words of Lowdham/
Tolkien, something strangely similar to Newman's imaginative apprehension, reinforcing the strong possibility of a Tolkienian application of the
illative sense to linguistic aesthetics.

The imagination initiated in Tolkien by these languages which were
so dear to him, certainly led him to an understanding of the *concreteness*
of language. Indeed, there is very little consideration in Tolkien for "language" in any abstract sense. In fact, in "A Secret Vice," Tolkien describes
his own understanding of language, and in particular of his "personal"
language. The flavor of words, their tone, their beauty is the basis for
Tolkien's literary work: a name gives birth to a language; from a language
a people rises, and then a culture, a story. If, as noted by Gregory Solari,
Tolkien "carved an adventure in language matters,"[71] it is with the matter
of a holistic imagination—an imagination that gave Tolkien the opportunity to grasp, with a single movement of imagination, the beauty of
language *and* the invention of new languages.

In conclusion, when Tolkien explains the invention of language
on the basis of an original language, phonetic preference, and personal
invention, we should turn to Newman. Obviously, it would be almost
impossible to claim an exclusive Newmanian influence since Tolkien
was eclectic in his reading, secretive in acknowledging influences, and
a linguistic genius in his own way. The fact remains that, in Tolkien, the
imagination, grasping in one single movement both the nature of language and its beauty, can also create new worlds.[72] Here, the workings
of Newman's illative sense can be discerned. The most vivid form of
imagination is creating things that have never been seen or heard. Only
by recalling—with the illative sense—the permanence of the past, but

70. HoME, IX:236.

71. Solari, "Réévangéliser l'imagination," in Caldecott et al., *Tolkien*, 79.

72. See Newman, *The Idea of a University*, 306. See also Godfrey, "Imagination,"
133.

always actual, beauty of Finnish, Welsh and other languages, did Tolkien succeed in creating new languages and embodying them in his "Faërie."[73]

---

73. Even though this spelling might be less used, Faërie is a generic term describing the land of fairies or elves. See Clute and Grant, *The Encyclopedia of Fantasy*, 328.

Conclusion

————— *Part One* —————

IN THIS FIRST COTTAGE, of language and words, we have heard a story, that of an English philology professor, and his life-long love of language creation. We have unearthed tales about the origin of his love for language, and the stories about how he formulated his theory of language. We have also contemplated the hidden source of Tolkien's apprehension of language. Maybe, however, this will not clarify all issues. Where does Tolkien clearly demonstrates himself to be a Thomist writer? The question is legitimate, but wrongly stated. His Thomism will not appear beyond the foundational level. Tolkien does not offer a distinctively and explicit Thomist theory of language. To discern the place of Tolkien's Thomism, we must first see Tolkien as a philologist: a difficult task indeed, for those who are not immersed in this field. And, as Lowdham in "The Notion Club Papers," he could probably say: "Well, I'm a philologist, . . . which means a misunderstood man."[1] Languages inhabit Tolkien's world as much as his sub-created races. Each has its language, and each has its nature.

If Tolkien could display such a high view and love of words, it is in great part because he was the child of intense academic debates that had taken place during the middle and late nineteenth century. However, Tolkien was not merely the result of the old Müller-Lang debates. He was also the representative of a different way looking at language, one

---

1. HoME, IX:233.

that would not accept that utilitarian or evolutionary perspectives dictate the use of language. On the contrary, Tolkien followed the intuition of Owen Barfield, specifically his *Poetic Diction* which promoted a view of the original unity of words. This provided the ground for Tolkien's opposition to Müller's view of myth as a disease of language. But, ironically, it also provided him with the firm basis for a slight disagreement with Barfield himself over the importance of words. While Barfield located their importance in the creation and recovery of meaning, Tolkien always valued words for words' sake. They did not depend on any other element than themselves for finding their beauty and integrity.

Through his academic and theoretical interactions, Tolkien became a true "wordsmith," a creator and lover of words. He was stricken by their rhythm, enamored of their form, fascinated by their sound. He was as spellbound by the meaning of one word, "Sigelhearwan," as he was by the script of Elvish. And through Tolkien's love of words, language led to stories that connected people to their history. The beauty of his invented languages made possible the depth and richness of his fiction. In fact, "Tolkien's invented world is presented with such authenticity and depth of detail that readers can easily imagine his having collected and transcribed the histories of Arda from ancient sources."[2] For Tolkien words and languages were the essential foundation of history, and thus were of crucial importance to human beings.

In Tolkien's theory of words and language, the Thomist foundation is not explicit. However, this same Thomism will become clearer as we proceed to our next part devoted to Tolkien's view and use of myth, history, and truth. In the same manner that myths and legends became the embodiment of previously created languages, Tolkien's theory of myth is a clearer embodiment of his theological convictions. It is time to take up our journey again, and go higher up, towards the land of myth.

2. Petty, "Identifying England's Lönnrot," 81.

Part Two

Myth, History, and Truth
——— *Tolkien's "Mythopoeia"* ———

To England; to my country

—J. R. R. TOLKIEN, *Letters*

LIKE EVERY TRAVELER IN Tolkien's realm, our walk continues with a song. And as we begin the second stage of our journey, towards the valley of the gods, we sing along with Tolkien about their City:

> There slow forgotten days for ever reap
> The silent shadows counting out rich hours;
> And no voice stirs; and all the marble towers
> White, hot and soundless, ever burn and sleep.[1]

We start with this poem, because it echoes a profoundly tolkienian quest, that of a true mythology. In fact, Tolkien's interest in, and love for, languages was further reinforced by his deep regret of the lack of a distinctive English mythology that would serve as the embodiment of the distinctive English language.[2] In fact, Tolkien once described himself as a "discoverer of legends," and as an "explorer" he dared enter the "Perilous

---

1. Tolkien, "The City of the Gods," in *The Book of Lost Tales*, 1:136.
2. L, 144.

Realm" of fairyland.[3] In his wanderings, he came to ponder the mythic quality of fairyland and the relation between myth and the Creator God. In Tolkien's works of fantasy, we have in fictional form a journal of his wanderings in fairyland, and we find the answers to questions regarding truth, history, and myth. Mythological terminology is pervasive in Tolkien, indicating the high regard he had for mythical language, stories, and life. This importance of the mythological motif indicates the relevance of the theory of myth to his fantasy.

Books on Tolkien's mythology abound; most of them are concerned with a presentation of the aesthetic, the significance, the structure, the intertextuality, or the sources of his mythology. Tolkien wrote a "mythology for England," and his works have been evaluated, praised, and criticized as a mythical story. However, it is notable that while Tolkien has been described as a mythologist and as a theoretician of mythology, he has rarely been ranked as one of the great mythographers. This is quite unfortunate for, as we will argue in the following chapters, Tolkien comes from a long line of British mythographers and folklorists. Tolkien sometimes used the term *legendarium* to refer to his overall mythical compendium. His goal was a wide set of interconnected stories and legends where his language could live.[4]

In order to present Tolkien's theory of myth, chapter 5 will open with a consideration of Tolkien's "mythological" context, focusing on the historical setting for nineteenth-century mythological studies. This is crucial to the figure of Tolkien as mythographer, especially in the context of the Grimms' work on their German tales and Elias Lonnröt's reconstruction of Finnish oral mythology. Later, in chapter 6, we will consider how language and myth relate through the concept of "mythical language." Here, the influence of Owen Barfield's *Poetic Diction* and his theory of the "ancient semantic unity" will be brought into consideration. Finally, chapter 7 will evaluate Tolkien's theory of myth, looking again at both the academic debate of Tolkien's days as well as his classical theological understanding of the relation between myth and truth.

3. OFS, 27.

4. L, 144.

5

Historical Mythologists

THE NINETEENTH CENTURY WAS a complex period of political, theological, and scientific turmoil. The Napoleonic wars, the new scientific theories and numerous theological controversies, both on the Continent and in Britain, provided fertile ground for a reevaluation of the meaning of history, the nature and origin of humankind, and the uniqueness of traditional Christianity. It was during this troubled period that scientific theories of language and literature flowered, especially in the new fields of mythology, folklore, and fairy tales, owing much to the labors, insights, and new directions given by two German scholars, Jakob and Wilhelm Grimm. The Grimms embodied their insights in a corpus of mythological and academic writings the range of which goes beyond what most scholars had previously achieved. This body of writing makes up more than fifty books including the comprehensive dictionary *Deutsches Wörterbuch*. As such, they rank as the founders of "German studies." A detour through the work and significance of the Grimm brothers is crucial here for it provides the connection between Tolkien and the common goal of many similar projects. Mythology-creation was embodied in a specific historical context and had linguistic-historical purposes, as will become clearer.

A "German" Landmark: The Brothers Grimm

Jakob and Wilhelm Grimm truly represent a landmark in the way nine-teenth-century scholars came to see and experience their world. What is found in the Grimms' scholarship is a historical tradition based on a Romantic approach to history and cultural identity, with a particular national perspective. The German brothers are best known for their collections of tales, among which *Children and Household Tales* (German *Kinder-und-Hausmärchen*), commonly known as *Grimm's Fairy Tales*, is the most read.[1] However, the Grimms published other collections of tales, notably *Heroic Germanic Tales* (German *Deutsche Sagen*), and translated collections of foreign tales like Croker's *Fairy Legends and Traditions of the South of Ireland* translated as *Irische Elfenmärchen*. But the Grimms were not only concerned with the collection and study of fairy tales, and their interest and expertise go far beyond what we commonly imagine.[2]

In fact, their influence on the study of the German language is at least equal to their influence on fairy tales study. Jakob Grimm published the impressive and groundbreaking *Germanic Grammar* (German *Deutsche Grammatik*), as well as the two volumes of *Germanic Mythology* (German *Deutsche Mythologie*).[3] One of the great followers of Jakob Grimm was Swedish scholar Viktor Rydberg, who readily acknowledged his debt to Jacob Grimm, saying that his name "will always be mentioned with honour as the great pathfinder in the field of Teutonic antiquities."[4] Wilhelm Grimm translated foreign tales and published a scholarly study of the *Germanic Runes* (originally *Über deutsche Runen*). Together the brothers undertook the publication of the monumental *German Dictionary* (German *Deutsches Wörterbuch*), not achieved in their lifetime.[5]

Though their publications largely contributed to their fame, the significance of the Grimms lies in their combination of linguistic and mythological studies. In fact, a people's language and mythological literature has never been so closely brought together as it was by the Grimms. Their new approach to the study of popular tales and language follows a common method and leads to the convictions and commitments typical

---

1. Grimm and Grimm, *German Household Tales*.

2. See, for example Hartland, *The Science of Fairy Tales*, 23.

3. Grimm, *Deutsche Grammatik*.

4. Rydberg, *Researches in Teutonic Mythology*, 9.

5. Wilhelm Grimm also translated some Danish ballads. See Grimm, *Old Danish Ballads from Grimm's Collection*.

of the Romantic tradition. Among these commitments, a strong histori-cal sensitivity is the most striking one. As a late nineteenth-century re-viewer said, "The leading traits in the character of the brothers Grimm are reverence for history, keen poetic sensibilities, and a warm love for all that is German and patriotic."[6] This summarizes in a nutshell the direc-tion of the Grimms' scholarship, a direction that was copied and adapted in Europe—especially in Britain at the end of the nineteenth century. It is crucial to see that this characteristically nineteenth-century method was born during the twilight of the last of the old empires' conquest wars and the initial collapse of a sentiment of cultural unity. This crumbling of the old world help us to understand why the Grimms' work was of such social and political significance.

The period in which the Grimms lived was in truth a turbulent one. To begin with, Germany was "a loose conglomeration of petty principali-ties, duchies, and kingdoms, some as large and powerful as Prussia, some so tiny that an oft-related satiric tale tells of one ruling prince who ac-cidentally dropped his realm out of his pocket and lost it forever on an afternoon's stroll."[7] Paradoxically, the Grimms expressed a strong sense of "national" unity and desired to give this "conglomeration" a common identity and origin. Moreover, when the *Kinder-und-Hausmärchen* was published in 1812, the soldiers of the Napoleonic armies were on their way back from the debacle of the Russian campaign from which only 5 percent returned. Morale was at its lowest, but the climate was surprisingly favor-able to an upsurge of patriotic and national enthusiasm, probably because the Russian debacle nourished the need for a national identity.

Because it was also a sociopolitical undertaking, the Grimms' work attracted strong criticism. Scholars charged the Grimms with academic deception and with having created all the tales. For example, Finnish folk-lorist Kaarle Krohn (1863–1933) charged the Grimms' work with being "unscientific," even though he recognized their national significance. The tales were accused of being merely the fruit of the writing of the Grimms, rather than the compilation of an oral tradition. Thus, what was supposed to be a national folklore unity was thought to be a mere farce. However, a large part of the charge of deception brought against the Grimms came from a misunderstanding of their purpose. Indeed, "Grimm philologists and folklorists have criticized the brothers for merging oral and literary

6. Von Raumer, "The Study of the German Language," 456.

7. Peppard, *Paths through the Forest*, 1.

traditions indiscriminately."[8] However, their goal was not to produce an academic work, nor was it to be a collective work crediting each and every author of tales. Rather, it was a holistic work produced by the "German spirit." In addition, the criticisms totally underestimated the processes of collection and revision undertaken by the Grimms.

Another original characteristic of their scholarship was that for the first time, scholars invested popular and plain speech with the value that was previously ascribed only to Greek, Hebrew, Latin, and, to a certain extant, Sanskrit—supposedly the "noble" languages. For the Grimms, popular tales were not only children's tales or old nursery tales; rather, they were the property, heritage, and foundational identity of a people. This second characteristic illustrates the Grimms' conviction that the study of past history was necessary to a right understanding of the origin of a people and of a nation. Here again, the Romantic and national ideal of the Grimms is visible in their view of the origin of language and tales. To begin with, Wilhelm's *Heroic Tales* defended the Germanic origin of the most famous old German text, the *Niebelungenlied*, against the commonly held theory of an older and more genuine Scandinavian origin. Of course, both Grimms in their respective fields of study were aware that languages and tales could be distinctly national while at the same time be similar to languages and tales from other nations. In addition, their works had theological implications. For example, Jakob Grimm's *On the Origin of Language* "refuted the theory that language had been 'revealed' to man by some higher power, thus putting to rest a widely held theological interpretation."[9] Jakob Grimm's rejection of this traditional theological explanation of the origin of language was the result of the method both brothers used in their folklore and linguistic studies.

Assessing the overall significance of the Grimms is a complex issue since their work covers different fields of study and is imbedded in a complex historical and philosophical period. A study of the influence of the diversity of the German romantic traditions would point to some essential characteristics of the Grimms.[10] A theological critical study might also benefit our understanding of the Grimms' significance for the founding of a new folklore scholarship. However, such an analysis is not possible within the limits of this book, and we have been concerned

8. McGlathery, *The Brothers Grimm and Folktale*, 69.

9. Peppard, *Paths through the Forest*, 238.

10. Williamson, *The Longing for Myth in Germany*.

here only with the areas in which the Grimms have significantly influenced British scholarship.

Lönnrot and the Kalevala

The Grimms were by no means the only ones to have launched such a grand project. Further north, another man had undertaken a similar project and, due to the mythology and culture involved, he would have a more direct influence on Tolkien's own motivation. The *Kalevala* was a cultural and literary project undertaken by Elias Lönnrot (1802–84), a Finnish physician and mythographer. Lönnrot is particularly significant because of Tolkien's reference to his work. Tolkien's indebtedness to Lönnrot is well-recorded in his letters, especially when it comes to his influence on parts of *The Silmarillion*. In particular, the *Kalevala*'s Kullervo story became one of the inspirations for the Túrin cycle. Tolkien confirmed that he was "immensely attracted by something in the air of the Kalevala"[11] and that "the germ to my attempt to write legends of my own to fit my private languages was the tragic tale of the hapless Kullervo in the Finnish."[12]

In fact, Tolkien recognized early on the influence of Finnish mythology. As early as 1914, in one of his earliest letters to Edith, he referred to his attempt to turn one of the stories of the *Kalevala* "into a short story somewhat in the lines of Morris' romances with chunks of poetry in between."[13] But Tolkien's fascination with the *Kalevala* was not merely due to its stories. Undoubtedly, there was something else at work, something intriguing, an attempt to recover the great loss of myth.[14]

The grandeur and universality of the *Kalevala* indeed attracted Tolkien. But even more than its universality, what attracted him was its historical, cultural, and linguistic distinctiveness, for the *Kalevala* was unmistakably Finnish. This he clearly expressed in one of his famous letters to Milton Waldman, dated late 1951, in which he regrets that England had not a distinct English mythology as there was a Finnish one.[15] This deep regret sprang from the feeling that "his true culture had been

11. L, 214.

12. L, 345.

13. L, 7.

14. Rateliff, *The History of "The Hobbit,"* 1:278.

15. L, 144.

crushed and forgotten; but characteristically, [Tolkien] saw things on a vast timescale, with the Norman Conquest as the turning point."[16] The Norman influence was, to Tolkien, a tragic one, a view he held very early. For example, during a meeting of the King Edward's School Debating Society, he supported the motion: "This House deplores the occurrence of the Norman Conquest."[17] Even though his defense seemed not to have been quite convincing, it is crucial to note that this was not a sentimental juvenile's opinion: Tolkien would never change on this matter. The heart of the issue was the importance of language and stories in "formation of nationhood and culture."

Tolkien shared further with Lönnrot one particular philosophical feature: a proximity with a typical nineteenth-century romanticism. Certainly, romanticism was influential in Victorian England. But it would be a mistake to think that this philosophical and aesthetic movement took root only there. It was also quite rooted in Germany and in France, but also in Finland. In fact, romanticism had reached Finland through poetical works such as *The Poems of Ossian* by James Macpherson. Rapidly, the same romanticism nourished the need for national identity as leading Turku romantic figure Adolf Ivar Arwidsson famously said: "Swedes we are not, Russians we can't become, let us then be Finns."[18] Finnish conveyed a sense of antiquity, of old aestheticism, that is, a true identity. In its turn, the *Kalevala* would become the symbol of the late Romanticism.

The relevance of Romanticism, particularly the kind of those known as the Turku Romantics, should be noted. Before Lönnrot, the great collector of Finnish poetry and folklore had been Henrik Gabriel Porthan (1739–1804), who was the teacher of many Turku Romantics. Sometimes called the "father of Finnish history," he was instrumental in creating interest in the aesthetic value of the runes. This resulted in the recognition of the literary value of Finnish folk tales and poetry.[19] This was so, even though Porthan demonstrated his indebtedness to the Enlightenment when he concluded that the runes were the consequence of ignorance and illiteracy.[20]

---

16. Garth, *Tolkien and the Great War*, 52.

17. Scull and Hammond, *Companion and Guide*, 1:21.

18. Quoted in Pentikäinen, *Kalevala Mythology*, 17.

19. Honko, "The Kalevala: The Processual View," in Honko, *Religion*, 183.

20. Pentikäinen, *Kalevala Mythology*, 6.

But more crucial to Lönnrot was the scholarship and theory of priest and compiler Christfrid Ganander (1741–90) who, in 1789, published the contemporary reference book on folk religion, *Mythologia Fennica*. Ganander was among the first to use the comparative mythology method to study Finnish mythology. He argued that "a knowledge of mythology is absolutely essential in order to be able to devote oneself to ancient Finnish poetry, to be able to read our Finnish runes for pleasure and benefit and with appreciation, and to perceive their nobleness, beauty, and attractiveness."[21] Hence, Ganander did not focus on explaining the myths and legends like his predecessors. "Rather . . . he attempted to understand the runes by examining beliefs and customs related to them."[22]

Building on Ganander's effort to recover tales and myths as they were told, without the urge for Enlightenment rationalistic interpretation, Lönnrot set out to compile the "pre-Christian religion" of the Finns in the form of stories and tales. As such, Lönnrot should be placed alongside comparative mythologists such as Jacob Grimm and Max Müller. They set themselves apart from the evolutionary, "developmental-historical" method that had been the basis for early Finnish folklore scholarship. In fact, fundamental to both Ganander and Lönnrot was the conviction that the basis of folklore was *not* paganism or an "underdeveloped" theology, as Renaissance and Enlightenment scholars had come to believe.

Thus, Lönnrot's main focus was the tales themselves and not the people. Whether the people retelling the tales were still superstitious or not was not of primary concern.[23] This might explain Lönnrot's refusal to record anything but the tales. So, for example, he did not record the context in which the tales were traditionally told, nor did he record, or only on very rare occasions did he record, the names of the "singers." Maybe it is possible to discern, behind Lönnrot's attitude, an attempt at an unbiased recording of ancient tales. Their integrity could then be seen as one of Lönnrot's major concerns. This would also be reflected in the evolution of the *Kalevala* from the "old Kalevala" to the "new Kalevala." Telling is the fact that the impulse to write the *New Kalevala* came from Jacob Grimm's 1845 lecture to the Berlin Academy, leading Lönnrot to give a slightly different perspective to the *New Kalevala*. In fact, "if, in constructing the *Old Kalevala*, Lönnrot was a mythologist in the spirit

---

21. Pentikäinen, *Kalevala Mythology*, 5.

22. Pentikäinen, *Kalevala Mythology*, 5.

23. Honko, "The Kalevala: The Processual View," in Honko, *Religion*, 195.

of Grimm and Ganander (with a view to creating a construct of Finnish mythology), in the *New Kalevala* his is the conscious role of Finnish
mythographer in writing the 'sacred history' of the Finns."[24] Collecting an
oral tradition was not the ending point of the mythographer's vocation.
Rather, the written exposition and transmission of the mythology is at
the heart of what Lönnrot set out to accomplish with the *New Kalevala*.

The Challenges of British Mythographers

The influence of the Grimms was by no means limited to their native land
but soon crossed the Channel and deeply affected British mythographers
and folklorists. The decades 1820–50 saw the emergence, or possible
revival, of fairy tales as popular literature. At the same time, Victorians
appropriated fairy tales into a very different sociopolitical context, giving them a distinctive flavor. In fact, the nineteenth-century's romanticism helped infuse a "folk" tonality to the tales, one that took the reader
back to ancient and popular poetry. British folklorists did not escape the
Grimms' influence but to different ends. While the Germans reflected
a national and romantic ideal, their efforts was only partially replicated
in England. Radically different from its German counterpart, the direction of the British study of fairy tales was to understand them mainly as
stories for children and not as scholarly materials.

This explains Tolkien's sarcastic comment in his "On Fairy Stories"
when he noted that "it is usually assumed that children are the natural or
the specially appropriate audience for fairy-stories."[25] This, he argued, was
a gross mistake typical of adults. By contrast, Tolkien encourages his audience to read those stories for what they are—tales and not as a weird cu-
riosity from ages past.[26] But rather than to collect such random oddities,
adults should better appreciate fairy-stories in and for themselves because
they are not made for children. Fairy-tales are not children's literature.

The difference in the British approach to the tales' function and
genre nonetheless paved the way for the appropriation of the German
Märchen scholarship.[27] Influenced by a different cultural and philosophical context, British folklorists adapted this scholarship to specific

24. Pentikäinen, *Kalevala Mythology*, 239.

25. OFS, 49.

26. OFS, 49.

27. Schacker, *National Dreams*, 19.

social needs. These needs were the reflection of the distinct social issues of Victorian society. Thus, the pervasive "class structure" characteristic of Victorian England became one of the main social problems addressed by British folklorists. While "Germany" wanted to regain the past in order to assert its national identity, Britain was undergoing rapid and radical industrialization that affected the very structure and cohesion of society. Fairy tale collection and scholarship in Britain were developed to answer the question of the unity of society rather than its identity.

Consequently, the fairy-tale genre in Britain assumed a relatively independent form, providing a fertile ground for the British Romantics who "commonly took part in developing a new genre which had its roots in the changing social configuration that stamped the character of the social order in its transition from feudalism to early capitalism."[28] The concerns of this distinctively British fairy-tale tradition were less about the identity of the "British spirit" than they were about the nature and origin of humankind, culture, and societies. By addressing these concerns, the emerging industrial empire could find a renewed social cohesion. Even though Zipes and Schaker disagree whether the English used them to assert their national identity, it is clear that fairy-tales were primarily a literary vehicle for societal criticism than a means for achieving national identity. In fact, "the folklore studies, not entirely pure or disinterested research, were closely connected to the ancillary search for national and cultural identity."[29] The emphasis on the themes of societal order, renewal, hierarchy, and structure of a given society in which the tales are received has been abundantly commented upon.

Regarding mythology, the British evolutionary school presented myths as nothing but the product of human activity and thus could be simply abandoned. To the rationalists, myth was fiction and was hardly connected to human history. For example, David Friedrich Strauss, a significant representative of the theological method known as "higher criticism," stated that myth was not history but "fiction, the product of the particular mental tendency of a certain community."[30] Interestingly enough, Strauss was not an extreme rationalist and maintained that mythical forms, if not historical, were still valuable to an understanding of the interpretation and development of history. As for the Romantics,

28. Zipes, *Breaking the Magic Spell*, 75.
29. Flieger, *Interrupted Music*, 13.
30. Strauss, *The Life of Jesus*, 87, quoted in Burstein, "Journey beyond Myth," 7–8.

with their stress on antiquity and delight in the "unsophisticated," they could only delight in the significance of ancient myths and "folk" traditions. Through a "renewed appreciation of the classics, translations from many lands and cultures, exotic literature from India, and adventures in literary ideas and philosophy," they gave the Victorian period a chance to expand its horizons.[31] To the Romantics, the grandeur of the past was the main means for interpreting and regaining the present.

Unable to choose between the Romantics and the Rationalists, most of the British mythographers used the theory of evolution to maintain the significance of the past for the present. In fact, English anthropologist Edward Clodd summarized the implication of evolutionary theory in the following way: "Thus the study of myth is nothing less than the study of the mental and spiritual history of mankind. It is a branch of that larger, vaster science of evolution which so occupies our thoughts to-day, and with it the philosopher and the theologian must reckon."[32] Through the application of Darwin's theory of evolution to the romantic past, mythographers were able to maintain both the relevance of myth and the superiority of human progress. In this way, nineteenth-century British mythographers partly succeeded in reconciling the rationalist and romantic traditions.[33]

Our consideration of Victorian mythography also requires us to be aware of the main issues it addressed, such as the origin, role, and function of folk and fairy tales and of myths. Shippey, in commenting on two influential mythographers, the German Jakob Grimm and the Danish N. F. S. Grundtvig, defined three main problems faced by mythographers.[34] The first was "to rediscover the lost unity of belief, along the lines of the linguistic science of 'reconstruction' in which they all firmly believed"; second, "to press this into the service of their own major or minor language groups: German, Danish, Frisian, Scottish, etc."; and third, to reconcile it with their own Christian professions.[35]

---

31. Peppard, *Paths through the Forest*, 43.

32. Clodd, *Myths and Dreams*, 138.

33. Burstein, "Journey beyond Myth," 17.

34. Nikolaj Frederik Severin Grundtvig was a Danish philosopher and pastor whose scholarship covered a wide range of subjects. There has been a renewed interest in Grundtvig in the last decade as shown in the publication of two biographies in English: Bradley, *N. F. S. Grundtvig*; Allchin, *N. F. S. Grundtvig*.

35. Shippey, "Grimm, Grundtvig, Tolkien," 12.

Shippey's summary of the mythologists' challenges similarly presents the same questions faced by the scholars of language. The problem of the "unity of belief" begs the question of the common origin of tales and myths—a problem also left unresolved by the scholars of language. In fact, the application of the comparative method led to the disturbing discovery of the close parallels between mythologies. Further, it was not only the mythologies from related peoples and languages like Greek and Latin that could be related, but also those from Polynesia, Persia, China, etc. A broader theory was needed, which would explain the unity and the diversity of *all* world mythologies.

Shippey's second challenge echoes the problem of the diversity and distinctive cultural nature of tales and myths. How was it that fairy-tales, myths, and legends could be so similar and, as the Romantics argued, so distinctive of a language, a culture, and a nation? This question all the mythographers faced, and each gave an answer of his own. Interestingly, Shippey recognizes that in Grundtvig, Grimm, and Tolkien, we witness similar mythographical and mythological concerns. Not only are fairy tales a means to understand one's culture and past, but they can also serve to support national identity, centered on a common language or dialect. Further, this specific linguistic concern serves to flesh out the problem of the "unity of belief" of different peoples. Of course, Tolkien himself does not seem to have been much concerned about that particular challenge of the mythographers. That being said, this importance of the "unity of though" is found in Barfield's own development of the concept of the "ancient semantic unity," that had been influential on Tolkien.

As for Shippey's third challenge, it is characteristic of Victorian society that the Christian faith was challenged to reassert both its uniqueness and its universality. Fairy tales became crucial in the way the relationship between Christianity and other forms of literature was defined. Moreover, fairy tales were not merely literature, but seemed to have higher aspirations about human thought and the human soul. The desire to find common ground between the oftentimes pagan origin of fairy tales and the Christian tradition pushed mythographers to investigate the question of the parallel origin of tales and of humankind.

Tolkien's Status as "English Mythographer"

The status of Tolkien as a mythographer for England is mostly the result of a single influence. In fact, Tolkien himself gives us a clue as to what that influence was. In July 1964, Tolkien sent a letter to Christopher Bretherton asserting that "the germ of my attempt to write legends of my own to fit my private languages was the tragic tale of the hapless Kullervo in the Finnish *Kalevala*. It remains a major matter in the legends of the First Age (which I hope to publish as *The Silmarillion*), though as 'The Children of Húrin' it is entirely changed except in the tragic ending."[36] Tolkien's fascination for the epic Finnish work dates to his early days at Oxford.[37] His discovery of a Finnish grammar could even have occurred as early as fall 1911, as he recounted in a letter written June 7, 1955 to W. H. Auden.[38]

While Tolkien's first reading of the *Kalevala* cannot be dated with absolute certainty, we know that as early as October 1914, Tolkien was already so fascinated by the *Kalevala* that he was recommending it to others. That very month, he wrote his then fiancée, Edith Bratt, that he had shared his delight of the Finnish ballad, part of which Tolkien was working on turning into a short story.[39] The influence of the *Kalevala* on Tolkien is by no means surprising. To Michael Branch, Emeritus Professor of Finnish at University College London, the attractiveness of the *Kalevala* is essentially found in its storyline and its poetical narrative, the very qualities that Tolkien engaged with and gave life to in his mythological corpus.[40]

The *Kalevala* thus led Tolkien on his march forward to writing a mythology for England. Hence, most of the questions raised by Victorian mythographical and mythological scholarship find an echo in Tolkien's project of writing a mythology for England. He answered Shippey's three challenges on his own terms. Though Tolkien can be seen as one of the great English mythographers, it is also notable that he answered the three previously mentioned challenges on his own terms. For example, while the tension between recorded myths and Christian truth is a constant challenge for mythologists, this issue is never clearly manifest in Tolkien.

36. L, 345.

37. Additional parallels between Tolkien and the *Kalevala* are documented in Helms, *Tolkien and the Silmarils*, 42–44; Himes, "What J. R. R. Tolkien Really Did," 69–85.

38. L, 214.

39. L, 7.

40. Branch, "Finnish Oral Poetry," 4.

In regards to this problem of reconciling heathen mythologies with a specific Christian tradition, Shippey comments on the fact that Tolkien's predecessors had faced a relatively easy conflict. Being Protestants they could easily reject the problem of reconciling pagan myth by simply denying the relevance of traditional natural theology. Shippey concludes: "This was clearly not an option open to Tolkien, and here I can only say that he seems to me to have turned the problem of reconciliation from one of belief to one of literary temper."[41]

Shippey is indeed correct in arguing that the anti-Catholic charge against Tolkien was a simplistic one. As we will see in the last section, Tolkien's theory of myth is a theological answer to the problem of the reconciliation of pagan myth and Christian faith. Even though Shippey is right on the evaluation of Tolkien's anti-Catholic critics, it is an overstatement to say that Tolkien was concerned more with literature than belief. Shippey well understands that Tolkien was not really as concerned about the "genuine" faith of the pagans as he was about their literary value. Tolkien's own perspective on this particular question will be explored further in chapter 7.

Even less obvious is Tolkien's treatment of Shippey's first challenge, that of the unity of belief, unless this recovery of unity is what Tolkien partly had in mind when he wrote that his attempt to create a mythology for England was an attempt "ostensibly to replace that which was lost during the Norman invasion and onward."[42] Whether it was or not, this unity of belief and mindset was not the primary preoccupation of Tolkien the myth-maker. It is possible that Tolkien was conscious of the three aforementioned challenges since for Lönnrot, the *Kalevala* was "mythology" in two regards: "It was, on the one hand, a collection of pre-Christian, mythological subject matter, mediated by folklore, and, on the other hand, a synthesis achieved by him as its compiler, the result of his own scholarship.

If Tolkien faced the same challenges, he was particularly concerned by the second one. Language and stories are a true means of asserting and discovering a sense of "national" or cultural identity, as in the case of Lönnrot for whom a nation's language was recorded through folk-tales and legends and transmitted through literature until it "became a means

---

41. Shippey, "Grimm, Grundtvig, Tolkien," 14.
42. Petty, "Identifying England's Lönnrot," 81.

of defining the identity of the nation."[43] In this approach, Tolkien is a descendant of Lönnrot. He tried—whether successfully or not, time will tell—to do for England what Lönnrot had done for Finland, and then say: "I, too, have a history!"[44] If "the *Kalevala* provided literary as well as linguistic stimulus to the young Tolkien," it was also with a similar goal and achievement. The *Kalevala* was truly a triumph of philology, and that certainly pleased Tolkien, captivated as he was by the sound and script of Finnish. As *The Lord of the Rings* was being published, Tolkien wrote in 1954 to the "doyenne of Scottish literature," Naomi Mitchison, that one his Elvish language, Quenya, gave him "phoaesthetic" pleasure, in particular because of his integration of *Finnish* and Greek.

The *Kalevala*, however, was no mere work of philological mastery. It was also a work of mythopoeic imagination. As such, the great Finnish tale was a rediscovery of Finland. Following in its footsteps, Tolkien also became a discoverer of legends, an explorer of a lost part of English history. So, when Tolkien expressed the will to dedicate his legendarium to "England, my country," he was actually setting out on a quest for history.

This is not to say that Tolkien had "nationalistic" motivations, in a socio-political fashion. Rather, he was going after the historic-cultural consciousness of a people, and was concerned about a myth that embodied "the quest for meaning in an otherwise random universe."[45] In many ways, the nationalistic debate of the early twentieth century is thus largely irrelevant to Tolkien. He was much less concerned about whether his country was "right" or "wrong" than he was about the foundation of the country itself, reflecting the conclusion of Chesterton: "'My country, right or wrong,' is a thing that no patriot would think of saying except in a desperate case. It is like saying, 'My mother, drunk or sober.'"[46] There is only "England."

So even though Tolkien was a "writer," in the popular sense, he saw himself as the re-teller of a lost history, or as others have said, a "mediator" of language and history. Thus, he was a true "philologist-creator" of the stature of Lönnrot. His legendarium is, properly speaking, a collection of poems, historical and personal accounts from different countries and times. Eventually, these were assembled "as the Quenta Silmarillion

---

43. Kvideland and Sehmsdorf, *Nordic Folklore*, 4.

44. Francis P. Magoun, quoted in Flieger, *Interrupted Music*, 27.

45. Flieger, *Interrupted Music*, 11.

46. Chesterton, *The Defendant*, 125.

and the Red Book of Westmarch. In this way, the poetry of Middle-earth supplies the depth of authenticity required in Tolkien's mythmaking process."[47] In this again, Tolkien shows great proximity with the *Kalevala*. One distinctive of Tolkien's project is his conscious reframing of the historical setting in a pre-Christian history. In doing so, Tolkien became a the keeper of an ancient knowledge, the scribe of an ongoing tradition, and transmitter of lore. But there is more.

Indeed, one of his less developed but most fascinating characters, Ælwine becomes the literary bridge between Tolkien's sub-created history and Anglo-Saxon history. Particularly, Ælwine can be seen as a bridge between Tolkien's legendarium and the "Matter of Britain." Even more precisely, the presence of Ælwine in the history of Middle-earth means that myth and history become deeply interwoven: the geography of Eärendel slowly evolves into the geography of England through the story of Eriol/Ælfwine, an Anglo-Saxon citizen of tenth-century England. Maybe here lies the historical significance of the "missing link" of Tolkien's corpus: the Arthurian cycle. This could sound at first surprising since Tolkien himself was highly critical of all things Arthur-connected.[48] Until the publication of *The Fall of Arthur*, most people would not have considered Tolkien as being of real value to Arthurian studies.[49] One could have even argued that Tolkien's complete disinterest in the Arthurian matter was because of his insistence that this material was British rather than distinctly English.[50] Maybe he could have simply said with Chesterton: "rightly or wrongly, this romance established Britain for after centuries as a country with a chivalrous past. Britain had been a mirror of universal knighthood."[51] However, while Chesterton was content to accept this as a matter of fact, Tolkien tried to remediate this in providing England with a true *English* mythology.

The significance of the Arthurian material for the particular challenge Tolkien faced as a mythographer lies in its historical dimension. The importance of the Arthurian material is highlighted by the fact that David Doughan pointed out that while Tolkien tried to avoid explicit use

---

47. Petty, "Identifying England's Lönnrot," 76.

48. Flieger, *Interrupted Music*, 35–37.

49. For the significance of Tolkien's *The Fall of Arthur*, see Higgins, *The Inklings and King Arthur*.

50. L, 144.

51. Chesterton, *A Short History of England*, 27.

of Arthurian material, the latter keeps "breathing through" in his work.[52] Again, the presence of the character of Ælfwine provides the ground for considering Tolkien's mythology as a discovery of England's past history. If, as we have already noted, Tolkien was a discoverer of legends and a discoverer of the lost part of English history, this "mythological history" encompasses the Arthurian cycle. One thing is clear: Tolkien's interest in the "Matter of Britain" demonstrates his lifelong project of writing a substantial Arthurian poem. As such, *The Fall of Arthur* is a failure given that it was left unfinished. However, it reveals Tolkien's deep interest in myth and history. In fact, the "mythological" material contained in *The Fall of Arthur* is much more historical than many other accounts of the Arthurian cycle published during the late nineteenth century. The historical connection Tolkien made between "England" and his own mythology came through his own rendering of the "Atlantis" story, his personal rendition of a time-travel legend.[53] If Tolkien did actually reject everything Arthur-related as unfit for the creation of a distinct *English* mythology, he was nonetheless quite ready to allow a certain significance for the Arthurian material. This is shown not only by the publication of his poem *The Fall of Arthur* but also, in its time, by *Gawain and the Green Knight*.[54] Moreover, the previous quote indicates that Númenor "became" English history.

Bilbo's own hand, writing the initial version of what would later become *The Hobbit*, reminds us that "men changed the language that they learned of elves in the days when all the world was wonderful."[55] With this simple sentence, Tolkien remains faithful to the mythologist's expressed conviction that language was crucial to the understanding of history. It is also distinctly Barfieldean reflecting, as we have seen previously, the conviction that language and meaning are deeply connected. All this is clearly evidenced in Tolkien's overall purpose of giving his country a mythological past, which had been strangely absent in comparison to the mythological depth of its neighbors like Ireland and Scotland, or in comparison to the Nordic countries. To Tolkien this lack was so lamentable that he set about to offer a mythology. As he wrote to Milton Waldman in late 1951:

52. Doughan, "An Ethnically Cleansed Faërie?," 21–24.

53. L, 347. Tolkien contributed another significant Arthurian writing, "The Notion Club Papers," which we will not explore at the moment. See the discussion of "The Notion Club Papers" by Flieger in her *A Question of Time*, particularly 61–88.

54. For Verlyn Flieger, the Matter of Britain even forms the essential model for Tolkien's own legendarium. See Flieger, "J. R. R. Tolkien and the Matter of Britain," 53.

55. H, 215.

I was from early days grieved by the poverty of my own beloved country: it had no stories of its own (bound up with its tongue and soil), not of the quality that I sought, and found (as an ingredient) in legends of other lands. There was Greek, and Celtic, and Romance, Germanic, Scandinavian, and Finnish (which greatly affected me); but nothing English, save impoverished chap-book stuff. Of course there was and is all the Arthurian world, but powerful as it is, it is imperfectly naturalized, associated with the soil of Britain but not with English; and does not replace what I felt to be missing.[56]

Tolkien's desire to invent a mythology for England paralleled the German thirst after a national spirit, but unlike many Victorian mythologists, Tolkien was not primarily concerned about class, social order, or cultural criticism. In the way he approached the purpose of myth-making, Tolkien was more "German" than many of his fellow British mythologists and folklorists. Moreover, there are striking parallels between the character and work of the Grimms and Tolkien's. Both of them, due to their romantic nature, were deeply affected by a love of history and delight in the past. Moreover, like the Grimms, Tolkien's literary success paradoxically contributed to the failure of his academic, philosophical, and theological perspectives.

One scholar commented on the Grimms, saying that their "dream of recapturing for the nation its ancient heritage was in great part defeated by their successful methods of scholarship, for their loving devotion to detail and historical accuracy made them inaccessible to many readers."[57] The same sort of conclusion applies to Tolkien. Even though he became an important and unavoidable part of popular culture, his academic theories never came to have a significant impact on language or fantasy. It could be argued that, in fact, Tolkien exerted an influence on the writing of fantasy but that he never had a theoretical influence on the way fantasists came to write their stories. Most fantasists look to Tolkien for inspiration or model, but very few question the validity or the possibility of a fantasy methodology. This failure pushed Tolkien to address even more effectively his goal of giving a lasting mythological cultural heritage to his country, England.

56. L, 144.

57. Peppard, *Paths through the Forest*, 32.

6

Mythical Language

THE DESIRE FOR A mythology, the sub-creation of a historical myth was the material outcome of Tolkien's mythological quest. However, the quest could not have succeeded without a clear view of the relation between myth and language. As it turns out, Tolkien's place among the British mythographers and mythologists is further reinforced by the connection between his theories of language and myth. In fact, most of the debates occurring in nineteenth-century Britain were related to the debate regarding the relation between languages and mythologies. Furthermore, the questions regarding the origin and function of language were transferred into mythological studies. As we have seen, the question of the origin of language was hotly debated by British scholars, and "mythology" also became a theoretical battlefield. One particular topic soon became the heart of the matter. In many ways, the appearance of mythical language in the history of humankind came to be considered the key to understanding both language and myth. Tolkien himself was part of this late-Victorian debate, and interacted with the three scholars who contributed to the main theories developed in the middle of the nineteenth century—Müller, Lang, and Barfield.

Myth and the Development of Language

Among the many theories of mythical language, Max Müller's theory of myth as a "disease of language" stands out as one of the most debated. As is well known, Tolkien vehemently rejected this explanation of the parallel development of myth and language. Müller's theory is based on the view that the development of mythology demonstrates the essential division of human history between metaphorical and literal forms of language and culture. While studying the history of religions and myths, Müller was confronted with two main problems: their origin and their irrational elements. In approaching these issues, Müller was careful to start with basic observations. This was important for Müller, especially because he himself had never traveled outside Europe. Many of his critics would point out this fact. It turned out to be a significant factor in the 1860 election to the Boden Professorship of Sanskrit. The supporters of his rival, Monier Williams, did not hesitate to use Müller's German origin (even though he had become a citizen of Her Majesty in 1855) and his lack of first-hand knowledge of India. Their own candidate was favored by the Englishmen in India and by the Natives.

Monier Williams was indeed known by the "Natives" from India, who further had continuing close communication with him. Why then, they asked, should the electors disregard the opinions of those directly concerned by the choice at hand? Moreover, Müller's opponents considered the German-born scholar was only that: a scholar. But, "the Professorship is not for Oxford alone," they exclaimed—implying again that Müller's lack of direct knowledge of India was a serious impediment to his choice as professor of Sanskrit. Their conclusion was without appeal: "Let us then vote for the man who is well-known and loved in India."[1] In the end, Müller was passed over in favor of Monier Williams but was in 1868 elected to the Professorship of Comparative Philology. Despite the controversies regarding his actual knowledge of India, Müller defended the validity of his study of Sanskrit myth and language. This led him to one fundamental observation. The apparent irrationality of myths was hiding the irrepressible rationality of the human mind.[2] The most crucial element necessary for the "Professor" was not so much actual knowledge of India as knowledge of its myths and language.

---

1. Beckerlegge, "Professor Friedrich Max Müller," 197.
2. Müller, *Life and Religion*, 151.

For Müller, the world could only be rational. To believe otherwise would imply that mind and thought could merely be the outcome of matter. Such an option was at best impossible, at worst ridiculous. Quite the contrary, Müller contended, there was primacy of mind and thought over matter; mind was the *prius* of all things. This was the first of Müller's three main premises to the approach of history and myth. His second premise was that language and thought are identical, thus establishing a strong connection between the history of language and mythology. The third premise was that, if languages possessed common origins, so did religions and mythologies. Thus he could explain, through language, both the unity and diversity of myths.

From these three premises, Müller found himself confronted with the dilemma of how irrational myths could arise from the mind of rational human beings. Indeed, if the origin of myths, tales, and legends was to be found in the rational origin of humankind, the irrational tendency of myths required an explanation. One of the ways scholars resolved this dilemma was to rely on evolutionary theory. They argued that the irrationality of myths was the fruit of the primitive savage's mind and the irrational condition of humankind. Of course, Müller could not accept the evolutionary explanation founded on the conviction that man's nature was initially similar to that of lower species. Instead, he sought an explanation for the irrationality of myths in the development and interpretation of myths themselves. In his view, the problem of the interpretation of myths resulted from a decay and misinterpretation of language. In Müller's view, our ancestors thought in words and elaborated languages around natural figures. And while "we speak of the sun following the dawn, the ancient poets could only speak and think of the sun loving and embracing the dawn. What is with us a sunset was to them the Sun growing old, decaying, or dying."[3] Müller believed that "primitive" thought was based on natural images that man used to explain his world. However, while some scholars thought that our ancestors used this language in a literal manner, Müller argued that our ancestors knew that the true meaning of mythical language was not literal.

Over the course of time, the original meaning of language and words was partly lost due to two factors. The first reason was the ascription of a fixed meaning to words that had originally conveyed a multilayered richness of meaning. For example, while the term "wind" used

3. Müller, *Selected Essays*, 1:369.

to have a diversity of meanings, such as "spirit" and "breath," only one meaning was retained, remembered, and attached to an individual god, thus giving rise to the mythologies we know. Müller follows the same line of thought in his article "Comparative Mythology" (1856), in which he argued that the diversity of meaning contained in mythical language was achieved with "polyonymy" and "synonymy." The same object could be represented and described with different names. However, confusion arose because of the many names given to the many different attributes of the same thing, so that "in the course of time, the greater portion of these names became useless, and they were mostly replaced in literary dialects by one fixed name, which might be called a proper name of such objects. The more ancient a language, the richer it is in synonyms."[4] As a consequence, mythical language, which intended to convey something about the world in the form of a story, came to be seen only as accounts about natural and personal deities.

The second factor for the loss of the original meaning of language was the loss of original etymologies. Greek myths are typical examples of how the Greek language at first provided all that was necessary to make mythical literature intelligible and rational. However, over time, some Greek words became etymologically separated from their meaning. More pointedly, Müller argued that Greek words became alienated from their etymologies after losing their reference to the original Sanskrit. Thus, they became rationally inexplicable from an exclusively Greek point of view. To make sense of the words, the Greeks adopted a literal reading of mythical literature. For example, the "sunrise was the revelation of nature, awakening in the human mind that feeling of dependence, of helplessness, of hope, of joy and faith in higher powers, which is the source of all wisdom, the spring of all religion."[5] However, this rather simple and rational approach was soon lost. Man adopted a metaphorical and then a literal reading of myths, thus confusing the thing signified and the sign, the word and the concept behind it.

For Müller, confusion in the reading of myth resulted from a confusion in language, thus leading to his famous statement that myth was indeed a "disease of language." Because man misinterpreted language, mythical stories became interpreted through non-metaphorical human rationality. This was a dramatic error because it made it impossible to go back

---

4. Müller, *Selected Essays*, 1:377.
5. Müller, *Chips from a German Workshop*, 96.

to the origin of humankind. To the German-born scholar, myths revealed, when correctly interpreted, the origin and rational nature of humanity.

Andrew Lang and the Evolutionary School of Mythology

Andrew Lang (1844–1912) was a famous Scottish poet, novelist, and literary critic, as well as an historian. His interests ranged from anthropology to psychic research and the study of fairy tales, for which he is now best remembered. He produced the famous twelve colored fairy books, republished by Dover between 1965 and 1968. Lang studied successively at Edinburgh, St. Andrews, and finally Balliol College, Oxford. Towards the end of his career, he was made an honorary fellow of Merton College, where Tolkien taught from 1945 to 1959. In 1891, *Men and Women of the Time* wrote of Lang that he was "one of the most pleasant writers of the time." Indeed, he belonged to a new class of literary critics that dominated British journalistic life from the 1880s until the end of World War I. Over the course of his career, he published over eighty books and numerous journal articles and collaborated on over a hundred other works. Because he was so prolific, he was charged with intellectual superficiality and even naive romanticism. Despite this criticism, Lang represents a very different manner of studying mythology.

Lang's overview of this field of study took a different direction than Max Müller's because he saw three main schools of mythology. The first school was the one defended by Müller, which relied on a philological approach to the study of myths, thus being labeled "the philological school of mythology." Because its main thesis is that myths are primarily the result of the savage man's contemplation of nature, this school has also been labeled "the naturist school." Müller was associated with the naturist school, and stood in a specific branch of it, which some called the "solar myth school." The second school of mythology was the "anthropological school," also known as the "ritualist school" because "its central focus was the belief that rituals were undertaken to manipulate, largely rejuvenate, the universe and that myth was merely the narrative accompaniment to such rituals."[6] The third school referenced by Lang, and probably the oldest one, was based on an historical and degenerative approach to the study of myth. The roots of this school

---

6. Mallory and Adams, *Encyclopedia of Indo-European Culture*, 117.

go back to the Greek philosopher Euhemerus; it was revived by the nineteenth-century philosopher Herbert Spencer.[7]

Lang, as a fierce defender of the anthropological school, constantly opposed Müller's position. Three main areas of disagreement can be determined. The first concerns Müller's theory of myth as a "disease" of language, mainly because, as we have seen, such a notion implied a degenerative view of history. Because of his own evolutionary bias, Lang held the opposite view regarding the development of history. From that perspective, to regard myth as a "disease" or degeneration was to consider that man was on the same degenerative path.

Secondly, he thought the philological school was deeply mistaken in its very method when narrowly focusing on the similarities among *related* language families. For example, Müller's approach was fundamentally misguided in focusing exclusively on the Aryan language as an explanation for the alleged degeneration of myths and history. Furthermore, Lang added that relying on the priority of names and etymology was a methodological danger because no consensus could be reached regarding which language was to be considered as key to etymological reconstruction. Some argued for the Semitic family of languages, others for Greek, and finally others, led by Müller himself, for Sanskrit. Because of its characterization of myth as a disease of language and its narrow scope, "philological mythology" was, in Lang's opinion, self-contradictory and was discredited by its very adherents.

Finally, Lang pointed out that the philological school began by investigating the *names* of myths rather than the myths themselves. Their mistake was to consider that the titles of myths were original, while they were for Lang an obvious late addition. His criticism of the philological school certainly does not lack clarity, arguing that "the philological method is inadequate and misleading, when it is a question of discovering the *origin* of a myth, or the physical explanation of the oldest myths, or of accounting for the rude and obscene element in the divine legend of civilized races."[8] In contrast to the philological school, Lang's understanding of folklore reveals two main assumptions about the human mind and the progression of human history.

Lang, on his part, always affirmed the uniformity of the human mind throughout cultures at any given time. The mind of the savage in

7. Lang, *Custom and Myth*, 199.
8. Lang, *Myth, Ritual, and Religion*, 1:27.

India, in Africa, or in northern Europe was identical, thus leading to his statement that "the uniformity of human fancy in early societies must be the cause of many other resemblances"—that is, myths. Lang's stress on the evolution of the human mind is also seen in his "Ballade of the Subconscious Self":

> Who suddenly calls to our ken
> The knowledge that should not be there;
> Who charms Mr. Stead with the pen,
> Of the Prince of the Powers of the Air;
> Who makes Physiologists stare–
> Is he ghost, is he demon, or elf,
> Who fashions the dream of the fair?
> It is just the Subconscious Self.
> He's the ally of Medicine Men
> Who consult the Australian bear,
> And 'tis he, with his lights on the fen,
> Who helps Jack o' Lanthorn to snare
> The peasants of Devon, who swear
> Under Commonwealth, Stuart, or Guelph,
> That they never had half such a scare–
> It is just the Subconscious Self.[9]

The commonality between peoples and civilizations was not based on language but on an identical mental condition, their "subconscious self." Lang pointed out that "while languages differ, men (and above all early men) have the same kind of thoughts, desires, fancies, habits, institutions."[10] The savage's mind was further characterized by Lang as "childlike," which led him to argue that tales were most fit for children because they had a mental condition most similar to that of the savages. This commonality of the savage's mental condition was reflected in their myths. Thus, Lang's assumption of the uniformity of the human mind can be seen as a form of anthropological and trans-historical *analogy*. As Lang said, *Humani nihil a se alienum putat*, "nothing human is alien to me."[11] This was true even for our primitive ancestor.

To explain his own method of folklore-study, Lang first compared his science of mythology—folklore—to archaeology. In his master work *Custom and Myth*, he explained the connection: in a similar way that

9. Lang, *New Collected Rhymes*, 62.

10. Lang, *Modern Mythology*, xvi.

11. Lang, *The Making of Religion*.

archaeology "collects and compares the material relics of old races, the axes and arrow-heads, there is a form of study, Folklore, which collects and compares the similar but immaterial relics of old races, the surviving superstitions and stories, the ideas which are in our time but not of it."[12] As such, folklore attempted to go back through the "layers of history" to humankind's initial state of mind in order to teach "civilized" man. The first element of a proper method of folklore is to confront the myths as they are found, either in oral or written form. Then, "when an apparently irrational and anomalous custom is found in any country, [the method is] to look for a country where a similar practice is found, and where the practice is no longer irrational and anomalous, but in harmony with the manner and ideas of the people among whom it prevails."[13] Lang was convinced that such an irrational, anomalous, and "barbaric" belief or rite will be found in every myth, and on this point Greek myths are not superior to the myths and tales of the Bushmen, the Hawaians, or the Eskimos. This consideration thereafter leads to the necessity of gathering, or "collecting," data from myths and tales, data concerned with unveiling the incongruous elements of myths.

Once this data was gathered, the next task was comparison. It was precisely regarding this task of gathering and comparing that Lang, once again, faulted Müller's school. To him, one of the problems of the philological school was that it confined itself to a certain family of languages and forgot that the whole human race was *one*. The main flaw of this school was thus its lack of scope. It was often assumed that the study of myth should be traced back to the origins of the Indo-European culture and language, thus focusing almost exclusively on the "Aryan" family. There lay the stumbling-block. The "mythologists" and "folklorists" could never come to agreement on this issue because their methods of investigation were so different. Lang complained that mythologists of the philological school were "averse to the method of folklore. They think it scientific to compare only the myths of races which speak languages of the same family, and of races which have, in historic times, been actually in proved contact with each other."[14] The difference between mythologists and folklorists is also seen is the personal attitude of Müller and Lang towards myths. As Lang himself clarified, Müller explained Greek

12. Lang, *Custom and Myth*, 11.
13. Lang, *Custom and Myth*, 21.
14. Lang, *Custom and Myth*, 22–23.

myths by Aryan and Sanskrit etymologies, whereas he "kept finding myths very closely resembling those of Greece among Red Indians, Kaffirs, Eskimo, Samoyeds, Kamilaroi, Maoris, and Cahrocs. Now if Aryan myths arose from a 'disease' of Aryan languages, it certainly did seem an odd thing that myths so similar to these abounded where non-Aryan languages alone had prevailed."[15]

For Lang, the disdainful attitude of the philologists towards "primitive" races was the sign of their failure. Lang argued that the difference between the myths of the Greeks and that of the Bushmen was not one of essence but of having advanced out of a savage state of mind and society while retaining "their old myths, myths evolved in the savage stage, and in harmony with that condition of fancy."[16] This easily leads to the general conclusion that every time we are confronted with an "anomalous" element, we can say with confidence that it merely represents the survival of a previous stage in the evolution of humankind.

However, Lang realized that he had not yet answered the main questions, that of the origin of the mythical and anomalous element as well as the origin of the mental condition of the savages. This was a complex and difficult question that could prove the downfall of the anthropological-ritualist school, and the answer proposed is a repetition of the central tenets of evolution. Thus Lang asked: "'But how did this intellectual condition come to exist?' To answer that is no part of our business; for us it is enough to trace myth, or a certain element in myth, to a demonstrable and actual stage of thought. But this stage, which is constantly found to survive in the minds of children."[17] His conclusion was obvious: men created myths and tales because they were the fruit of their "natural" mode of thinking at a particular stage of evolution.

Here, Lang faced the same problem every anthropologist and mythologist had to struggle with. How could the "savages" entertain the same irrational ideas that were transmitted over and over in myths? Lang's answer is here again decidedly evolutionary. This is so, he answered, because "their intellectual powers are not fully developed, and hasty analogy from their own unreasoned consciousness is their chief guide. Myth, in Mr. Darwin's phrase, is one of the 'miserable and indirect

---

15. Lang, *Modern Mythology*, 4.

16. Lang, *Modern Mythology*, 54.

17. Lang, *Myth, Ritual, and Religion*, 1:157. See LoTR, Appendix B, 298–303.

consequences of our highest faculties."[18] This mythological mode of thinking and writing was shaped by a mental condition characterized by two main elements. The first was the incapacity of savages to distinguish between animate and inanimate objects, thus leading to the rise and prevalence of fetishism and animism along with beliefs in ghosts, the soul, and other such notions. As Lang said, "The savage tendency is to see in inanimate things animals, and in animals disguised men."[19] The second element of the "savage's thinking" was a strong belief in sorcery, accompanied by a conviction in the rationality of the sensible world.

This mode of thinking was, first, rational, in the sense that they did have a view of causation. The sensible world made "causal sense," so to speak. Evidently, this did not mean that the savage was thinking in the same way we do. One notable difference is the savage's view of causation. To Lang, "*Post hoc, ergo propter hoc* [after this, therefore because of this], is the motto of the savage philosophy of causation."[20] This phrase *post hoc, ergo propter hoc* is not used by Lang without a reason. It served to express the following logical fallacy: because event B follows event A; then event A is the cause of event B. For example, imagine that you did not pray for the blessing of a certain god on the occasion of the birth of your child and that this child dies a few days after. From this succession of events, you will conclude that the god punished you for not offering prayers to him. However, there might not be any direct cause from one to the other. That is the essence of the *post hoc, ergo propter hoc* fallacy. Lang summarized this difference in the following manner: "Another way to put it is that causal connection pertaining to thought is made into causative relation pertaining to facts."[21] Thus natural causation became a personified causation by agents such as gods, heroes, or demons.

But the "savage's thinking" was also, secondly, mostly irrational and superstitious because it turned natural causes into supernatural ones. The consequent belief is what Lang called spiritualism, that is, the belief in the persistent existence of the souls of the dead. Finally, Lang affirmed that the savage man is by nature curious, never ceasing, like the child, to

18. Lang, *Myth, Ritual, and Religion*, 1:36n1.

19. Lang, *Myth, Ritual, and Religion*, 2:344. See also Lang's further comment: "By the 'savage condition,' is meant the mental condition of men who did not draw the line between man *and* the animate or inanimate objects (all nature is in a way *animate*)." Lang, *Myth, Ritual, and Religion*, 2:346.

20. Lang, *Myth, Ritual, and Religion*, 1:94.

21. Lang, *Myth, Ritual, and Religion*, 1:96.

ask questions. Far from being fundamentally afraid, he is fascinated by what surrounds him, and this awe-inspired contemplation leads him to reflect on the workings of the world. Such were our "primitive ancestors": credulous and demonstrating a confused state of "mental indolence."[22] This led Lang to affirm the evolution of savages from their initial state of mind and thought toward "civilization." Savages really were our distant ancestors. The relevance and significance of the theory of evolution was such that "we are enabled to examine mythology as a thing of gradual development and of slow and manifold modifications, corresponding in some degree to the various changes in the general progress of society."[23]

As we come to the end of our survey of the British study of myths, tales, and folklore, it is interesting to turn to Chesterton who entertained a rather negative attitude towards folklorists of either school. According to him, all committed the same mistake in believing that man and the world could provide the ultimate meaning and ground for the study of folklore. But to Chesterton, man cannot study himself from the "outside": "The truth is that the science of folk-lore has suffered terribly from oblivion of one fact: that folk-lorists also are folk."[24] To study man, what was absolutely needed was a vantage point from which to observe and study. Not only that, one needed an "observer" that could actually study man "from the outside." To the English journalist, man could not pretend to study mankind as a neutral scientific observer could. Man could not be the "observer" and the "object of study" without the risk of accepting all sorts of mistaken assumptions about himself. Regarding comparative religion Chesterton commented in a like manner: "Comparative religion is very comparative indeed. That is, it is so much a matter of degree and distance and difference that it is only comparatively successful when it tries to compare. When we come to look at it closely we find it comparing things that are really quite incomparable."[25] This criticism is right to the point.

Chesterton's criticism could imply that theories of folklore held essentially to a materialistic philosophy for which all that exists is material. However, we should proceed with caution. In fact, Lang should not be considered as a materialistic thinker. For him, the study of myths had a double purpose, that of demonstrating the savage's mental condition and

22. Lang, *Myth, Ritual, and Religion*, 1:54.

23. Lang, *Myth, Ritual, and Religion*, 1:39.

24. Chesterton, *Collected Works*, 34:248.

25. Chesterton, *The Everlasting Man*, 85.

that of demonstrating the surviving belief in the fundamental existence of a super/supra-natural world. His evolutionary theory does not lead to a materialistic world. In that, Lang differentiated himself from many other Darwinians who rejected the mere possibility of the non-material aspect of reality. Through his interest in psychic research—in *The Book of Dreams and Ghosts* (1897) or *Magic and Religion* (1901)—Lang showed that his theory did not require the denial of the supernatural. Although presented in a very different way, this evolutionary conclusion was echoed by Barfield.

Barfield's Theory of "Ancient Semantic Unity"

We presented Barfield in the previous chapter, but left his theory of "the ancient semantic unity" unexplained. This chapter will define this theory and draw out the implications of Barfield's anthroposophy for the study of myth. As Flieger affirms, Barfield's theory is one with "far-reaching philosophical implications," so it is necessary to become familiar with its basic argument, especially in light of its potential influence on Tolkien. Barfield's theory of the ancient semantic unity has been well summarized by different scholars, notably Verlyn Flieger, who has shed light on Tolkien's re-appropriation of Barfield's theory. In her book, *Splintered Light*, she summarizes the theory of the ancient semantic unity as the notion that "myth, language, and humanity's perception of the world are interlocked and inseparable."[26] This is but a different way to summarize Barfield's argument for the "ancient" unity of meaning, words, and perception. Therefore, Barfield's theory is one of historical and cultural fragmentation, something that is implied in the very notion of an "ancient" unity. Thus Flieger can summarize *Poetic Diction*, pointing to two important points made by Barfield. The first is that according to him, "language and perception are interconnected and interdependent. Perception gives rise to language, which then houses and further develops perception." Secondly, he proposed that, "in its beginnings, language did not separate between the literal and the figurative or metaphoric. Each word embodied an 'ancient semantic unity' of meaning that has over time divided and subdivided into ever narrower, more precise, and often more abstract unity of meaning."[27] The "mythological" implication of Barfield's theory

26. Flieger, *Splintered Light*, 37.

27. Both quotes are from Flieger, "Owen Barfield," 50.

is that "he examined the history of words, and came to the conclusion that mythology, far from being (as the philologist Max Müller called it) 'a disease of language,' is closely associated with the very origin of all speech and literature."[28] Moreover, his theory is concerned with the development of human consciousness toward a full and exhaustive awareness and participation with the wholeness of existence. Myth demonstrates this development in the initial period of humankind's history.

This view of the evolution of human consciousness is evidenced in Barfield's analysis of the mythical unity between abstract and metaphorical language. To him, the history of human consciousness demonstrated the initial unity of different forms of thinking in one mythical language. In fact "Barfield has pointed out again and again in a dozen books and numerous essays that, when we look back into the history of any so-called abstract or immaterial word, we come to a period when it also had a concrete or outer meaning as well, like 'gravity' or 'focus'–meaning 'heavy' or 'weighty' and fire-burning hearth,' respectively."[29] R. J. Reilly, in his survey of Barfield's philosophy, defended the same point in commenting on Barfield's notion of the poet as a master of metaphors: "What the true poet grasps, then, and expresses by metaphor, is the ancient unity of thought and perception . . . or that the percept and the meaning were one and the same apprehension; the whole of reality, not only the percept or only the concept, was taken in as a kind of meaning figure."[30] In presenting his own interpretation of the evolution of language, Barfield was opposing a common view that considered the development of language as a progress towards more complex and abstract thought. This was further considered to imply a greater richness of language, including poetical language. Thus, Barfield remarked, "Shelley said that metaphorical language, some would say mythical language, marked 'the before unapprehended relations of things and perpetuates their apprehension until words . . . become . . . signs for portions or classes of thought.'"[31] This of course was to Barfield pure nonsense. In fact, the linguistic observation proved the contrary: ancient languages possessed a richness and beauty that did not depend on their correspondence to a more abstract form of thought. Worse, Shelley's position was self-contradictory. Despite all its

---

28. Connolly, *Inklings of Heaven*, 41–42.

29. Carpenter, *The Inklings*, 34.

30. Reilly, "Anthroposophical Romanticism."

31. PD, 67.

proclaimed "poeticism," the argument of Shelley and like thinkers did not value poetical and metaphorical language at all. They valued poetical language insofar, said Barfield, as they equated it with reason. Thus, the general argument that "from the primitive meanings assumed by the etymologists, we are led to fancy metaphor after metaphor sprouting and solidifying into new meaning"[32] is false. Far from becoming more and more poetic, language is becoming more fragmented, and the multiplicity of meanings, in becoming fixated, leads to an impoverishment of language. All this, contends Barfield, was because the original unity between thought and perception of poetical language was lost.

However, it seems that Barfield goes further than the mere unity of thought and perception. For him, the "unity" was not merely between thought and perception but also between metaphorical and literal meanings. In Johnson's words, "Barfield argued that initially for man, there had been no distinction between 'literal' and 'metaphorical.'"[33] Indeed to him the blowing wind was not similar to, or somewhat like, someone breathing, but it *was* the breath of a god. This pointed to the fact that nothing was then "abstract" or "literal," or rather that there was no difference between them. This unity of "metaphorical" and "literal" was explained by Barfield's belief "that this unity of consciousness had become fragmented as conceptual thinking developed and he looked forward to man being better able to reconcile the literal and the abstract again some day with a renewed perception informed by the past, rather than reverting to it.[34] This is clearly seen in the previous example of the word *pneuma*, in which we saw that Barfield's point was not merely the unity of percept and meaning but the unity of the word's various meanings. Thus, for a greek word like pneuma, the various united meanings ranged from "spirit" and "wind," to "breath," "breath of god," or even "principle of life." Some of those meanings are literal and others metaphorical, but they are all integrated in an ancient semantic unity.

This is the first of Barfield's two governing principles regarding the evolution of language. Percepts and meanings have become fragmented, and the real meaning of metaphors has been lost. "Primitive men" reported metaphors "as direct perceptual experience. The speaker has observed a unity, and is not therefore himself conscious of *relation*. But we, in the

---

32. PD, 67.

33. Johnson, "Tolkien's Mythopoesis," 27; see Chen, "A New Periodization," 399.

34. Chen, "A New Periodization," 399.

development of consciousness, have lost the power to see this as one." This power of unity, according to Barfield, was essential, almost inherent to human language, but was rapidly lost. He located this dramatic turn of human history early on during the fourth and fifth centuries BC At this point "the old, instinctive consciousness of single meanings, which comes down to us as the Greek myths, is already fighting for its life by Plato's time."[35]

In constructing his own theory, Barfield interacted, and debated with, other scholars, including Müller. Flieger even contends that he was the "first serious student of words" to contest Müller's interpretation. This is quite an overstatement since, as we have seen, William Whitney had already debated the very same issues with Müller well before Barfield's birth. Still, Barfield's interaction with Müller in particular is significant, but also symptomatic of disagreements he entertained with all mythological schools. Barfield's diagnosis of their failure serves as an explanation of the relevance of his theory. He faulted them for two basic mistakes. The first was the separation between metaphorical and literal language. Whereas for Müller, myth was the fruit of a "literal misunderstanding" of metaphorical language, for Barfield, "the word *myth* in this context must be taken to mean that which describes humankind's perception of its relationship to the natural and supernatural worlds."[36] So, for example, "*Pneuma* initially meant neither 'wind' nor 'breath' . . . but had its own peculiar meaning, which has since, in the course of the evolution of consciousness crystallized into the three meanings specified.[37]

Barfield's point is that all language is radically metaphorical. He explains that words originally had several meanings, and that this richness of meanings is the essence of mythical language. Here again, he separates himself from scholars such as Müller and Lang. Of course, Barfield does not want to reject the metaphorical nature of mythical language altogether. In fact, he tries to maintain a careful balance between two extremes. On the one hand, he is cautious not to reject all forms of metaphorical language, since this would be a dissociation of words and meaning. On the other hand, he avoids considering metaphorical language as a disease of human history, discarding language as altogether purely evolutionary. The latter view is of course that of Müller. Barfield commented that Max

35. PD, 95.

36. Flieger, *Splintered Light*, 37.

37. See Connolly, *Inklings of Heaven*, 120.

Müller "perceived very clearly the intimate bond connecting myth with metaphor and meaning, [and] was actually obliged to characterize the myth as a kind of *disease* of language. Such a point of view is barely worth discussing, or rather, to the genuine critic, it is *not* worth discussing."[38] This is echoed in Tolkien, who probably follows Barfield without interacting directly with Müller himself, at the expense of intellectual honesty, when he affirms that "Max Müller's view of mythology as a 'disease of language' can be abandoned without regret."[39] Barfield's third way was that "these poetic, and apparently 'metaphorical' values were latent in meaning from the beginning."[40]

Moreover, Barfield vehemently rejected any explanation founded on a degenerative evolutionary approach. It is here that Barfield's anthroposophy enables him to bring positive elements to the study of myth. Barfield's rejection of accepted evolutionary explanations does not mean that he denied any relevance to "evolution." In fact, his own theory of the "evolution of consciousness" is a rare combination of humankind's evolution of consciousness with a positive appraisal of the development of anthropocentric history. But, Barfield always maintained, there was at no point an idea that primitive language was less rich than our modern ones. The mistake of evolutionary theories regarding language, indicates Barfield, is that "the naturalist is right when he connects the myth with the phenomena of nature, but wrong if he deduces it solely from these."[41] Thus, the process of evolution truly explains the differentiation of modern language out of mythical language. In fact, the complexity of our language is the result of a fragmentation of the unity of metaphoric and concrete language leading to differentiation of meanings. This understanding led Barfield to state that "mythology is the ghost of concrete meaning."[42] Mythology reveals the shadow of an original, ancient, concrete meaning; this crucial aspect of mythical language is demonstrated in Barfield's defense of original participation. The first principle is thus a principle that observes the difference (the "fragmentation") of things.

The second Barfieldean principle is what he called the "living unity," which is concerned with knowing what things *are*. As Barfield

38. PD, 89.

39. OFS, 41.

40. PD, 85.

41. PD, 91–92.

42. Flieger, *Splintered Light*, 33.

himself describes, "it observes the resemblances between things," and thus attempts to discover what things are.[43] This also is a poetical principle enabling the poet to make connections between similar things and recombining them. As Barfield writes: "the poet is Zeus; he has swallowed the heart of the world; and he can reproduce it as a living body."[44] This second principle requires less explanation for it plays a less important role in Tolkien, which explains why it has received much less attention from Tolkien scholars.

The combination of these two principles gives humankind the possibility of knowing what things *are* and *are not*, thus giving life and meaning to the surrounding world. Barfield's conclusion defines the importance of metaphor and myth. Barfield asserts that myths are relevant and that "to the poetic understanding myth presents an altogether different face. These fables are like corpses which, fortunately for us, remain visible after their living content has departed out of them."[45] For Barfield, myth is but the means to regain the older, original, and undivided meaning of words. Thus, the meaning of myths is not primarily in the mythical cycles and stories themselves but in the meaning of their words. But now is the time to turn more specifically to Tolkien.

Tolkien and Mythical Language

Evidently, Tolkien entertained a fascination with Barfield's theory of an original unity of meaning giving rise to a proper theory of myth. Tolkien certainly agreed with this aspect of Barfield's theory. In fact, Arundel Lowdham, one of the main characters of "The Notion Club Papers," defends a Barfieldean view of language. The metaphorical dimension of language was "inherent" to language, would declare Barfield. To use Lowdham's words, "it is not only the way language is changed, it is how it was made."[46] The point is stressed further and made more explicit when Lowdham adds that this inherent working of language is paramount to the contemplation, in a single action, of "sound: sense; symbol: meaning."[47] This of course is a truly Barfieldean statement. This should

43. PD, 87–88.
44. PD, 88.
45. PD, 91.
46. HoME, IX:225.
47. HoME, IX:225.

not be surprising given the influence Barfield's theory seemed to have on Tolkien's own theory of language.

Tolkien commented that Barfield had an important influence on *The Hobbit* and that in fact Barfield had "modified his whole outlook." Many have commented on this expression. The first thing to note is that this expression is a second-hand report, that of Lewis about Tolkien. This very expression is usually taken from an undated letter Lewis reportedly sent to Barfield in 1928. However, the undated letter has not been located in Lewis's *Collected Letters*, and only Carpenter, in his official biography of Tolkien, reports the same words. Even so, Barfield's influence on Tolkien is clear. In August 1937, Tolkien wrote to Allen & Unwin about the only philological remark present in *The Hobbit*, noting that it was "a point that will (happily) be missed by any who have not read Barfield (few have), and probably by those who have."[48] Many will be surprised to hear that there even is a philological remark in *The Hobbit*. And those same will probably look for it without success. The elusive philological remark is in chapter 12, "Inside Information." As Bilbo entered the lair of the dragon Smaug, his "breath was taken away." Tolkien adds, in an already quoted passage of *The Hobbit*, that this was "no description at all. There are no words left to express his staggerment, since Men changed the language that they learned of elves in the days when all the world was wonderful."[49] Men had changed the language, and the initial unity between thing perceived, language, and thought was fragmented. This is evidence that Tolkien largely accepted Barfield's insight of an ancient "semantic unity." However, Tolkien was not as focused as Barfield was on the essential drive to discover meaning. To Tolkien, stories could be valued for stories' sake, and not primarily for their meaning. In that, Tolkien demonstrates some definite differences with Barfield. If Tolkien could have agreed with Barfield that myths were the way to recover ancient meaning, he probably would have been as obsessed with meaning as Barfield ever was.

Thus, if Tolkien followed Barfield in significant ways, it is nevertheless an overstatement to affirm, as Flieger does, that Tolkien's works of fantasy as well as his more theoretical "On Fairy-Stories" are "pure Barfield."[50] Johnson provides a better appreciation when she concludes that "there were aspects of Barfield's argument with which Tolkien and

48. L, 22.

49. H, 15.

50. Flieger, *Splintered Light*, 178n3.

Lewis would never agree, but his 'theory of how words originally embodied an ancient, unified perception' inspired them both."[51] In fact,
there are different ways to look at Barfield's impact on Tolkien. Rather
than assume that they agreed on every point, it is possible to argue that
they agreed on a main direction. Tolkien stood in close agreement with
Barfield regarding "some important interests and attitudes," and in presenting their relationship in this way, Flieger is perfectly right. However,
this does not require a philosophical and theological agreement. Tolkien
certainly agreed that the history of humankind evidences a refinement in
the use and meaning of words, as Barfield explained, but this was apparently not due to an evolution of consciousness.

Tolkien also sided with Barfield in his opposition to the thesis of
the richness of poetical language. Ancient poetry was, for Barfield, but
ancient language, and Tolkien would heartily agree: ancient language is
"endued with an extraordinary richness and splendour."[52] This, Tolkien
clearly shows through his love of the aesthetics of archaic words and
languages. Of course, it is not without finding an echo in Barfield's con-
testation of the complexification of poetical language. In fact, if the "rationalists" were right, how were we to explain the aesthetic pleasure felt at
the sound of ancient words? Tolkien had felt such an aesthetic experience
at the reading, not of a work, or of a poem, but of a single word, "éarendel," from the Crist poem of Anglo-Saxon poet Cynewulf:

> Éalá Éarendel engla beorhtast
> ofer middangeard monnum sended!
> Hail Earendel, of angels brightest,
> above Middle-earth sent unto men![53]

"Éarendel," a name Tolkien thought "entirely coherent with the
normal style of [Anglo-Saxon], but euphonic to a peculiar degree in that
pleasing but not 'delectable' language."[54] And Lowdham, after encoun-
tering these words in the dictionary "felt a curious thrill, as if something
had stirred in me, half wakened from sleep. There was something very
remote and strange and beautiful behind those words, if I could grasp it,

---

51. Johnson, "Tolkien's Mythopoesis," 28.

52. PD, 71.

53. This very same line is quoted by Tolkien's Lowdham, from the "Notions Club
Papers," in *Sauron Defeated*, 236.

54. L, 297.

far beyond ancient English."[55] As for Eriol, to whom we will return in a moment, the first mention of Eärendel opened for him what seemed to be a new world. "Éarendel" (or more often "Eärendel") is highly significant in Tolkien's mythical corpus. Indeed, the poem "The Voyage of Eärendel the Evening Star," marked the beginning of Tolkien's own mythology, and was dated 1914. As for "The Notion Club Papers," Tolkien mentioned it in a letter dated July 21, 1946, to Stanley Unwin that he had put it aside to concentrate on *The Lord of the Rings*. At this point, Tolkien has worked on his own mythology for more than thirty years. What was consistent in all the works related to the burgeoning richness of Middle-earth was the aesthetics of words and their definite role for the formation of his mythical history. In fact, words are the distinguishing characteristic of Elves, who loved making words—and that is the real cause of the diversity of their tongues.[56]

From these Barfieldean considerations, it is natural to move on to Tolkien's own approach to mythical language. Of course, from a self-professed linguistic inventor we should not expect a philosophical treatise or a somewhat analytical book, but a fictional embodiment. As with the philology taken from Barfield in *The Hobbit*, we must look in Tolkien's mythological corpus for his view of mythical language. We can begin exploring Tolkien's relation between language and myth by looking at a passage of "The Etymologies," an invented "historical dictionary" of the Elvish language, later published in part three of *The Lost Road*. What is interesting in this particular piece is that it was essentially written in 1937–38, before Tolkien started working on the Hobbit-sequel. In this very unusual dictionary, Tolkien remarks about his Elvish languages that they were to be embodied in stories, and in the history of the Elvish race.[57]

However, the best place to go is one of the most intriguing pieces Tolkien ever wrote, "The Notion Club Papers." The connection between language and myth, that is, the creation and function of a mythical language, is most manifest in this work. It begins during a meeting of a fictionalized "Inkling" meeting. In the course of the meeting, one of the main characters, Arundel Lowdham, discusses his dreams about a mysterious "Atlantis." During the meeting's first reported minutes, "suddenly Lowdham spoke in a changed voice, clear and ominous, words in an

55. HoME, IX:236.
56. HoME, V:168.
57. HoME, V:341.

unknown tongue; and then turning fiercely upon us he cried aloud: *Behold the Eagles of the Lords of the West! They are coming over Númenor!*[58] Lowdham spoke in Elvish, a language unknown even to himself. The surprise was general, more so for Michael Ramer, for "Númenor" was his name for "Atlantis." And as far as Éarendel was concerned, Lowdham felt something quite similar to Tolkien, albeit expressed in different words. Éarendel, "a queer name, and a queer end," was the name of Lowdham's father's ship.[59] The importance of words for history does not stop here however. Lowdham was called Alwin Arundel by his mother, while his father had chosen Ælfwine Éarendel. It is also no accident that Alwyn (Arundel) Lowdham is "Éadwines sunu," the son of Éadwine. A very significant fact lies in the name of Lowdham's father: Edwin (Éadwine). It must be noted the closeness of "Edwin" to "Oswin," a name taken directly from another of Tolkien's often enigmatic writings, "The Lost Road."

"The Lost Road" reports on a series of recurrences of several father-son duos, like "Eädwine-Ælfwine" and "Audoin-Alboin." Ælfwine, also called Eriol, is the Elf-friend *par excellence*. The character Eriol ("One who dreams alone") appears in the first book of *The Lost Tales* when, lone survivor of a wrecked ship, he reaches the Cottage of Lost Play on Tol-Eressëa, the Lonely Island of the Elves.[60] The cycle of Eriol, also named the Eriol-Saga is highly significant within the Tolkien corpus. In fact, Christopher Tolkien even says that "the story of Eriol the mariner was central to my father's original conception of the mythology."[61] The role the Eriol-Saga should have played, if *The Lost Tales* had been completed, was to form the groundwork for the connection between actual England and Tolkien's mythology. It sill plays this function in part today, despite being "among the knottiest and most obscure matters of the whole history of Middle-earth and Aman."[62] Originally, indicates Christopher Tolkien, the Eriol-Saga was supposed to connect Middle-earth to the invasion of Britain by Hengest and Horsa in the fifth century—which forms the background to *Beowulf*. Even when the original name ("Ottor" before becoming "Eriol") and setting had changed, the mythical function remained. The connection between Tolkien's Middle-earth and England

58. HoME, IX:231.
59. HoME, IX:234.
60. HoME, I:13–14.
61. HoME, I:22.
62. HoME, I:23.

would have been so clear as to allow the identification of Kortirion, the town at the center of Tol-Eresseä, as Warwick.[63]

All these mythical-historical connections have one thing in common: languages, words, Elvish. It was through his father's notebooks that Lowdham became fascinated with languages. It is through Elvish tales that Eriol comes back to England to tell the tales that would be transmitted in English (a new "common tongue"). And it is through dreamed language that Lowdham again finds his connection to the mythical past. Lowdham's eruptions of memory from the "far Past" are through language and mythical language, serving as a bridge between history and myth. As Flieger makes clear, these manifestation of memory into the present are "mythical co-incidents," neither looking forward nor looking backward. Both are concurrent. We must then conclude that the connection between, notably, related names is evidence that the recovery of language can lead to the recovery of history, especially ancient (or mythical) history. Through language, we can indeed go back to the past, as we see from many discussions in "The Notion Club Papers." The minutes of the meeting reports: "Thus spake Ælfwine the Fartravelled son of Éadwine. Those names connect distant points in history. This, explains Flieger, "should immediately be recognized as the same verse remembered by Alboin Errol from his dream and quoted with some chagrin to his father, Oswin."[64] This connects his own mythology to England via the Atlantis cycle. As Lowdham says after bringing fragments of a story in both Avallonian and Adunaic languages reported in the minutes of the Notion Club, this longer fragment is a record of a catastrophe of the Atlantis type.[65]

So to the question "If you went back would you find myth dissolving into history or history into myth?," Wilfried Trewin Jeremy comments: "Sometimes I have a queer feeling that, if one could go back, one would find not myth dissolving into history, but rather the reverse: real history becoming more mythical—more shapely, simple, discernibly significant, even seen at close quarters. More poetical and less prosaic, if you like."[66] More clearly, "perhaps the Atlantis catastrophe was the dividing line?" And indeed it was. The Atlantis story was the point where history and

---

63. HoME, I:25. Moreover an early poem by Tolkien, "Kortirion among the Trees," was dedicated to Warwick.

64. Flieger, *A Question of Time*, 146.

65. HoME, IX:246–47, 249.

66. HoME, IX:228.

myth (Númenor) touched. England's history would then be taken up into myth. The Atlantis joined the Eriol-Saga: myth and history fused within Tolkien's corpus. Mythical language has given life to mythical history.

7

Tolkien's Theory of Myth

IN 1961, AS *THE Lord of the Rings* was becoming increasingly a commercial success, Tolkien wrote a very annoyed letter to his publisher, Allen & Unwin. It was not with the respectable publisher, however, that Tolkien was displeased, but with comments made in the introduction to the Swedish translation of *The Lord of the Rings*. There Åke Ohlmarks suggested that the Ring was "in a certain way the 'Nibelungen Ring,'" the ring from the famed Scandinavian Saga known through the *Niebelungenlied*. Tolkien rather sarcastically commented in his letter that "both Rings were round and there the resemblance ceases."[1] Whether Wagner's Ring, or the atomic bomb, Tolkien's "ring of power" has been much allegorized, despite his claim that his work had its own integrity and should be read for itself. Such is the plight of every myth-maker. It seems quite impossible for a new "creation" to avoid being socially or politically interpreted, allegorically or not. This might even be the result of the nature of myth-making itself, being "an original enterprise that can range from the very personal to the overtly political."[2]

Very personal or very political, it seems that all myth-making is faced with this tension. Clearly Tolkien did not escape this "fate" and his work has often been politically and socially allegorized. In the previous chapters,

1. L, 306.
2. Blumenfeld-Kosinski, *Reading Myth*, 171.

Tolkien has been considered in the context of the British mythographers and mythologists, but he is also an example of myth-making, which "is a less well defined activity than mythography. The term can suggest anything from a creative rewriting of mythological material (see C. S. Lewis' *Till We Have Faces*) to a radical shifting of the ideological bases of society (see Sir Thomas More's *Utopia*)."[3] With Tolkien we have undoubtedly a very personal enterprise that has had profound and lasting social and cultural repercussions. To understand the impact Tolkien's mythology had, and to understand the meaning this could have had for him, we must proceed first by looking at Tolkien's theory of myth in the academic mythological debate. This debate, of which Tolkien was a part, poses important questions such as the origins of myths and their relation to "truth."

The Mythopoeic Debate

Tolkien's place in twentieth-century literature is due almost exclusively to his myth-making ability. The artful imagination of his mythological writing has had more influence than the theology behind his theory of aesthetic fantastic creation. This emphasis on his fantasy writing, at the expense of its theological foundation, is the result of failing to read Tolkien in his intellectual and theological milieu. This can be seen in the misleading popular idea that Tolkien coined the term "mythopoeia" to refer to literature of a mythical tone.

The blame for such a cliché cannot be placed solely on the popular reading of Tolkien. Even Tolkien scholars, without explicitly arguing that Tolkien coined the term "mythopoeia," reinforce the Tolkienian specificity of this concept. Other scholars adopt a more balanced view, arguing that Tolkien's mythopoeic faculty functions in the same way described by mid twentieth-century anthropologists of the University of Chicago.[4] But the fact remains that the reference to a mythopoeic faculty is already evidenced in the nineteenth-century debate on mythology. All schools used it not only to describe the nature and abilities of "primitive" man but also to justify an "archeological" study of humankind. Once again, the two most important schools in the debate were the philological and the anthropological, led by Müller and Lang respectively. Like the theory of language, the theory of myth was derived from the study of the nature, origin,

3. Blumenfeld-Kosinski, *Reading Myth*, 171.
4. Lobdell, *The World of the Rings*, 28–29.

and development of fairy tales, themselves originating in the mythopoeic faculty, based on which Victorian anthropologists and philologists were able to explain the nature, origin, and development of humankind.

Therefore, if we trace our mythological steps back to the nineteenth century, we encounter the two familiar figures of Max Müller and Andrew Lang. Both had much to say about the mythopoeic nature of humankind. While the purpose here is not to give an exhaustive summary, a basic presentation of the pertinent views of Müller and Lang is necessary. Given the disagreement Tolkien voiced regarding Müller, more attention will be given to him. As became clear after our investigation of Müller's view of language, he postulated a development of mythopoeic man in three different epochs. The first one was that of agglutinative grammar, of the slow, systematic organization of language. Müller also labelled this epoch "empirical."[5] Second came what Müller called the rhematic period during which man began to form expressions to render the most necessary ideas. Then came the mythological or mythopoeic age, with which we are most concerned here. Myth-making came only after a long and slow process of language formation, intimating that man had no myths before he could express them in a particular and organized form. The mythopoeic age, then, was an age of accumulation of materials, but not properly an age of myth-making.

When examining the intellectual and social conditions of the mythopoeic age, Müller again uses philology and relies on his conviction that the origin and common trait of all myth-making was the motif of the sun conquering the night. Hence Müller read every myth invoking "the shining one pursuing the burning one," as signifying "the sun follows the dawn." From that, and from that only, he deduced the apparition and development of myths and the practice of myth-making, always finding commonalities between myths. Writing to the Reverend G. Cox on November 10, 1863, Müller made this point quite clear. To his opponents who criticized him for concluding that the "myth of the Sun" was found in every culture, Müller replied in his letter, "and yet it is not our fault if the Sun has inspired so many legends and received so many names. And what else do you expect at the bottom of mythology if not the reflection of heaven and earth in the mind and language of man?"[6] Myth-making then has but one origin but many embodiments; numerous versions of

5. Müller, *Lectures on the Science of Language*, 116–17.
6. Müller, *The Life and Letters of Max Müller*, 1:299.

the same stories, myths, were transmitted. In conclusion, for Müller, the mythopoeic age was really the age when the original and sublime ideas of the Indo-Iranian people had been originally conceived.

Müller and Lang agreed that the history of mankind revealed such a faculty for myth-making and/or myth-believing. However, the two schools opposed each other over whether or not the mythopoeic faculty gave birth to a mythopoeic age characteristic of one period of human history. The philological school, led by Müller, affirmed that the mythopoeic faculty resulted in a confusion of thought, since man was unable to distinguish properly between literal and metaphorical language, leading to misinterpretation.[7] This confusion resulted in a mythical age in which man confused the metaphorical and literal interpretations of myths. Thus Müller's theory of myth as a "disease of language" was reinforced by his interpretation of the origin and development of the "mythopoeic faculty." For Müller, the mythopoeic age was primarily a linguistic one.[8]

Andrew Lang voiced the response of the anthropological school in several reviews of Müller's work and in his own *Custom and Myth*. In this latter work, Lang argued that if there were a mythopoeic age it should not be considered as a disease but merely as a demonstration of man's evolution. Lang had serious doubts, to say the least, regarding Müller's idea that man had just "forgotten" the meaning of myths, thus giving rise to an epoch of myth-making. The problem with that theory, thought Lang, is that it did not explain why man suddenly became a myth-maker. To Lang, the answer was rather simpler: "The truth is, that while languages differ, men (and above all early men) have the same kind of thoughts, desires, fancies, habits, institutions."[9] The mythopoeic mind was one of these evolutionary stages. For Lang, the mythopoeic faculty, in its historical development, was the result of the animistic stage of the development of human thought. He would himself summarize his position in the classic *Custom and Myth*: "Now the peculiarity of the method of folklore [that is, the anthropological school] is that it will venture to compare . . . the myths of the most widely severed races. Holding that myth is a product of the early human fancy, working on the most rudimentary knowledge

---

7. Lang, *Modern Mythology*, 6.

8. Müller, *Selected Essays*, 1:369.

9. Lang, *Modern Mythology*, xvi.

of the outer world, the student of folklore thinks that differences of race do not much affect the early mythopoeic faculty."[10]

Given the context of this mythological debate, Tolkien's reference to the "mythopoeic" power of man is a reference to the problem of the origin and nature of myth. It is also necessary to remember that, if the mythopoeic was the center of a difficult debate regarding the nature of humankind, Tolkien's use of the same terminology probably reflects the same concerns. Even though he clearly did not coin the term, its use in his writing points to the existence of a specific Tolkienian answer to this issue.

The Origin and Nature of Myth

During Trinity term 1929, Oxford, was the setting for an extraordinary event. C. S. Lewis, after long-lasting resistance, prayed to an unknown God and slowly became "the most dejected and reluctant convert in all England."[11] He was now a theist. His theological and spiritual journey, however, was not over. Incidentally, around that same time, Tolkien gave Lewis "The Lay of Leithian," a major part of his mythology, for him to read. Lewis had come a long way during the five previous years, from a strong rationalistic atheism to deism and finally theism, while still not acknowledging the singular significance of Christ's death and resurrection. It took about two years for Lewis to openly declare himself Christian. Significantly, Lewis wrote on December 21, 1941, to Bede Griffiths that he owed to the Inklings something "incalculable." He adds: "[Hugo] Dyson and Tolkien were the immediate human causes of my own conversion. Is any pleasure on earth as great as a circle of Christian friends by a good fire?"[12]

The precise process of Lewis's conversion is still somewhat conjectural. A few landmarks can be identified, though, among which was a discussion between Lewis, Tolkien, and Dyson. Beyond the conversion of Lewis, the significance of their interaction was the importance that myth came to have. That, of course, is surprising enough if we think in purely theological terms. We might be tempted to ask how myth, something in itself nonhistorical, could lead to the conversion of Lewis who so emphasized the historicity of the death and resurrection of Christ. Lewis himself

10. Lang, *Custom and Myths*, 23.

11. Lewis, *Suprised by Joy*, 229.

12. Lewis, *Collected Letters*, 2:501.

explained what had happened during this memorable night in a letter sent to Arthur Greeves in mid-October 1931. In his words: "Now what Dyson and Tolkien showed me was this: that if I met the idea of sacrifice in a Pagan story I didn't mind it at all: again, if I met the idea of a god sacrificing himself to himself . . . I liked it very much and was mysteriously moved by it: again, that the idea of the dying and reviving god (Balder, Adonis, Bacchus) similarly moved me provided I met it anywhere *except* in the Gospels." Lewis's dismissal of the Gospels was, to Tolkien and Dyson, quite irrational. But they were right! Lewis continues: "The reason was that in Pagan stories I was prepared to feel the myth as profound and suggestive of meanings beyond my grasp even tho' I could not say in cold prose 'what it meant.'"[13] What Lewis was ready to accept from any literature, he was not ready to accept from the Gospels, even only as literature. His reconsideration of his position led him to become a Christian theist.

Immediately following this discussion, where Lewis had denied all value and significance to the Christ of the Gospels, Tolkien began drafting his most influential poem, "Mythopoeia." Dedicated "To one who said that myths were lies and therefore worthless, even though 'breathed through silver,'" it is clearly addressed to Lewis. In "Mythopoeia," "Philomythus" argues against Lewis, "Misomythus," and points out the mythic function of Christ's death and resurrection. Tolkien's poem "Mythopoeia" encapsulates his ideas about the nature of myth, but it can also be read in the light of our previous discussion of Victorian mythology. It is the best primary resource available to answer the question Tolkien himself asks about the nature of myth: "whence came the wish, and whence the power to dream, or some things fair and others ugly deem?" (lines 73–74). This question Tolkien will answer with several arguments.

First, it is important to note that Tolkien's defense of myth is at the same time an attack on the relative materialism of most mythological schools, and not only the rationalism that Lewis was exemplifying. This is exactly what Philomythus is getting at in the opening lines of the poem: "You look at trees and label them just so, / (for trees are 'trees' and growing is 'to grow')" (lines 1–2). In the same way, he describes the stars as "some matter in a ball" (line 5), running on fixed trajectories and quite "inane" (line 7). The implication is clear. For Misomythus, the universe is one of scientific laws and quite devoid of all transcendent quality. For Philomythus, the world is not so. Rather:

13. Lewis, *Collected Letters*, 1:977.

God made the petreous rocks, the arboreal trees,
tellurian earth, and stellar stars, and these
homuncular men, who walk upon the ground
with nerves that tingle touched by light and sound.[14]

Against Lewis's rationalism and his contemporaries' materialism, Tolkien puts the discussion of myth squarely within the theological context of a doctrine of creation. If the natural world demonstrated the presence of God, it was quite logical to expect myths, ancestral tales about the world, to also reflect the presence of the Creator of the world and of stories.

Second, Tolkien argues in "Mythopoeia" that myth-making is testimony, not to an evolutionary dimension of human thought but to an intrinsic quality of human beings. Certainly, myth-making is historically embodied and myth displays a development "from dark beginnings to uncertain goals" (line 12). In fact, the myth-making power is so strong that it almost serves to qualify what being human means. The true nature of things perceived can equally be conveyed in myth. These, then, do not tell lies. They are the truth of the world. This is precisely why, continues Philomythus, naming is a decidedly mythic thing: "trees are not trees until so named and seen."[15] Naming, describing the world, not always as it is seen, but as it is: that is the calling of the myth-maker. Then we can say of the myth-maker: "Blessed are the legend-makers with their rhyme / of things not found within recorded time."[16]

Third, Tolkien is arguing in "Mythopoeia" that myth-makers created their myths looking backward in time. In fact, the activity of the myth-maker is similar to that of an imaginative archaeologist, as Tolkien poetizes in lines 38–39: "digging the foreknown from experience / and panning the vein of spirit out of sense." Man, because of his mythopoeic ability, digs out unknown, or forgotten things from memory, later producing spiritual ideas and thoughts. This is especially evidenced in the Elvish artistic sensitivity for language.

Tolkien's defense of myth in "Mythopoeia" is thus directed at a rationalism characteristic of the early twentieth century. Being directed at Lewis' doubts about the historical or truthful dimension of myths, particularly as relating to, Tolkien later argued in "On Fairy Stories," the myth that became fact: Christ's incarnation, death, and resurrection. As Tolkien

---

14. Tolkien, "Mythopoeia," lines 20–23, in *Tree and Leaf*, 86.

15. Tolkien, "Mythopoeia," line 29, in *Tree and Leaf*, 86.

16. Tolkien, "Mythopoeia," lines 97–98, in *Tree and Leaf*, 88.

maintains, myths are not by nature "lies" but contain an element of truth, a "splintered light" emanating from God's natural light. In this sense, myths are part of the traditional Catholic understanding of natural theology. Tolkien's second defense is directed at Lewis' doubts about the truth of Christianity. Here, Tolkien argued that we can see in all myths the same divine light, a reflection of the existence, creation, and natural revelation of the same God. Moreover, Tolkien's conclusion goes further in affirming that Lewis was intellectually dishonest in accepting the resurrection stories contained in myths while rejecting the story of the gospel on the basis of the impossibility of a resurrection. Again, here Tolkien demonstrated that Lewis was not the rational thinker he thought he was; otherwise, he would have made the essential connection between world-mythologies and the historical myth of the Bible. However, he was so blinded by his rationalism that he rejected the logical outcome of his rational thinking. It is interesting to notice that this way of reasoning, based on the irrationality of modern rationalism, is one of the methods in which Lewis later excelled. Tolkien himself probably learned of this apologetic tool through his reading of Chesterton, the master of paradoxes.

Tolkien's response to Lewis's charge that "myths are lies" is clear when he affirms that "the heart of Man is not a compound of lies, but draws some wisdom from the only Wise,"[17] indicating that myths are the fruit of man's heart, of man's creative activity. To Tolkien, myths are not primarily the inspiration of demons, some church fathers held, nor are they abstract lies, as Lewis held. In affirming that man's heart is not a "compound of lies," but that it takes its source from the "only Wise," Tolkien places himself squarely within the Roman Catholic tradition, holding that everything in man and every human activity reflects the source of all being, thus echoing St. Thomas. As the theologian wrote, "Since all things are destined and directed by God to good, and this is done in such a way that in each one is a principle by which it tends of itself to good as if seeking good itself, it is necessary to say that all things naturally tend to good."[18]

On the other hand, Tolkien is Catholic enough to acknowledge a problem with the nature and development of myth. According to Tolkien, myths are the result of both "use and misuse" (line 69), of man's "world-dominion by creative act" (line 59); they are both light and dark" (lines

17. Tolkien, "Mythopoeia," lines 53–54, in *Tree and Leaf*, 87.

18. Aquinas, *Truth*, 1:3–37. Aquinas also defends the theory that "Inasmuch as they exist, all things are good."

44 and 67).[19] Tolkien is well aware that myths are "mixed literature." In theological language, myths reflect the sinful nature of man, a nature that is not wholly changed. The dark aspect of myth comes from a misdirection given to the mythopoeic faculty by sin, and is not the result of the intrinsic nature of the mythopoeic gift. Here Tolkien defends the dignity and legitimacy of the mythopoeic power. He maintains that the mythopoeic creation is a right, that sowing the "seeds of dragons" (line 68) is a worthy and glorious activity, a right that "has not decayed" (line 69). Man's mythopoeic faculty witnesses to humankind's development and reflects the Source of all creative power, God himself, the Divine Artist. Myths are the "heraldic emblems of a lord unseen" (line 118), the flowing banner of God's artistic presence within man.

Moreover, Tolkien's reference to the "timid hearts" is significant since it is a clear reference to the Beatitudes (Matt 5:8):

> Blessed are the timid hearts that evil hate
> that quail in its shadow, and yet shut the gate;
> that seek no parley, and in guarded room,
> though small and bate, upon a clumsy loom
> weave tissues gilded by the far-off day
> hoped and believed in under Shadow's sway.[20]

One of the possible implications of Tolkien's reference to this verse in Matthew in connection with the mythopoeic power is that this faculty allows the poet, the myth-maker, to regain truth that has been perverted by sin. The mythopoeic believer is "blessed" in that he shall "see God." Even though the "timid hearts" that hate evil "quail" "under Shadow's sway," they shall have their reward.

The reference to the "timid hearts" can also be found in Isaiah 35:4 (Protestant Darby version): "Say to them that are of a *timid* heart, Be strong, fear not; behold your God: vengeance cometh, the recompense of God! He will come himself, and save you." However, the Douay-Rheims version possibly used by Tolkien reads: "Say to the *fainthearted*: Take courage, and fear not: behold your God will bring the revenge of recompense: God himself will come and will save you." It is possible that Tolkien, with his knowledge and interest in languages, sided with a more

---

19. See, for example, the importance of line 59, in which Tolkien refers to man's world-dominion, a dominion that is effected and actualized through man's creative activity.

20. Tolkien, "Mythopoeia," lines 85–90, in *Tree and Leaf*, 88.

literal translation of the Hebrew word and appropriated the English term "timid heart."

Further, it is possible to see the Thomist influence in this poem. Aquinas defends the position that man's tendencies are the result of a potential or actual/habitual appetite, which in turn is the result of man being created by God. In fact, "only a rational nature can trace secondary ends back to God by a sort of analytic procedure as to seek God Himself explicitly. In demonstrative sciences a conclusion is correctly drawn only by a reduction to first principles. In the same way the appetite of a rational creature is correctly directed only by an explicit appetitive tendency to God, either actual or habitual."[21] Moreover St. Thomas argues that an appetite is a special power of the soul, thus locating precisely the seat of human appetites. Tolkien's description of the mythopoeic faculty falls within this Thomist definition of the appetite, and more precisely within the parameter of the potential natural appetite, defined as that which is in accord with one's nature. To Tolkien, the mythopoeic is more than a mere power possessed by humankind but an *appetitus naturalis* of the soul, a legitimate thirst after myth itself, a thirst created and implanted by the Creator God.

The Relation of Myth and History with Truth

The origin of myth and of the mythopoeic was not the only challenge Tolkien tried to address. Myth-making, while being an appetite of the soul, raises questions about myth, history, and truth—especially questions about the identity of the pagan gods. Tolkien was acutely aware of the apparent contradiction for a pious Roman Catholic to re-invent pagan myths. For Tolkien, to defend the power of myth-making necessitated presenting an explanation of the historical development of myths and their relation to historical truth.

Different theories have been offered to explain the interrelation of myth and history. Edmund Spenser, for example, defended Euhemerism, a view affirming that the gods are merely divinized historical characters. Or in other words, that "behind the myths of pagan antiquity lay real and recoverable history." This theory has its roots in Cyprian, who expressed the opinion that the gods are not truly gods. Rather, they were at one time kings, "who, because of their memory as kings, began later

21. Aquinas, *Truth*, 3:42.

to be worshipped even in death. Thereupon, temples were established for them."[22] In this, Cyprian echoes Tertullian's response to the charge of atheism brought against the Christians: "As for your gods, then, I see in them merely the names of certain men long dead. I hear their stories and recognize the sacred rituals arising from these myths."[23] Later Tertullian is more specific and continues: "We cease worshipping your gods when we find out that they are non-existent. This, then, is what you ought to demand, that we prove that those gods are non-existent and for that reason should not be worshipped, because they ought to be worshipped only if they were actually gods."[24] For Cyprian, as for Tertullian, gods and mythological figures could only be historical persons that had been mythologized or deified in ancient times.

Opposite this historical explanation stands the position held by Justin Martyr, who is usually understood to say that pagan gods are demons worshipped by men, sometimes without men's knowledge. However, his position is more subtle. After writing that "we can now show that these myths were first related through the instigation of evil demons to deceive and seduce all men," he continues by noting that "for having heard the Prophets announce the coming of Christ and the punishment of sinful men by fire, they produced many who were reputed to be sons of Jupiter, thinking that they would be able to put the suspicion in men's minds that those things foretold of Christ were fabulous tales, just as were those related by the poets."[25] Here Justin falls short of equating the gods with the demons who are behind the poet's inspiration. In fact, he does not argue that gods *are* demons but that the demons inspire the invention of pagan gods. This reading of Justin does him more justice and is in agreement with his *Dialogue with Trypho*, in which he presented the Devil as a counterfeiter.

Tolkien took another approach, maintaining that a proper theory of myth should allow for both spiritual and historical significance. In doing so, Tolkien did not invent a new way to look at pagan mythology. Rather, he adapted a theological tradition that went back to the church fathers, particularly those of the Alexandrian tradition. One of the most significant Alexandrian figures is Clement of Alexandria who argued that

22. Cyprian, *Treatises*, 349.

23. Tertullian, *Apologetical Works*, 41.

24. Tertullian, *Apologetical Works*, 35.

25. Justin Martyr, *The First Apology*, 91–92.

pagan philosophy could render the human mind more subtle and ready to understand higher realities, including the gospel. God, in effect, had distributed "his blessings both to Greeks and to barbarians, and in their own time those were called who were predestined among the elect."[26] Clement could even go so far as to argue that God gave to the Hebrews the commandments, and to the pagans he gave philosophy. The significance of Clement is highlighted by the fact that, almost alone among the church fathers, he not only mentions the Greeks but also includes Eastern philosophers, those he called "indian gymnosophists."[27]

Further, as far as "pagan mythology" is concerned, Clement of Alexandria seems to have been a major influence on Newman. In fact, the Alexandrian church father is a recurring figure in Newman's writings, whether in *An Essay in the Development of Doctrine* or *The Arians of the Fourth Century*, and there is little doubt that Newman stood firmly in the Alexandrian tradition. In the *Apologia*, Newman said that it is Clement's, and Origen's, philosophy that "carried me away."[28] Throughout his writing, Clement shows a fascinating appreciation for pagan myths and religion. This sensibility was the direct consequence of the theological interpretation of myths as preparation for the gospel.

This notion of *praeparatio evangelium* is much discussed in Catholic theology, but also provides the background of many debates regarding one of Tolkien's favorite texts, the 3182 alliterative verses of the poem *Beowulf*. The Old English poem can even serve as a test case of the relation between the virtues of the "pagans" and the truth of the Christian faith. Writing some time between the eighth and the eleventh centuries, the "Beowulf-poet" recounts the epic tale of Beowulf, hero of the Geats, come to the aid of Hrothgar, king of the Danes. After battling the monster Grendel and its mother, Beowulf is proclaimed king of the Geats before, after some years, finding his death in heroic battle defeating a mortal dragon. The amount of writing regarding the tension of the "virtuous pagan" in *Beowulf* could itself be the topic for an entire book. It is sufficient here to say that Tolkien saw no particular irreconcilable tension between the "pagan" character of *Beowulf* and the potential Christian dimension of the poem.

26. Clement of Alexandria, *Stromata*, 524–25.

27. Clement of Alexandria, *Stromata*, 316.

28. Newman, *Apologia Pro vita Sua*, 36.

A first resolution comes through the use of the contrast of implicit and explicit Christianity. Horace Hodges's conclusion, in his study of *Beowulf* as typical *preparatio evangelium*, is well in line with Tolkien's own appreciation of the Old English poem. Hodges writes, "At the outset of this article, I mentioned minimal and maximal criteria for evaluating whether or not Beowulf is a Christian poem. Although methodologically, I prefer minimal criteria, if I am right about Christian typology in Beowulf, then the poem comes close to satisfying even strongly maximal criteria, falling short only by being implicit rather than explicit."[29] This will also be strangely familiar to Tolkien readers, so much Christianity being implicit in Tolkien's *corpus*, rather than explicit. A second resolution finds its roots in traditional natural theology, which sees the "divine light penetrating into the darkness of the heathen world" and will become an important direction in Newman's theological writing.[30] Tolkien, due to his long interest in Nordic mythologies and in particular given his interest in *Beowulf*, and due to his Newmanian Catholic upbringing, was most likely aware of the church fathers' resolution of the "virtuous pagan" conflict. There might also be another venue to explore on the subject, and that is the theology of John Henry Newman himself. The great English Catholic theologian had his own answer to the dilemma of the "virtuous pagan"—understandably so as both representing "natural theology" and being a Romantic well-versed in ancient writings.

The 2014 publication of Tolkien's *Beowulf* brings to light his view of the truth of myths, especially in a theological sense. In his commentary on the ancient tale, Tolkien displays the same concern over the "noble pagans" as the church fathers. His answer draws us back to the redeeming work of the incarnate God: "They too were 'damned' owing to the Fall, even if they were members of the chosen people. The redemption of Christ might work backwards."[31] And for him, backwards it did work indeed. The "noble pagans of the past" had of course not heard the gospel, but they knew of the existence of God, giver of all good things, even though the Fall had cut them off from God. Throughout his *Beowulf* edition, Tolkien shows empathy for the virtuous pagans such as Beowulf. It is quite understandable, then, that he stood quite opposed to the theory according to which noble pagans were just confused: "The old idea . . .

---

29. Hodges, "Praeparatio evangelium."
30. McGrath, "John Henry Newman," 29.
31. Tolkien, *Beowulf*, 160.

that all he [the author of *Beowulf*] had was a few bits of Old Testament story which he had remembered while actual Christian teaching was beyond him, is of course patently absurd."[32] This noble pagan's posture regarding the biblical God is not qualified by his knowledge—partial or not—of the Old Testament, but by a natural knowledge of God. This was further reflected in legend, myths, and tales. In so arguing, Tolkien demonstrates an essential theological posture, one very familiar to the natural theology of his Roman Catholicism.

This natural theology is well represented by Newman's notion of the "dispensation of paganism." This "positive" theology appeared for the first time in Newman's second university sermon in 1830. The concept is especially important in *The Arians of the Fourth Century* in which he talks about the "vague and uncertain family of religious truths, originally from God."[33] Newman's conclusion is based on his deep conviction that, contrary to what some rationalists were saying, no religion was the mere consequence of "unaided reason." On the contrary, religious knowledge can come only from God—and not only through his words in the Bible. In this, he was echoing the opinion of Thomas Aquinas defending the impossibility of anything to exist independently from God. Newman goes further than the great Alexandrian church fathers but felt free to adapt their insights to his particular context and sensibility. For example, he did not find it necessary to use the doctrine of the Logos. Instead, he focused on the natural religion of paganism which *in itself* had value, being merely the demonstration that "revelation, properly speaking, is a universal, not a partial gift."[34] Mythologies and "pagan philosophies" could then legitimately be seen as visible instruments of God, clearly echoing his view that "the visible world is the instrument, yet the veil, of the world invisible."

In *The Idea of a University*, Newman even affirms that God used pagan religion to advance his plan of salvation. God, he remarked, condescended to speak though he gave "no sanction, to the altars and shrines of imposture, and He makes His own fiat the substitute for its sorceries. He speaks amid the incantation of Balaam, raises Samuel's spirit in the witch's cavern, prophesies of the Messiah by the tongue of the Sybil . . .

32. Tolkien, *Beowulf*, 171.

33. Newman, *The Arians*, 89.

34. Newman, *The Arians*, 89.

and baptizes by the hand of the misbeliever."[35] This seems to suggest that pagan religions and myths could not that easily be discarded. Pagan mythologies indeed have meaning for, at the very least, they might display something of God's salvific will. This line of thought is typical of Newman's natural theology. The Oxford theologian argued that some "doctrines" were common to all dispensations, including pagan. Only doctrines that went "beyond reason" were part of the unique revealed dispensation of Christianity. As such, myths could demonstrate in prosaic, epic, and poetic manners pagan dispensations.

Further, divine origin of religion could be seen as a natural and experiential revelation of God to all men. In fact, Newman considered it certain that the experience of human conscience impressed on the human mind an "image" of God. Causes of emotions and feelings in intelligent beings, whatever their religious standing, did "not belong to this visible world"; rather "the phenomena of Conscience, as a dictate, avail to impress the imagination with the picture of a Supreme Governor, a Judge, holy, just, powerful, all-seeing, retributive, and is the creative principle of religion, as the Moral Sense is the principle of ethics."[36] The relation between "image" (of God) and human conscience is here interesting because it brings into the picture the necessity of imagination as a vehicle for revealed truth. The importance of pagan mythology lies in its potential conveying of truth, and also in its use of a kind of metaphysical imagination.

In the same manner, Chesterton's exposition of Thomism confirms that "the substance of all such paganism may be summarized thus. It is an attempt to reach the divine reality through the imagination."[37] In his famous book *The Everlasting Man*, Chesterton thus exposes the function of myths: "What are here called the Gods might almost alternatively be called the Day-Dreams. To compare them to dreams is not to deny that dreams can come true. To compare them to travelers' tales is not to deny that they may be true tales, or at least truthful tales."[38] Truth lies at the heart of a Thomist appreciation for mythologies, and so does imagination. In fact, mythology sought God through the imagination, argued Chesterton—or rather truth through imagination by means of poetic

---

35. Newman, *The Idea of a University*, 58–59.
36. Newman, *Grammar of Assent*, 83–84.
37. Chesterton, *The Everlasting Man*, 242–43.
38. Chesterton, *The Everlasting Man*, 233.

beauty. Thus, not only did mythology relate to truth, but also to beauty, which might have been a particularly convincing point for Tolkien.

Chesterton also then argues, in a fashion very similar to Newman, that the universal and active presence of God displayed in world mythologies demonstrates the existence of an intuitive apprehension of God in the phenomena of conscience. To Chesterton, the importance of the Catholic faith considered as an "historical mythology" lies in its reconciliation between mythology and philosophy: "It is a philosophy and in that sense one of a hundred philosophies; only it is a philosophy that is like life. But above all, it is a reconciliation because it is something that can only be called the philosophy of stories."[39]

The Catholic story of Christ is the true story that illuminates all others. There is something truly metaphysical lying at the heart of the Catholic story, something that was only dimly seen in mythologies and tales. This explains how Chesterton could rhetorically ask: "If the Christian God really made the human race, would not the human race tend to rumours and perversions of the Christian God? . . . If we are so made that a Son of God must deliver us, is it so odd that Patagonians should dream of a Son of God?"[40] Clearly the value of myth is here related to its truth-function. This was central to Tolkien's approach to *Beowulf*, both as a poem and as an author. If its essential theme was the tragedy and sorrows inherent to human nature and to the world, its overall significance was in the presence of truth within myth. As far as Tolkien was concerned, the *Beowulf*-poets's work was but "one step in a lifelong intellectual project of recovering [as Tolkien believed the *Beowulf*-poet had] the old, lost stories and harmonizing them with the new Christian truth."[41] This becomes evident throughout Tolkien's own *Beowulf*. As Christopher Tolkien remarks regarding his father's translation of *Beowulf*, the guiding idea is that the "noble pagans" of the past knew the Creator God as good, and benevolent.[42]

Faithful to this theological tradition, Tolkien thus held mythology in high esteem, especially Nordic mythologies. This led many scholars to discern an ambiguity in Tolkien, even wondering if there was not an irreconcilable dichotomy between the Christian and the pagan Tolkien.

39. Chesterton, *The Everlasting Man*, 378.

40. Chesterton, "The Blatchford Controversies," 1:374–75.

41. Drout, *Beowulf and the Critics*, 27.

42. Tolkien, *Beowulf and the Critics*, 170.

This, of course, is to be totally ignorant of Tolkien's basic theological stance. The ignorance of Tolkien's Thomism is probably one of the main reasons for this recurrent misinterpretation. Even Tom Shippey, one of the most cogent Tolkien scholars, considers that "Tolkien's problem as regards the heroic literature of antiquity was, I would say, on the one hand great professional liking, and on the other extreme ideological aversion."[43] Tolkien's Thomism provides the philosophical framework that allowed him to value mythologies, including his own, without downgrading the uniqueness of the biblical revelation.

Of course, Tolkien does not deny that mythology can contain veiled truths, which is the result of a misinterpretation of the subject of myths or a misinterpretation of the mythical persons. The fall of Númenor, as recorded in the Akallabêth, is a good example. After Sauron was vanquished for the first time, he was taken prisoner to the isle of Númenor, under the guard of its king. There, he ensnared the King.[44]

Thus it came to be that Sauron corrupted the king and his court, leading them to believe that his master Morgoth was the one god. Notice that Sauron does not hide the fact that Morgoth is the Lord of Darkness, but affirms that Darkness takes the place of Light, and that the Light is the perverting element of the world. Here we witness a complete reversal and perversion of the order of the world in the inversion of the place of God (Ilúvatar) and his angel (Morgoth). This perverted reversal is reinforced in the argument that the One God is but an invention intended to enslave men, thus ironically turning Justin's argument on its head.

That Morgoth uses the expression "folly of their hearts" is also significant in that it is a use of Paul's expression in Romans 1:21–22: "Because that, when they knew God, they have not glorified him as God or given thanks: but became vain in their thoughts. And their foolish heart was darkened. For, professing themselves to be wise, they became fools." This very verse of the epistle to the Romans points to the correct interpretation of the nature and origin of the dark element in myth. The origin is not to be found in a degenerated history, nor is it to be found in the childish stage of man's evolution, as Müller and Lang respectively argued. But this process is not, incidentally, the result of Barfield's "evolution of consciousness" either. Rather, it is to be found in the distortion and corruption of a spiritual truth—that spiritual beings exist, foremost

---

43. Shippey, "Heroes and Heroism," 282.

44. S, 279.

among whom is the One God. In fact, it is a mistaken view of God's nature that historically led to the rise of pagan gods and mythologies. The dark elements of mythologies thus lie in the historical dissociation of the nature, function, and "personality" of mythological characters. If Morgoth, instead of Ilúvatar, came to be worshipped as the "Lord of All," it is because the nature of Ilúvatar and his person have been dissociated from his function. Instead of a person, he came to be considered as an "invention," whose function was to enslave men, not provide them with free-will, gifts, and destiny. This spiritual dissociation and perversion is, in theological terms, one of the historical consequences of sin. The real problem comes from this dissociation, not from myth itself.

The account of Isildur's death is another example of Tolkien's historical view of the nature of myths and legends. After the battle of Dagorlad and the overthrow of Sauron, which occurred in the year 3441 of the Third Age, King Isildur took for himself the One Ring.[45] But the king was soon ambushed by some remaining forces of Sauron and drowned in the river Anduin, in which the Ring was, for the time being, lost.[46] In the later account of the disaster of Isildur's death and the loss of the Ring, "Isildur's bane," Tolkien demonstrates the close relation between legend and historical accounts, "So it was, as is told in the legends of later days, that the second year of the Third Age was waning when Isildur set forth from Osgiliath."[47] Here the legends are not legends in the sense of popular myths or unverifiable common stories. Rather they are historical accounts that, in the course of time, have been either lost or the origins of which have been forgotten.

Further in the account, Tolkien reports the sources of the legend of Isildur's death, beginning with the words: "There were eyewitnesses of the event." Tolkien again reveals his high historical view of the formation of legends.[48] The "legendary" aspect of Isildur's death is due to the oral tradition to which it gave birth, not to an invented account. For example, it is said: "The legend in its full form was not composed until the reign of Elessar in the Fourth Age, when other evidence was discovered."[49] It is implied here that the status of legend was already acquired by the result

---

45. LoTR, Appendix B, 1059.
46. Tolkien, *Unfinished Tales*, 3:271–75.
47. Tolkien, *Unfinished Tales*, 3:271.
48. Tolkien, *Unfinished Tales*, 3:275.
49. Tolkien, *Unfinished Tales*, 3:276.

of an oral tradition that was later "fixed" in written form after the final and complete victory over Sauron as reported in *The Lord of the Rings*.

Another example of legend-formation is given in the introduction to Appendix A of *The Lord of the Rings* on the "Annals of the Kings and Rulers," according to which legends and histories have the same goal—to illustrate an historical "origin"—which is of the highest significance.[50] It demonstrates that for Tolkien, legends and, by implication, the older mythical accounts are historical traditions recorded by eyewitnesses and transmitted in oral or written form to later generations.

Given the historical nature of the transmission of legends, lore, and myths, it is instructive to turn to the cosmogony of Middle-earth recorded in *The Silmarillion*. In this mythological work, Tolkien provides an historical account of the origin of both the gods and Middle-earth. In the Ainulindalë it is reported, "There was Eru, the One, who in Arda is called Ilúvatar; and he made first the Ainur, the Holy Ones, that were the offspring of his thought, and they were with him before aught else was made."[51] The myth of Middle-earth, transmitted through historical annals and records, presents the gods as personal and spiritual beings. Moreover, these spiritual beings are "historical" in that they are part of *time*, while not being, strictly speaking, material beings. Tolkien's interpretation of myth is "personalist" in nature, emphasizing both the personal and spiritual nature of the gods. Furthermore, the basis for Tolkien's *personalized* interpretation of myth is the person of Christ, the *person* of the Logos who gives myth its true historical meaning. This is precisely the reason behind Tolkien's qualification of the gospel of Christ as the true myth, the only one that has "entered History."[52] Against the deist Lewis, Tolkien and Dyson argued that in the story/history of Christ is the only true myth whose truth is rooted in its historicity. It is, literally, "myth become fact."

Interestingly, Lewis later wrote an essay entitled "Myth Become Fact," in which he argued that "as myth transcends thought, Incarnation transcends myth. The heart of Christianity is a myth which is also a fact. The old myth of the Dying God, without ceasing to be myth, comes down from the heaven of legend and imagination to the heart of history."[53]

50. LoTR, Appendix A, 1009.

51. S, 3.

52. OFS, 78.

53. Lewis, *God in the Dock*, 66.

Lewis concludes by saying that since God chose to be mythopoeic, we should not be afraid to be "mythopathic."

For Tolkien, myths demonstrate the presence in history of an incontrovertible spiritual reality. "Myth" is a form of historical account of the unity between metaphorical, literal, and also spiritual language and reality. Of course, not all myths reflect a true account of the historical past because of the blinding and corrupting power of sin upon the hearts of men. For Tolkien, true myth is found in the historical revelation of the *person* of the Logos, not in Barfield's impersonal Gnosticism, nor in the ahistorical or "aspiritual" view as developed by some of the church Fathers. Because Christ is the eucatastrophe of History, he can also, in his very person, convey the real and true meaning of all myths.

Conclusion

Part Two

IT IS TIME TO leave the valley of the gods. There, we have found that they were merely "fractured light" of the one knowing and creating God. From this valley, Tolkien gathered precious soil to plant the seed of English language that gloriously bloomed into a mythology for England for which he had so longed for. During his solitary journey to the valley of the gods, Tolkien had encountered many figures, and had seen many strange sights. All had pushed him to move forward. As a result, as with his view of language, Tolkien's theory of myth is dependent upon the influences and debates taking root in the growth of mythography and the relevance of comparative mythology. Here, Tolkien squarely places himself in the academic milieu of English mythology. As a fantasy writer whose goal was writing a mythology for England, Tolkien can be ranked among the most significant English mythographers. If this latter term is to be preferred, it is out of Tolkien's own conviction that his mythology was one to be *discovered*, it was one of fictionalized historical depth resulting from the interaction and mutual nurture of history, language, and truth. As such, Tolkien is a mythographer, not first and foremost a mythologist, one who created myth, but one who records them. Hence, the Red Book of Westmarch is seen as the main source of Tolkien's corpus, one that led to the writing of *The Lord of the Rings*. It is the result of an historical process.

This mythographic process of narrating and recording myths was for Tolkien possible because of his conviction that a myth could be a record since it remained a "splintered light," a veiled truth shining forth out of humankind's creation by God. If myth is a partly mistaken historical account, it nonetheless remains a human endeavor, fruit of the human ability to express something reminiscent of a long forgotten truth about God and creation. The profound unity Tolkien discovered, through Barfield, between the metaphorical, literal, and spiritual dimensions of myth led him to ascertain the validity of myth as a limited human knowledge about the world. Of course this spiritual nature of mythology was for Tolkien intimately connected with his view about language. It is utterly impossible to separate Tolkien's views about language and myth, since both relate to the human apprehension of truth as a created reality accessible both as a limited, creative, historical account—myth—and embodied through a human ability to express beauty and meaning—words and language.

It is this innate human capacity that indirectly, but surely, leads us to conclude that there is something more fundamental at work in Tolkien than merely language and myth. The soil in which they were planted was a religious, even a theological, one. Put differently, we can say that there were presuppositions at work in Tolkien's view of myth, as there were in his view of language. Of particular relevance is the notion of myth as a potential natural appetite that was spiritually "deceived" (distorted), a process that is demonstrated in Tolkien's view of the historical development and the literary creation of myths. To Tolkien, myth itself is not the consequence of sin but is the fruit of the separation between the gods' personal and historical nature.

As Tolkien maintains in "Mythopoeia," myth is, properly speaking, "refracted light" because the myth-makers themselves are a "refracted light,"[1] a true but limited refraction of their Creator. Myth takes its source from man, who himself derives his nature from the nature of God. This theological view of the nature of myth in relation to the nature of man points to the center of Tolkien's artistic vision, embodied in his theory of fantasy. But before reaching the summit of Faërie, we must go through a third stage of our journey.

---

1. Tolkien, "Mythopoeia," line 61, in *Tree and Leaf*, 87.

Part Three

Tolkien's Theory of Imagination

Eala Earendel engla beorhtast
ofer middangeard monnum sended!

—J. R. R. TOLKIEN, *The Book of Lost Tales, Part Two*

WE HAVE WALKED IN Tolkien's Faërie for some time already. We have considered Tolkien's love of language and myth and have become more acquainted with his lifelong literary ambition for England. We have walked far and climbed high on our journey towards the top of Tolkien's Perilous Realm. But on our path we come now to a major obstacle: the wall of the imagination. Before going further, we have to now ask: "What is the imagination?" If we have contemplated the God-given human capacity for sub-creation, we have yet to explain its inner workings.

We already know that sub-creation is nourished by human imagination. This, however, is not enough. To move forward and upward, we must probe deeper into the mysterious workings of the imagination. A vast topic, indeed, but a crucial one both for a deeper appreciation of Tolkien, and for reaching the end of our journey. To investigate Tolkien's view on the nature of the imagination is, yet again, a difficult enterprise. Not surprisingly, we find little in Tolkien himself that directly addresses this issue, for Tolkien was not a theoretician, at least not in the sense of formulating and publishing a precise theory. Rather, Tolkien's view of the function of imagination must be discovered indirectly.

But how? What are the clues available to us that could help us to gain a glimpse of Tolkien's own view of the imagination? The best path for us is through historical and personal connection, and this is the path we are now taking. Especially important to this investigation are three authors who had a significant impact on Tolkien: Owen Barfield, St. Thomas, and G. K. Chesterton. In this third part, we will begin, in chapter 8, by looking at Barfield, Thomas, and Chesterton's theory of the imagination. Then, in chapter 9, we will consider how Tolkien appropriated their views. Finally, chapter 10 will explore further Tolkien's notion of sub-creation.

8

The Nature and Purpose
of the Imagination

IN ORDER TO UNDERSTAND the richness and depth of Tolkien's own myth-ological corpus, we must look at the power of the imagination, the creative force behind Tolkien's masterful myth-creation. In this chapter we begin our investigation of the influences that must have nourished Tolkien's own thinking on the nature and role of the imagination. Throughout the preceding chapters, we have already identified the three most important authors to have influenced Tolkien, and we meet them again here as we approach this complex subject: G. K. Chesterton, Thomas Aquinas, and Owen Barfield.

Barfield's Coleridgean Imagination

The first, and in fact most obvious, influence on Tolkien was Owen Barfield. Given the complexity of Barfield's thought, a complete overview will not be possible here, though we must wrestle with the issues most connected to our riddle about the functions of the imagination. In mat-ters concerned with the nature of the imagination, Barfield built much of his own aesthetic philosophy on Samuel T. Coleridge. But approaching Coleridge's aesthetic philosophy is also, in turn, a complex one. Read-ing Coleridge, we are faced with three problems. First, he integrated the insights of many other philosophers in his theory of imagination. In fact, in his chapter on Coleridge, James Engell mentions that "in forming his concept of the imagination, Coleridge draws on nearly every other writer who discussed the subject."[1] If Engell's judgment is correct, this certainly makes the presentation and the evaluation of Coleridge's theory difficult. Second, the scarcity and the diffuse nature of his references to the imagination render the task of presenting a coherent and comprehensive picture of Coleridgean imagination hazardous. Finally, not only did Coleridge draw upon most of the writers who came before him, but he has also been at the center of later studies of imaginative power, adding another layer of difficulty to the task of interpreting his theory. Coleridge's concept of imagination crystallizes the insights of previous traditions and is the focus point of many subsequent theories of imagination.

Our best starting point to summarize Coleridge's investigation into the powers of the imagination is his observation, through Kantian philosophy, of the dialectical opposition between object and subject, and in particular the tension between man and his environment. During the nineteenth century, several philosophers consciously identified and addressed this issue as the most significant one faced by the industrialization of British society. This tension was most dramatically seen in the alienation of man from his environment. For many Victorians, especially those connected to the Romantic movement, rapid industrialization was the determining factor in their awareness of the growing separation between man and the natural world. Coleridge, along with Matthew Arnold, was one of the first English philosophers to ask this question with due seriousness. To Coleridge, who was at the same time a poet sensitive to natural beauty, a religious figure, and a philosopher, the necessity of regaining a view of the world as a comprehensive single unit appeared crucial—a typical concern of Barfield's. This implied establishing a reconnection between human understanding of the world and its self-conscious access to such knowledge. To make the reconnection Coleridge distinguished between reason and understanding, a distinction already present in Shakespeare, Milton, and Bacon, in the form of a contrast between the discourse of reason and the "intuitive exercise of this faculty."[2] Here already, the distinction between an organized, natural process of the mind and a more intuitive and educated one appears.

1. Engell, *The Creative Imagination*, 328.
2. Engell, *The Creative Imagination*, 65.

This kind of distinction is also applied by Coleridge to the imagination, leading to the distinction between primary and secondary imagination.

It is clear that for Coleridge imagination is *complex* (it is of one *kind*, is present in several *degrees*, and works through a single *process*) and serves to synthesize knowledge in order to provide the human connection with the wholeness and singleness of the world. It is in this context that Coleridge's famous distinction between primary and secondary imagination takes place. The primary imagination, he noted, was the "prime Agent of all human Perception," while the secondary imagination, echoing the former and co-existing with it, "dissolves, diffuses, dissipates, in order to re-create; or where this process is rendered impossible, yet still at all events it struggles to idealize and to unify. It is essentially *vital*, even as all objects (*as* objects) are essentially fixed and dead."[3] Apart from primary and secondary imagination, Coleridge also mentions fancy as being one "imaginative power." Fancy, by contrast to imagination proper, "is indeed no other than a mode of Memory emancipated from the order of time and space."[4] This is one of the most discussed passages in Coleridge and one of the most debated as well. The main difference Coleridge saw between the two degrees of imagination is explained in terms of their object and processes.

Primary imagination is about perception and repetition, functioning in a manner similar to memory in processing images already present in nature. For Coleridge, imagination and the power behind nature were essentially one. The structure of the natural world is thus constitutive of Coleridgean imagination. To Coleridge then, *natura naturans* or "nature in the active sense" is one with the power of imagination. As such, it merely receives and aggregates forms already existing in nature. As his interpreter Owen Barfield puts it, "Primary imagination, then, is an act, but it is an act of which we are not normally conscious. It becomes secondary, whether philosophically or poetically, when it is raised to, or nearer to, the level of consciousness and therewith becomes expressible."[5] Primary imagination thus stands between fancy and secondary imagination. Fancy, for Coleridge, is content to work with "fixities and definites," and in that capacity is very mechanistic. It deals with material memories, and in that sense could be considered a form of imagination. Of course

3. Coleridge, *Biographia Literaria*, 304–5.

4. Coleridge, *Biographia Literaria*, 304–5.

5. Barfield, *What Coleridge Thought*, 77.

Coleridge qualifies fancy to distinguish it from imagination—whether primary or secondary. Fancy exclusively deals with empirical phenomena. Compared to fancy, primary imagination is a "higher" imaginative power. But at the same time, it displays a lesser imaginative power than secondary imagination.

Secondary imagination works similarly and also processes images already present, not in nature, but to the human mind. A significant word used by Coleridge is the term "fixed," arguing that primary imagination deals with "fixities," that is, on realities that cannot be modified by or through the human mind. By contrast, secondary imagination works on the basis of these fixities and then "dissolves, diffuses, dissipates, in order to re-create." Imagination, "in creating new wholes, *wills* them into being, designs their totality, and acts not as an 'empirical phenomenon' but as a conscious desire for something not yet in existence, something to be created that, by definition, cannot be the subject of choice, which selects and combines images from those already perceived."[6]

In his lectures on Shakespeare, Coleridge provides, without naming them as such, another example of the distinction between primary and secondary imagination. The "common" imaginative power serves to picture a more precise view of the truths of nature, while the secondary imagination modifies and corrects them. This is done through the power of secondary imagination, aggregating the truths apprehended by primary imagination and creating new relations. In doing so, it re-creates the framework for receiving the truth of "first principles." Secondary imagination thus serves a greater purpose to the mythopoeist in allowing the secondary world to display truth itself: "Hence is produced a more vivid reflection of the truths of nature and of the human heart, united with a constant activity of modifying and correcting these truths by a sort of pleasurable emotion, which the exertion of all our faculties gives in a certain degree."[7]

Coleridge expressed this as being the imagination's *esemplastic* power, particularly significant with respect to secondary imagination— as some German philosophers had already discussed, using their native word *Einbildung*. As the editor's note to Coleridge's work explains, "the early meaning of *Einbildung*, which Herder points out in explaining his own usage of *Einbildung* and *Einbildungskraft* as forming a unity meant

6. Coleridge, *Biographia Literaria*, ciii

7. Coleridge, *Shakespeare*, 2.

to work into the soul of man, is to unify all perceptions by drawing them into one man's life and total experience."[8] This double outcome of the workings of the *esemplastic* nature of the imagination (unifying perceptions *and* integrating them to man's life) is also characteristic of Coleridge's concept of the imagination. Whether the esemplastic power is characteristic of imagination as such or only of secondary imagination is not clear. Coleridge used the word "imagination" in both senses, sometimes referring to the generalizing power of imagination, and sometimes referring to the specifically artistic nature of imagination. At the very least Coleridge is arguing that *secondary imagination* provides a further and clearer understanding of eternal truths. As such, secondary imagination provides the possibility for spiritual understanding.

Many scholars have commented upon Coleridge's few paragraphs on the power of imagination. Among these, Barfield holds a significant place especially because of his relation to Tolkien and his conviction that Coleridge's theory prepares and supports the teaching of anthroposophy and of his master, Rudolf Steiner. Moreover, the connection between Coleridge and Barfield with regard to the "creation of meaning" becomes obvious. Barfield, as one should expect, interprets Coleridge through the lens of anthroposophy. In this respect, it is important to identify the two main consequences of the discovery of Steiner's theory on Barfield. First, it serves to stress that the poetic and imaginative use of words actually enhances their meanings. Second, it implies that these enhanced meanings may reveal hidden aspects of reality. This is precisely Barfield's initial intuition, that "we find in abundance an instinctive *conviction*, and courageous *assertions*, that Poetry, that Imagination, as it is now understood, bears some special relation to Truth."[9] Barfield is correct in affirming that this conviction is central to Coleridge, in fact, central to the Romantics themselves.

Barfield's comments on the distinction between primary and secondary imagination now deserves mention. Barfield begins with repeating Coleridge's words affirming that imagination *dissipates and dissolves* the fixities that fancy can only *rearrange*. Fancy, continues Barfield, is merely an *aggregating* power; it is one with primary imagination—which Barfield calls the "seminal principle"—in that it modifies "sense" itself, this "common" sense. To quote again this relevant passage: "[Primary imagination]

8. Coleridge, *Biographia Literaria*, 170.

9. Barfield, *Romanticism Comes of Age*, 28.

is an act of which we are not normally conscious. It becomes secondary, whether philosophically or poetically, when it is raised to, or nearer to, the level of consciousness and therewith becomes expressible."[10] Secondary imagination becomes the conscious progress working from the information furnished by the primary unconscious process.

To be rightly understood, Barfield's study on Coleridge needs to be read alongside his *Romanticism Comes of Age*. Both works have one central concern, the most vital to Barfield, the question of consciousness. Barfield's reading of Coleridge brings in this very issue. Of course, the evolution of human consciousness is a distinctive Barfieldean theme. Whether it is as important to Coleridge as Barfield thought is unclear. Quite certain, however, is Barfield's own conviction regarding the power of the imagination. Barfield's Coleridge can then consider that "imagination *is*, and fancy is *not*, 'the very power of growth and production'; and we have seen how it is *this* power which, as its own two opposite forces, works at all stages of the process, at first of nature and then of consciousness leading to self-consciousness."[11] We should not, however, take consciousness in an abstract sense. To Barfield, the very act, the experience, of consciousness was the real preoccupation of Coleridge. Even if this assertion were true for Coleridge, it certainly reflects more Steiner's theory of the "evolution of consciousness."

Here, a few words on the place of imagination and fancy in the evolution of consciousness are necessary. In Barfield's view, imagination is not merely a means of cognition, nor even a necessary means of cognition, but is the unifying power between spirit and sense, the marriage of spirit and sense. From this initial observation of anthroposophy, Barfield develops his own concept of fancy and imagination. As to the former, "it has its proper and beneficent place in the genesis of consciousness as a whole and, particularly, in the conversion of perceptions into memories."[12] Fancy is hence passive, coming very close to being identified with human perception. Imagination is the means to go beyond this limitation. This understanding recalls Coleridge's distinction between primary and secondary imagination. However, there are some differences between Barfield and Coleridge, most clearly seen in the following sentence: "Above the level at which consciousness begins, the same principle

10. Barfield, *What Coleridge Thought*, 77.

11. Barfield, *What Coleridge Thought*, 88.

12. Barfield, *What Coleridge Thought*, 87.

continues to apply as between the lower faculties or manifestations of intelligence and the higher."[13] For Barfield, once again, the center is on the principle of the evolution of consciousness. Thus imagination, as an aesthetic category, is best understood as a felt change of consciousness.

Coleridge and his interpreter Barfield are important to the understanding of Tolkien's mythopoeic writing. In fact, if Tolkien has been influenced by Coleridge, it is certainly through his interaction with Barfield. Of course, such an influence is much less obvious than in the case of Barfield's theory of words. Barfield's intuitive notion of the imagination as being important, even vital, to the perception and creation of truth, might well be an inspiration for Tolkien's own imagination as seen at work in his theory of sub-creation. However, due to Barfield's re-reading of Coleridge along anthroposophical lines, it is also possible to argue that Tolkien recombined the insights gained from Coleridge. In any case, Coleridge's distinction between primary and secondary imagination would find an echo in Tolkien's categories of primary and secondary worlds. In this way, Tolkien might even come closer to Coleridge than to Barfield himself.

St. Thomas on the Sense of Imagination

If Barfield was the most obvious influence on Tolkien's theory of language, he was nonetheless not the only influential figure. Thomism, considered as a theological tradition, exerted a profound, powerful, and lasting influence on Tolkien. St. Thomas, even though he does not present a full-blown theory of the imagination, speaks directly about this faculty, and his influence on imagination and aesthetics should not be underestimated. Inkling scholar Bradley Birzer has noted that many prominent Thomists and neo-Thomists have neglected Thomas's stress on the powers of the imagination. This is rather surprising, however. It is unclear to which neo-Thomists Birzer is here referring but the two most prominent ones, Etienne Gilson and Jacques Maritain, have both taken their aesthetic clues from Thomas. Thomas, in his commentary on questions V and VI of the *De Trinitate of Boethius*, deals with the possibility of the use of the imagination in divine science. There, he repeats his constant affirmation that all our knowledge must begin with our sense, even though this knowledge is not sufficient by itself: "Again, as was said

13. Barfield, *What Coleridge Thought*, 85.

above, all our knowledge begins from the senses. But what we perceive by the senses is inadequate to reveal the divine form or even the other separate substances."[14] Moreover, St. Thomas continues on to define the way in which imagination can be used with respect to the investigation of divine science, mathematics, and the natural sciences.[15] This, however, has no direct bearing on the subject of "literary imagination" as presented in fairy-stories.

A more promising direction is to look at St. Thomas's exposition of the distinctions of the faculties of the soul. The starting point in St. Thomas's investigation is his threefold division of the human soul into vegetative, sensitive, and intellectual soul. Without expanding on the specific powers of the vegetative and intellective souls, it is necessary to mention those of the sensitive soul. St. Thomas, after having distinguished between the three kinds of souls, the five kinds of power, and the four modes of existence, moves on in article 4 to consider "whether the internal senses are correctly distinguished."[16] After his usual mention of pros and cons, he finally defines four powers of the sensitive soul, namely, "common" sense, fantasy [*phantasia*] or imagination [*imaginatio*], memory, and instinct, which in human beings is called cogitation.[17]

It is important to notice that St. Thomas's distinction regarding the different powers of the soul is guided by his consideration of their objects. For him, each power is distinct with respect to its object, and sense is defined by its acting on, and restriction to, the sense-world. Moreover, the sense-soul, as St. Thomas sometimes calls it, functions to receive and process the perception of sense objects. He goes even further, arguing that "receiving and conserving, however, must be traced to different principles in the physical order. . . . Hence since the sense power is an activity of a physical organ there has to be one power to receive sense forms and another to conserve them."[18] And so here we have St. Thomas's important distinction of the four powers of the sensitive soul, arising out of his consideration of the power and object of the sensitive soul.

To these three different categories of the soul, Thomas added the distinction between imagination and understanding, two different but

---

14. Aquinas, *The Division and Methods of the Sciences*, 81.

15. Aquinas, *The Division and Methods of the Sciences*, 79.

16. ST, Ia.77.4.

17. Kretzmann is of the opinion that *phantasia* should not properly be translated by "imagination." Kretzmann, *The Metaphysics of Creation*, 345.

18. ST, Ia.78.iv.

related inner senses. The diversity of inner senses is important to Thomas's theology of the imagination. In fact, Thomas uses a diversity of words to refer to our English "imagination," among which *phantasia* stands out. For example, he takes "phantasia" in his *Commentary on the De Anima* as being a generic term actually covering several distinct faculties of our inner senses. First is the *sense communis*, the common sense which functions as the receptive faculty of *per se sensibles*—things that are sensed directly. Second, there is the imagination proper (*vis imaginativa*), which is properly speaking the power to conserve or *retain* the sensible forms and objects *received* from the *sensus communis*—imagination is thus the retention of sensation. Third is estimation, the receptive faculty of "intentions," or things that are sensed indirectly. Fourth is memory (*vis memorativa*), which retains the information provided by the *vis cogitativa* and functions as the retentive power of intentions. Fifth, and finally, "compositive" imagination serves as the conjuring power of *per se sensibles*. Thus two powers serve as the retention of images: imagination and memory. These could then be used by the "compositive" or re-composing imagination as a faculty to create, to make, the power of imagination most properly related to the imagination.

Imagination (*vis imaginativa*), as one of the internal senses, also has a specific object and function. The process by which the sensitive soul receives and processes information from the sense-world implies the following activities: reception, retention, conservation, and what we could call reflection. Each of these activities is rendered possible by one of the powers, respectively, *"common" sense, imagination, memory*, and instinct or *cogitation*. Imagination specifically is defined in the following way: "Just as one power arises from the soul through another as intermediary, as said above, so the soul is a subject for one power through another as intermediary. This is the way imagination and memory are described as receptive at the level of primitive sensation."[19]

The function of imagination is further explained in the seventh article of question 84: "Can the intellect, using only the species it has and not turning to sense images, actually understand?" On the one hand, St. Thomas argues that "the imagination is more dependent on the senses than is the intellect upon imagination. But the faculty [*potest*] of imagination can exercise its act in the absence of sensible objects. Therefore *a fortiori* the intellect can actually understand without turning to sense

19. ST, Ia.78.iv.

images."[20] It would seem, following this line of thought, that the imagination is a sense providing the possibility of understanding without sense images. On the other hand, true to the scholastic method, St. Thomas ultimately embraces the contrary argument, built on Aristotle's opinion: "the soul never thinks without an image."[21]

On this matter, St. Thomas is inflexible and affirms that "it is impossible for our intellect, in its present state of being joined to a body capable of receiving impressions, actually to understand anything without turning to sense images."[22] When confronted with the problem of the human understanding of incorporeal things, St. Thomas relies on one form of analogical reasoning and explains that we actually "know incorporeal realities, which have no sense images, by analogy with sensible bodies, which do have images, just as we understand truth in the abstract by a consideration of things in which we see truth."[23] It seems that for St. Thomas the understanding relies on perception of images. In other words, the power of the intellective soul relies on the working of the sensitive soul, the imagination.

In this connection, we also need to ask whether or not falsity—that is, false judgment—arises from the intellect or from the imagination. To solve this matter, St. Thomas starts with arguing that falsity arises from the connection between the faculty and its object. Turning first to the intellect, St. Thomas remarks that the proper object of the intellect is the essence of things. As such, the intellect yields knowledge of first principles and therefore can never give rise to falsity. With regard to the imagination and the senses, the issue for St. Thomas is clearly that falsity arises out of the absence of any referent in the actualized world. Our imagination cannot make or "create" things out of nothing. If it did, or tried, it would lose itself. To take the example of Tolkien's "green sun," human imagination does use a referent in the actualized world: "green" and "sun."[24] What the imagination does is to recombine and fuse two pre-existing realities into a new entity, the "green sun."

Further, it is necessary to consider the place of imagination with respect to other powers, especially the intellect. As said above, for St.

20. ST, Ia.84.vii.

21. ST, Ia.84.vii.

22. ST, Ia.84.vii.

23. ST, Ia.84.vii.

24. MC, 219.

Thomas "the kinds of power in the soul are distinguished through their objects. The higher a power the more extensive its scope, as we noted above."[25] The obvious conclusion is that the intellect is the highest power because it has a higher object, that is, universal ideas. However, St. Thomas does not conclude that the imagination is useless in matters of understanding. For, even though the intellect is concerned with first principles, in order to know them it must be informed by data about the sensuous world (the sense-forms) and in this, the intellect needs the imagination. For St. Thomas, then, imagination is one of the powers of the soul that informs other faculties like the intellect—while being below it.

Finally, we must notice that Thomas does not provide a complete explicit foundation for Tolkien's use of the imagination. One particular instance of such incompleteness is that imagination for Thomas does not have the power to create new worlds, while it certainly can for Tolkien. This being said, Thomas allows the imagination to be a power of composing new forms. In his *Summa*, as well as in other places scattered through his writing, Thomas gives the example of a "golden mountain." The argument runs like this. The power of *imaginatio* helps to separate the "goldness" of the golden chalice from the chalice itself that the priest uses during Mass. Through distinction and separation, imagination is able to join this quality to the picture of a mountain that was seen previously. Thus imagination can help me form the image of a golden mountain, an image that I "experience" with my inner senses even though I have no exterior sensual experience of it.[26] In that specific sense, but in that *limited* sense, Thomas also argues for a recombining power ascribed to the imagination.

Chesterton on the Imagination

Finally, it is impossible not to mention Chesterton among the influences that shaped Tolkien's creativity. It was actually difficult for anyone not to come under the spell of Chesterton, through agreement or debate. In fact, Chesterton biographer Michael Ffinch reports the following comment by one of Chesterton's contemporary: "Mr. Chesterton's extravagances have none of this quality [self-conscious, bound to his time]. He is not a rebel. He is a wayfarer from the ages, stopping at the inn of life, warming himself at the fire and making the rafters ring with his jolly laughter."

25. ST, Ia.78.i.

26. For the "golden mountain" example, see ST, I.12.ix, *De veritate* VIII.5.

Someone has even humorously noted, "I can conceive him standing on his head in Fleet Street in sheer joy at the sight of St. Paul's."[27] However, the task of exploring and evaluating this influence is difficult, especially since Tolkien rarely commented on, or even directly acknowledged, the influences behind his vision. Thus, Chesterton's influence on Tolkien is a silent one, unseen but ever present.

Chesterton comes as the latest influence on Tolkien's already fertile mind. One of the main differences between Chesterton and the previous authors mentioned is that he does not try to build a theory of imagination. Certainly, it could be argued that neither did St. Thomas, but there is in the Angelic Doctor's writings a lengthy discussion about the imagination. As for Coleridge, he was directly concerned about the powers of the imagination, as was his re-interpreter Barfield. But Chesterton does not have a precise, full-blown theory of imagination. Some of his most important points are found in *Orthodoxy*—especially in the chapters "The Maniac" and "The Ethics of Elfland"—and in the Father Brown story "The Blue Cross," as well as in related journal articles written for the *London Illustrated News*.

Chesterton, while a defender of the imagination, was also a defender of "common" sense, owing much to the Catholic doctrine of natural theology, particularly in its Thomistic tradition. Chesterton, in his biography of St. Thomas, argues that the loss of common sense is behind his contemporary society gone wrong. Only the loss of common sense could explain the fact that his fellow countrymen did not "see" the obvious. And to him, such was the strength of Thomas's theology: it helps us recognize that reality is real. Common sense is thus the natural and obvious fabric of the world; it is that which belongs to all mankind. In his introduction to Aesop's fables, Chesterton notes that "the firm foundations of common sense, the shrewd shots at uncommon sense, that characterise all the Fables, belong not to him but to humanity. In the earliest human history whatever is authentic is universal: and whatever is universal is anonymous."[28] At the heart of Chesterton's common sense is the conviction that the world itself is infused with meaning, and not with just any meaning, but with the Creator's meaning.

The stress on common sense is reinforced by Chesterton's appreciation of St. Thomas, about whom he wrote a biography. Always delving

27. Ffinch, *G. K. Chesterton*, 105.

28. Chesterton, Introduction to *Aesop's Fables*.

deeper in St. Thomas's thought, Chesterton's own thinking became a typical example of applied Thomism to the point that Etienne Gilson, the noted Thomist scholar, said that Chesterton in his biography of St. Thomas was "nearer the real Thomas than I am after reading and teaching the Angelic Doctor for sixty years."[29] It would be impossible here to summarize Chesterton's humorous prose, though we can note one of the central points: "the fact that Thomism is the philosophy of common sense is itself a matter of common sense."[30] It is from St. Thomas, then, that Chesterton borrows the conviction that the world *is*, and that to recognize it as such is just a matter of common sense. For Chesterton, as for St. Thomas, there was no point in asking the question of the reality of cognition and recognition. This meant that what was needed was to present, picture, and defend the world as it is. Chesterton constantly argued that his fellow countrymen suffered from blindness, from alienation, from insanity, not because they did not convert to a different way of looking at the world, but because they did not see the world as it actually was.

In this context, Chesterton's "madman" is relevant. In *Orthodoxy*, he argued that the madman is "commonly a reasoner"; it is man with only reason. The madman is the person who exercises insane reason when not seeing what is "too plain to see."[31] The difference between the madman and the rest of humankind is precisely one of *kind*, not of degree. It is not that the madman sees things in a different degree, but that he does not see at all. In fact, "the mad are not a minority because they are not a corporate body; and that is what their madness means. The sane are not a majority; they are mankind. And mankind (as its name would seem to imply) is a kind, not a degree. In so far as the lunatic differs, he differs from all minorities and majorities in kind."[32] The madman's reason is actually not reason at all but rather a combination of rational insanity and spiritual delusion. It seems that on this matter, there is no commonality between the madman and humanity.

Fortunately, there is common ground, a common desire affecting both the sane and the insane, both "everyman" and the "madman." Chesterton says that this common ground is the desire for "an active

29. Hunter, *G. K. Chesterton*, 173.

30. Chesterton, *St. Thomas Aquinas*, 171.

31. See Chesterton, *Collected Works*, 1:230.

32. Chesterton, *Collected Works*, 4:315.

and imaginative life."[33] The significance of Chesterton's understanding of imagination lies in an attack on the alleged rational mind of modern man, and takes the form of an argument for fairy tales and for fairyland. Chesterton takes his insights about the nature of imagination from his conviction about the *strangeness* of the world in which he lived. In fact Chesterton was, much like Tolkien would be, anachronistic to his times. He was unabashedly traditional in his religious conviction, and constantly at odds with the main opinions of his time. The first lines of Chesterton's autobiography describe, with his usual humor: "Bowing down in blind credulity, as is my custom, before mere authority and the tradition of the elders, superstitiously swallowing a story I could not test at the time by experiment or private judgment, I am firmly of opinion that I was born on the 29th of May, 1874, on Campden Hill, Kensington."[34] The blend of autobiography and philosophical criticism is, of course typical of his engaging writing temperament. This strange blend of familiar and unfamiliar in his writing, though, is not merely a matter of style but reflects something quite deeper. In fact, throughout his whole life, Chesterton fought for "the need for that mixture of the familiar and the unfamiliar which Christendom has rightly named romance," the only possible answer to England's spiritual need. The unity of the ordinary and the unordinary was both an imaginative statement and a theological one.

Chesterton constantly argued that to answer the spiritual need of the modern world, it was crucial to see the world in its renewed strangeness, contrasting it with the madman's tyranny of reason. Chesterton makes the case for the essential queerness of the world, even in his evaluation of Dickens.[35] To see the world in such a fantastic manner does not mean reinventing the world as something it is not, but rather to look at the world as God's theatrical creation in which everything is infused with God's gracious, surprising, and joyful presence. Chesterton describes the world as one of "fantaisie" infused with God's *magic* actions, which are magic because they are God's own act. Indeed, for Chesterton, because God is an artist, the world itself is artistic:

> I had a rather funny dream
> intense, that is, and mystic;
> I dreamed that, with one leap and yell,
> The world became artistic.[36]

33. Chesterton, *Collected Works*, 4:315.

34. Chesterton, *The Autobiography of G. K. Chesterton*, 1.

35. Chesterton, *Charles Dickens*, 290.

36. Chesterton, *Greybeards at Play*, 83.

Furthermore, nature, for example, is not purely *law* in itself, is not merely scientific, but is itself artistic. Natural law is not merely the rationalistic expression of human investigation, but rather, magic: "The only words that ever satisfied me as describing Nature are the terms used in the fairy books, 'charm,' 'spell,' 'enchantment.' They express the arbitrariness of the fact and its mystery. A tree grows fruit because it is a *magic* tree. Water runs downhill because it is bewitched. The sun shines because it is bewitched."[37] We can compare this with Tolkien's observation that "it was in fairy-stories that I first divined the potency of the words, and the wonder of the things, such as stone, and wood, and iron; tree and grass; house and fire; bread and wine."[38] The wonder of the things is that they are both natural and unnatural. For both Tolkien and Chesterton, the natural world is not controlled by mere scientific and natural laws but by the unseen presence of something much more fundamental to the world: the active presence of the Creator-God. In another of his works Chesterton argues again that the so-called "laws of science" are not all there is about our world. In his play *Magic*, Chesterton made the very same point, contrasting unstable scientific "laws" and the fixed beauty of the starry sky. Debating the "doctor's" remark that the red lamp standing over his door is not beautiful but simply a lamp, a young woman, Patricia, asks: "But don't you think there may be floating and spiritual stars which will last longer than the red lamps?" To which another character, Smith, answers: "Yes. But they are fixed stars."[39]

Magic is thus an embodiment of Chesterton's philosophy of reason and imagination. The world is scientifically fixed: it is the fruit of God's moving imagination. The world, seen through this sane and reasonable imagination, becomes the heavenly window of the communion between God and his creation, and between man and his Creator. This leads Chesterton to affirm that "imagination does not breed insanity. Exactly what does breed insanity is reason."[40] Reason alone, concludes Chesterton, leads to the suicide of thought, and similarly imagination without proper reason leads to suicidal fantasy.

What happens then, if fantasy is *really* allowed to live? What happens when common sense imagination runs free? We will discover,

37. Chesterton, *Collected Works*, 1:256.
38. OFS, 69.
39. Chesterton, *Magic*, 29.
40. Chesterton, *Collected Works*, 1:219.

argues Chesterton, that fairyland is freedom from observable laws. He argued this point again in *Orthodoxy*, where he sounds like St. Thomas, who argues that "although the intellect is superior to the senses, it does in a manner also receive from them; its primary and principal objects have their foundation in sensible objects. Thus intellectual discernment is necessarily hindered when the senses are bound."[41] To Chesterton, "freedom of observable laws" does not mean absolute freedom, but the absence of bondage to these observable laws. This is the essential nature of Chesterton's view: fairyland is founded upon sensible objects but not bound to their structure. In arguing so, Chesterton is in effect saying that the imagination is—or should be—the mightiest and brightest of the natural pleasures of man. Imagination displays the unity between the actual world and the sub-created forms, through imagination. As Chesterton puts it, "the trumpet of imagination, like the trumpet of the Resurrection, calls the dead out of their graves."[42]

Conclusion

Three writers were highly influential for Tolkien's own understanding of the nature and workings of the imagination. While Tolkien never fully acknowledged how these three authors specifically contributed to his writings, his personal interests and milieu demonstrate that Barfield, Thomas, and Chesterton were all significant, on different levels, as we will continue to explore in the next chapter. There is, of course, a consistent line of thought uniting these three authors: a profound conviction that human beings are not first and foremost rational beings, but both rational and imaginative. While they all granted human imagination a more or less primary importance, the union of reason and imagination is nonetheless clear. At the end of the nineteenth century, and as the twentieth century opened with all its social and scientific promises, this was to prove a powerful response to the tragedies of the two world wars. We have now reached the point where one final question must be asked. A very simple one, with a complex answer. How did Tolkien himself appropriate the influences of these three major thinkers?

---

41. ST, Ia.84.viii.

42. Chesterton, "A Defence of China Shepherdesses," in *The Defendant*, 60.

9

Tolkien's Appropriation of the Theories of Imagination

IN TOLKIEN, THE THREE figures of Barfield, Thomas, and Chesterton come out as one, making it rather difficult, if not utterly impossible to determine where the influence of each should be precisely located. What is certain is that Tolkien, like these three other aesthetes, highly valued the power of the imagination and the existence of Faërie. He, for example, stated that "the magic of Faërie is not an end in itself, its virtue is in its operations."[1] As will become clear in part four, Tolkien will embody the full force of the aesthetic imagination in Faërie and its three functions of Recovery, Escape, and Consolation. All these will become manifest in Tolkien's mythological corpus, his trues work of imagination. It is appropriate that, before turning to Tolkien's Faërie, we first explore Tolkien's appropriation of Barfield's, Thomas', and Chesterton's theories of imagination. Tolkien's view of the imagination is a complex association of all previous influences, having matured in an already fertile mind until it was able to birth a mythological world.

1. OFS, 34.

Revisiting the Barfieldean Tolkien

Even though it is difficult to prioritize the influence of either Barfield, Coleridge, and Chesterton on Tolkien, we should recognize that, at first sight, Tolkien seems closer to Barfield, than anyone else. As we have already noted, his use of the expressions "primary world" and "secondary world" obviously echoes Coleridge's distinction between primary and secondary imagination. Also, much as been said about Barfield's influence on Tolkien, especially with respect to Tolkien's comment to the effect that Barfield has transformed his whole outlook. This is usually enough to defend a definite Barfieldean influence, to the point of, perhaps, considering Tolkien as being Barfieldean at every point. However, the Barfildean Tolkien might be less obvious than usually assumed. For example, we might be surprised to find no reference to the distinctively Barfieldean aspect of Coleridge's theory of the imagination. Further, Tolkien never even mentions the "evolution of consciousness," or the possibility that imagination might give insights into the coming stages of this evolution. Where is then the Barfieldean Tolkien to be found? He is there, but he is often silent, and must be found in Tolkien's imaginative writings.

For example, the working of fancy and primary imagination can be found in the poem "The Road Goes Ever On," especially if we compare two versions, one sung by Bilbo and the other spoken by Frodo. Bilbo, in *The Hobbit*, sings the following on his way back from his "adventures." While Bilbo had always been a most regular hobbit, full of uneventful hobbit common-sense, a poetical revelation dawns on him as he sees "the country where [he] had been born and bred, where the shapes of the land and of the trees were as well known to him as his hands and toes."[2] Faced with this familiar, but now poetical landscape, Bilbo's thoughts turn into poetry:

> Roads go ever ever on,
> Over rock and under tree,
> By caves where never sun has shone,
> By streams that never find the sea;
> Over snow by winter sown,
> And through the merry flowers of June,
> Over grass and over stone,
> And under mountains of the moon.
> Roads go ever ever on

2. H, 302.

Under cloud and under star,
Yet feet that wandering have gone
Turn at last to home afar.
Eyes that fire and sword have seen
And horror in the halls of stone
Look at last on meadows green
And trees and hills they long have known.[3]

When Bilbo bursts into poetical song, his imagination is working out of the things seen and known, a landscape so familiar that to create a poem from this scenery is but an example of imaginative memory. Here, Coleridgean fancy is most likely at work. In *The Lord of the Rings*, three versions of the poem are found. The first time we hear the poem, it is again chanted by Bilbo as he leaves the Shire for Rivendell. The second time the poem appears, it is spoken aloud and slowly, almost in a whisper, by Frodo on his way to Crickhollow:

The Road goes ever on and on,
Down from the door where it began.
Now far ahead the Road has gone,
And I must follow, if I can,
Pursuing it with weary feet,
Until it joins some larger way
Where many paths and errands meet.
And whither then? I cannot say.[4]

Only one difference appears in line five with the replacement of "eager" by "weary." The change of term is in itself not significant. More indicative is Frodo's comment upon being asked if it was "a bit of old Bilbo's rhyming." Whether it was or not, Frodo does not know. But what he does know is that "it came to me then, as if I was making it up; but I may have heard it long ago."[5] Frodo's primary imagination is unconsciously working with what he has heard and knows, recombining memory and new forms to give birth to the second version of the poem. Even if it presents but one small difference, Frodo's comment is telling, especially in the light of Coleridge's distinction between fancy and primary imagination.

This could leave us wondering how much of Coleridge Tolkien actually interacted with. An interesting question at first, but misdirected. In

3. H, 302.
4. LoTR, I.1.iii, 82.
5. LoTR, I.1.iii, 82.

fact, it is not at Coleridge that we should look, but at Barfield. And here we face one of the greatest challenges in understanding Tolkien: the attempt to articulate his relationship with Owen Barfield. There is no doubt that, as we have seen in previous chapters, Barfield exerted an immense influence on Tolkien. However, the question before us is whether he had a determining influence for Tolkien's understanding of the nature of imagination.

The intellectual and philosophical relationship between Barfield and Tolkien has already been investigated, especially by English professor Verlyn Flieger. She has published a book specifically concerned with Tolkien's view of language, *Splintered Light*, the subtitle of which is telling and reads, "Logos in Language in Tolkien's World." In her opinion, "the effect of Barfield's work on the fiction of J. R. R. Tolkien, and consequently on the present study of Tolkien's fantasy, would be hard to overestimate."[6] Despite numerous comments to the effect that Barfield was the most influential thinker for Tolkien's overall philosophy of language and myth, a detailed study of Barfield's influence on Tolkien has yet to be published. Most studies, including Flieger's groundbreaking work, tend to downplay the irreducible differences between Barfield and Tolkien.

Thus, Flieger herself is not concerned with the main differences that could subsist between Barfield and Tolkien. Nor does she qualify the influence Barfield had on Tolkien. Therefore, caution is crucial here. To affirm that Tolkien and Barfield stood together in opposing erroneous views about language does not imply that they shared the same solutions to the problem. Other linguists relied on a complete separation between man and the world while arguing for the exclusive human origin of language, and thus were opposed by Barfield who affirmed the "participation" of man in the world, and the connection between meaning and word. Tolkien shared this particular point, as well as the notion of the poet as maker of worlds and meaning. What Tolkien found in Barfield is another way to approach the problem, a way that would integrate his beliefs about the structure of the world. Barfield and Tolkien turned away from the dominant theory of their time, but arrived at different destinations, reaching different conclusions regarding language.

This entails that while Barfield and Tolkien shared a general outlook, they also had major differences. Even if Tolkien and Barfield shared a common interest in "language," there was a profound difference in the

---

6. Flieger, *Splintered Light*, vii.

way they approached the relation between language and history. For Barfield, the relation between language, words, and their meanings is the path to knowledge, the path to the next stage of human consciousness. The value of words and language is relative to their benefit for man's consciousness. For Tolkien, on the other hand, words are not a mere *medium*; rather, words in themselves are imbued with meaning and beauty. The relevance of language lies in the historicity and delight of words themselves. We will come back to this difference when approaching the nature and role of philology for Tolkien. Furthermore, there is a difference in their appropriation of Coleridge's concept of the Secondary Imagination. For Barfield, who was probably the closest to Coleridge's original intent, the Secondary Imagination refers to a next stage of participation, or stage in man's consciousness of his participation. The Secondary Imagination serves to rescue our phenomena. For Barfield, words and language are the means of regaining true representations and they must be reclaimed in order to lead man to a greater understanding of his "evolution of consciousness." But for Tolkien, true representations of and about the world are already present to man because they are part of the created structure of the world. The real problem is to regain a correct understanding of what the world is. For Tolkien, it is the perception of the observer that changes, not the "phenomena." It is not the structure of the world that changes but the cognitive structure of man.

Here there might be an important difference in how Barfield and Tolkien understood the nature of man's view of reality. For Barfield, the way we see the world reflects a collective construction, which he labels "representation." This construction can change parallel to the evolution of man's consciousness. For Tolkien, however, the way we see the world does not change the representations present in the world. These remain always the same because they are part of an unchanging created reality. The change is due to man's interpretation of this reality, and, in theological terms, to a distorted view of the created reality. The center is on the created structure of our world, which has an important connection with the fundamental structure of the Secondary Imagination. This explains why, for Tolkien, the Secondary Imagination is imbued with the structure of the Primary World. For Barfield Secondary Imagination is only a means to interpreting the Primary World, to the point that Secondary Imagination even tends to create a Secondary World truer than the Primary World.

For Tolkien, by contrast, the Secondary Imagination is no doubt a means of interpreting the Primary World, but not to the point of creating truer meaning. Rather, it leads to the *recovery* of meaning. Indeed, for Tolkien the Primary World itself furnishes the structural framework of the Secondary World, which can in turn *enlighten* our understanding of the Primary World. Moreover, at this point one should note that Barfield's philosophical approach is specifically an anthropocentric one. Following his "master," Rudolph Steiner, Barfield saw the process of the "evolution of consciousness" as essentially, if not exclusively, an anthropocentric process.[7] As a consequence, the development of language was essentially anthropocentric. Tolkien, of course, did not deny the human element in the development of language.[8] However, he also refers several times to the innate, or birth-given, capacity for language. Here Tolkien stands in the tradition of the Christian faith for which God the Creator governs and ordains everything that comes to pass, including the development of language. For Barfield, the development of language points first to man, while for Tolkien, it points first to God. The references to the divine element within language are rare and look like a shadow hovering over the rest of Tolkien's theory of language, but they are more than just a footnote to his overall theory. This reflects an essential difference in how Barfield and Tolkien apprehended the structure of the world. For Barfield, the foundation is found in *anthropology* while for Tolkien it is found in *theology*. In Tolkien, the anthropocentric element in the development of language, of myth, and of history, is included in a divine governance of both Primary and Secondary worlds. However, even Tolkien's disagreements with Barfield serve to point to the essential aspects of his view of language, for after all, Tolkien always remained first and foremost a philologist.

Common Sense Imagination

Barfield definitely stands as the most obvious influence on Tolkien. However, it would be far too simplistic to regard him as having the one definite influence on the author of *The Lord of the Rings*. In fact Chesterton, this other great influence on Tolkien, helps us understand Tolkien's disagreement with Barfield regarding the Primary World. If Tolkien valued Secondary imagination only with respect to the integrity of the Primary world, it is probably because of a determinant theological conviction, in line with Chesterton's own view. In fact, the great English theologian and

---

7. Flieger, *Splintered Light*, 35–40.
8. As convincingly argued by Flieger, *Splintered Light*, 73–106.

journalist, in his great work on Thomas Aquinas, relied on one of the angelic doctor's main three tenets: "the primacy of the doctrine of being."[9]

This partly explains the importance of paradoxes in Chesterton's writings. Under his pen, they are used to reveal a fundamental dimension of reality: that we are never aware of the fulness of reality. Chesterton scholars have commented on this limited human apprehension of reality. In fact, they have noted that even his buoyant, witty, and colorful style, incrusted with wordplays, should not be seen as mere fireworks of rhetorical devices. Quite the contrary! The style demonstrates his ontological conviction. There is always much more at play. In the same way that reality is always larger, fuller, than what we can experience, there is always more behind his rhetorical devices.

One of the best example of this is the use of nonsense. As a literary genre, nonsense was increasingly relevant in the literature of the end of the nineteenth century. While superficially nonsense could be too easily dismissed, there is much more at work than mere sensationalism. There is a double purpose in nonsense. Its first purpose is to manifest the writer's knowledge of, control over, and foundation on logic. Here, nonsense is not a denunciation of logic and rationality, but a manifestation that reality is larger than our own limited understanding. The second purpose of nonsense is a direct consequence of the previous point. It denounces the inadequacy of a supposedly absolute and complete human rationality. If the first purpose is positive, this second is its negative counterpart. And if these are the functions of nonsense, the former purpose is shared by fantasy, hence Chesterton's conclusion that those who inhabit fairyland are "the most reasonable of all creatures."[10] By contrast the madman, and the materialist, who have only reason, are "in the prison of one thought."[11] Tolkien is in full agreement with Chesterton regarding the rational dimension of imagination, and so also with the affirmation of the rational nature of fantasy. In a footnote to a comment on the relation between Fantasy and Dream, Tolkien writes that "fantasy is a rational not an irrational activity" and adds, nor does it "insult reason."[12]

However powerful Chesterton's influence might have been, Tolkien differed in one major aspect regarding the nature of imagination and

9. According to Dennehy's introduction to Chesterton's biography of Aquinas in *Collected Works*, 2:414.

10. Chesterton, *Collected Works*, 1:253.

11. Chesterton, *Collected Works*, 1:265.

12. MC, 139n2, 144.

fantasy. In "On Fairy Stories," when he comments on the first function of Faërie, Recovery, Tolkien makes an important note on Chesterton: "And there is (especially for the humble) *Mooreeffoc*, or Chestertonian Fantasy."[13] This is the clearest summary of Chesterton's fantasy one could hope to write. It encapsulates the very nature of Chesterton's attitude towards fantasy, and more broadly, towards life. For Chesterton, our attitude towards life, and the world, should be one of thanks. And the proper dimension of thankfulness included humility. This Christian virtue was not meant to function in and of itself, without proper direction. Chesterton's humility is not humility for self-pity or morbid depreciation, but humility for the nourishment of thankfulness.

Tolkien appropriated this connection between humility and fantasy in one of his most debated short stories, "Leaf by Niggle." Written in 1938–39, this intriguing piece was first published in the Dublin Review in January 1945. About the circumstances of its writing, Tolkien confessed that he did not remember much, and was not really sure about the year it was written.

The manner of its writing—including the fact that Tolkien's own recollection might not be as clear as he remembers—is the first of the many peculiarities of this story—a story over which Tolkien agonized in the process of writing it. To begin, it is the least fantasy sounding. Forget about elves, Secondary World, or dragons. Nothing in the plot or characters indicate the possible presence of a Secondary World. Further, it has been highly commented on with respect to Tolkien's comment about his dislike of allegory. While Tolkien repeatedly denied that "Leaf by Niggle" was an allegory, it has regularly been read as such.[14] Finally, the interpretation of this piece is complicated by Tolkien's own qualification of "Leaf by Niggle" as his "purgatorial story."[15] While we can grant Tolkien the denial of the allegorical nature of this story because Niggle does not represent a "single voice," the label "purgatorial fantasy" has an allegorical tone.[16] Regarding the allegorical nature of "Leaf by Niggle," the jury is still out. Even though this point is relevant to the interpretation of this short story, its Chestertonian nature is as relevant.

13. MC, 146.
14. L, 321.
15. L, 195.
16. L, 321.

In fact, *Leaf by Niggle* is the quintessential Chestertonian fantasy. The story tells the struggles of Niggle, an artist so completely taken up in his task of completing the painting of a tree, that the world around him often seems to disappear. Typical of Tolkien's own struggles, Niggle finds it difficult to finish his tree, concentrating on the perfection of a single leaf. Then, the story takes its strangest turn. In the process of helping his neighbor, a gardener named Parish, Niggle is plagued by an unknown sickness. Sent to an unnamed institution, with an unnamed end, the case of Niggle's life and accomplishment is brought before two voices. The first one, pointing to Niggle's forgetfulness, procrastination; the second, pointing to his humility, to his self-effacement, to his goodwill, and to his heart that was "in the right place."[17] As a treatment for his past failures, Niggle is sent off to a garden country.

And then it appears before his eyes: his tree. The Tree. Finished, alive. The Tree was exactly the one he had imagined, even thought he had not "made it" himself. Seeing this, Niggle exclaims: "'It's a gift!' he said. He was referring to his art, and also to the result; but he was using the word quite literally."[18] The thankfulness of Chestertonian Fantasy is here, in Niggle's words. But Niggle also discovers more than a Tree. The tree that he imagined through the exercise of his subcreative ability, is larger, more complete than he could have dreamed of. In fact, it was alive, growing and blossoming, in the image of what Niggle had imagined, not made.[19]

This is good example of Tolkien's imagination at work. Niggle's act of painting, is a "partially successful attempt at what Tolkien considers sub-creation" but also a demonstration of the nature of the imagination. Tolkien's view of Imagination, or image-making, combining with Art to produce Fantasy, could hardly be exemplified more clearly than in "Leaf by Niggle." In fact, in this story, as in "Mythopoeia," it is also clear that this 'elvish craft' is combined with the Divine. Imagination is not purely that of the crafter, but comes from the image in which the crafter was originally created. We always create, concludes Tolkien in "On Fairy-Stories," in the same way we were created. We also imagine only as far as our creator has imagined us. We are imagined beings, and we thus become sub-creative beings.

17. Tolkien, *Tales from the Perilous Realm*, 132.

18. Tolkien, *Tales from the Perilous Realm*, 136.

19. Tolkien, *Tales from the Perilous Realm*, 136.

However, there is here at work more than mere sub-creation. It is also humility at the final contemplation of a life's work that was merely imagined and never created. It is precisely this nature of Chestertonian Fantasy that permeates the story. Humility directed at thankfulness, and manifested in Niggle's collaborative work with his neighbor Parish—who in the past had "seldom showed any gratitude at all."[20] Together, they give form to Niggle's vision of the Forest Spring, that Niggle here again had only imagined but never drawn. "Leaf by Niggle" can then surely be read as a Chestertonian Fantasy. But it is not merely a Chestertonian Fantasy. For if Tolkien discerned great power in this fantasy imbued with humility-like quality, it had "only a limited power."[21] In which respect did Tolkien think Chesterton's fantasy to be limited? Two complementary answers are possible.

While there is no clear indication of it, Tolkien probably thought Chesterton's fantasy limited in its scope. The relative absence of focus on language and myth creation in Chesterton likely left a bitter taste of something unfinished. Given his deep love for language, Tolkien was certainly looking for an imaginative ability that nourished the capacity for creating language. In that way Chesterton's Fantasy was probably too limited. Moreover, the embodiment of language in myth is also somewhat lacking in Chesterton. It is no wonder, then, that Tolkien's personal taste in words and myths led him to conclude to the relative limited relevance of Chestertonian Fantasy. There is also a second reason, directly reported by Tolkien. It is a rather simple reason. Chestertonian Fantasy is defined merely by Recovery, it is "its only virtue."[22] This form of fantasy is thus not mistaken, or misdirected, merely insufficient in itself. Here, "Leaf by Niggle" also points to the far too limited nature of Chestertonian Fantasy which does not provide enough room for the concept of sub-creation to fully blossom.

"Leaf by Niggle," by contrast, is yet another embodiment of Tolkien's essential anthropological concept. In fact, someone has written of this short story that it "clothes that concept [sub-creation] in a narrative in which God appears only thinly disguised as two Voices and as the Giver of the gift embodied in the Tree."[23] Put another way, "Leaf by Niggle"

20. Tolkien, *Tales from the Perilous Realm*, 133.

21. MC, 146.

22. MC, 147.

23. Hanks, "Tolkien's 'Leaf by Niggle,'" 27.

represents the same perspective on myth as Tolkien's "Mythopoeia." It is "both a springboard into fantasy and the end result of fantasy."[24] This short, unusual, story is a good example of the manner in which Tolkien has appropriated and formed a theological view of the imagination: "In short, Imagination and Art have resulted for Tolkien and for Niggle in sub-creation—in Fantasy, for Tolkien. Again from the close of the essay: '[an author] may now, perhaps, fairly dare to guess that in Fantasy he may actually assist in the effoliation and multiple enrichment of creation.'"[25] Of course, this enrichment of creation was only possible to Tolkien because of a strong view of both *creation* and *imagination*.

Tolkien's Thomist Imagination

Strangely, Chesterton seems to go much further than St. Thomas in arguing that fairyland provides liberation from the observable laws of this world. In turn, Tolkien echoes both St. Thomas and Chesterton in defining Faërie as that "which combines with its older and higher use as an equivalent of Imagination the derived notions of 'unreality' (that is, of unlikeness to the Primary World), of freedom from the domination of observed 'fact,' in short of the fantastic."[26] It is not certain whether St. Thomas would have wholeheartedly agreed or not, should he have been faced with the question, since he seems to entertain a dual view on this matter. Of course, he allows for the creative powers of the imagination as seen in the *Summa Theologiae*. But St. Thomas also argues that the imagination cannot create something standing at the opposite of God's creation. It seems therefore that there is a binding aspect to the imagination, according to St. Thomas, balancing the freedom of imagination "from observable facts."

This distinction is at the heart of the Thomists' understanding of the nature and workings of the imagination, and thus, is also at the heart of both Chesterton's and Tolkien's theories. To borrow the words of Jacques Maritain, another well-known twentieth-century Thomist, "Art, then, remains fundamentally inventive and creative. It is the faculty of producing, not of course *ex nihilo*, but from a pre-existing matter, a new

---

24. Hanks, "Tolkien's 'Leaf by Niggle,'" 29.
25. Hanks, "Tolkien's 'Leaf by Niggle,'" 41.
26. Tolkien, *Tales from the Perilous Realm*, 139.

creature, an original being, capable of stirring in turn a human soul."[27] This new thing created by art could be construed as being a translation of forms into matter through the imagination. As McIntosh explains, this translation of form to matter implies the future actualization "of those forms in and through the material substances which they are the forms of."[28] Or, as Flieger puts it using similarly scholastic terminology, "the Music is not the physical act of creation, but only its blueprint. It is the pattern for the world *inpotentia*."[29] Thus, says St. Thomas, the imagination does not copy but *imitates*. A copy is merely a reproduction of the exact original while an imitation is a creative work based on the model. The Ainulindalë—the account of the creation of Tolkien's mythological world, Arda—should be seen in this light. True imagination is not content with merely (re)-producing perceived images but also creates images based on pre-perceived ones. This is seen in Chesterton's previously quoted comment on the connection between the actual world and the imagined world. This connection exists and is set forth by Chesterton in terms of the moral nature of all possible worlds, a moral nature that reflects that of the Creator. As we have already said, this demonstrates that for the Thomists, imagination is not unbridled but is bound by the nature of the universal Being.[30]

We can now see the implication of St. Thomas's explanation of the working of the imagination for Tolkien's theory of the imagination. Faërie is not a land completely abstracted from the nature of the primary world. Certainly, it is independent in its form, but it corresponds to the nature of the primary world. As we have said, the view that imagination functions analogically to the sense-forms perceived by the sensitive soul is central. Significantly, Tolkien said that "creative Fantasy is founded upon the hard recognition that things are so in the world as it appears under the sun; on a recognition of fact, but not a slavery to it."[31] This perception-freedom is seen in the evolution of Tolkien's languages, an evolution that is based on the framework learned from the philological study of actualized languages. Another example is Tolkien's creativity in the matter of

---

27. Maritain, *Art and Scholasticism*, 63.

28. McIntosh, *The Flame Imperishable*, 227.

29. Flieger, *Splintered Light*, 58.

30. Or, more properly, sensation leaves an imprint on *phantasia*. *Phantasia* is thus bound by pre-existing matter, as existing and/or perceived. Kretzmann, *The Metaphysics of Creation*, 346. See SCG, II.liivi.

31. OFS, 65.

descriptions, which is always based on a first "exemplar," our actualized world, as imagination works out new mental images based on existent and substantial ones. Tolkien's descriptive skill is a demonstration of Maritain's assertion that "artistic creation does not copy God's creation, it continues it."[32] Thus, the order of Faërie is an imaginative continuation of our created order. The appeal of Faërie is that it *is* both a continuation and extension of the appeal of God's revelation on nature.

This also illuminates Tolkien's reaction against allegory. It is rather well-known that Tolkien "disliked allegory." He forcefully rejected any such reading of his work. Thus Arwen is not Mary and Sauron is not Stalin, nor even Hitler. The Ring is not the nuclear bomb, and Gondor is not Western Europe. Tolkien's imagination ran much deeper than allegorical associations. There was no need of allegory because the imagination could muster new forms to the service of art. In fact, he recognized dislking allegory, preferring the applicability of the story which gave the reader more freedom.[33] We see here again Tolkien's concern with the freedom nourished by the imagination. His rejection of allegory, if caused by his value of the reader's freedom, was also reinforced by his stress on the integrity of the re-composing powers of the imagination. The practice of the artist had no necessity for allegory for it could compose beauties, forms, and meanings through the active working of the imagination.

Rather, in Thomist terms, the imagination is similar to the intellect in that it serves as an analogical relation to universal being. As St. Thomas affirms: "For the intellect is in potency or in act according to the relation it maintains with universal being. In considering the nature of this relation, we find, at its highest degree, an intellect whose relation to universal being consists in being the very act of being taken in its totality."[34] There is no doubt that this firm conviction was shared by Chesterton and Tolkien, who were both convinced that the Source of imagination was ultimately the Creator God.

Further, commenting on the powers of sub-creation, Tolkien made the following point: "I should have said that liberation 'from the channels the creator is known to have used already' is the fundamental function of 'sub-creation,' a tribute to the infinity of His potential variety, one of the ways in which indeed it is exhibited, as indeed I said in the Essay

---

32. Maritain, *Art and Scholasticism*, 63.

33. LoTR, foreword, vii.

34. Gilson, *The Philosophy of St. Thomas Aquinas*, 234.

['On Fairy Stories'].”[35] This recalls St. Thomas's view that the fruits of the imagination are based on the information furnished by the senses. Imagination does not work out of a vacuum, but with pre-existing elements. Regarding the question of the origin and material on which fairy-stories are invented, Tolkien made the same point. In fact, he argued that true fairy-story is creative but *not* illusory.[36]

Faërie can only be the fruit of a human imagination that is nourished by the Primary world. Tolkien thus manifests what is for Chesterton an intrinsic quality of Thomas's common sense philosophy: that things are as they are, and could not be otherwise. As Tolkien writes: “creative Fantasy is founded upon the hard recognition that things are so in the world as it appears under the sun; on a recognition of fact, but not a slavery to it.”[37] This is common sense in its purest Thomist form. Because the world is one thing and not another Fantasy, or for Tolkien, Faërie, can be fully understood. Tolkien's grounding in Thomas' common sense also explains how Faërie can be imbued with the three qualities of Recovery, Escape and Consolation, which we will discuss in the last chapters. There is no doubt that Tolkien's Thomist understanding of the nature of the imagination is in the background of his concept of sub-creation and in his mythopoeic writings. It is also evident that this potent influence was often more indirect than Barfield's, while probably more profound.

Conclusion

Whether Tolkien's theory of imagination stands closer to Thomas, Chesterton or Barfield is an extremely difficult question. While Barfield's theory of the “ancient semantic unity” had a clear impact on Tolkien's own vision, it was certainly not the only imaginative perspective that nourished Tolkien's own thinking. Of course, if one asks which of these three thinkers was the most influential, Barfield stands as the most obvious and direct influence, giving Tolkien a new perspective on language and myth. However, Tolkien did not follow Barfield completely because it would have taken him to places he is not comfortable to go. When it becomes necessary to relate the imagination and the Primary World, Tolkien displays a more Chestertonian understanding of the imagination.

35. L, 188.
36. OFS, 35.
37. MC, 144.

It could actually be argued that there is a broader Chestertonian influence behind Tolkien's approach to Faërie—at least initially. Of course, given Chesterton's personality and the imaginative nature of his writings, it is quite understandable that Tolkien would have partly grown under his shadow and be one of his "descendants." One dimension of Chestertonian fantasy that most likely had a lasting impact is the essential property of freedom, but not independence, from the facts.

Of course, the undercurrent of this latter view of the imagination can only be called Thomist. That does not necessarily imply that we should only read Tolkien as a Thomist writer, nor that we should do so lightly. Thus, while there is a Thomist coloration to Tolkien's sub-created world, it is largely re-formed through Tolkien's own understanding of the nature and purpose of the imagination, embodied in "Faërie." If the Thomist nature of his sub-creation remains the most fundamental dimension that accounts for the final "product" we have become so familiar with, the process that led to its creation makes room for Barfield, Chesterton, and Thomas. In a way, all three thinkers are necessary to understand what Tolkien was doing in his imaginative sub-creation. Tolkien, always his own man, combined the intuitions of these three major thinkers in a manner very much personal to his own taste, thinking, and overall mythological project for England.

10

Literary Creation under God

——— *Man as Sub-creator* ———

TOLKIEN'S MYTHOLOGY, WHILE A great work of imagination, could not have become the great mythological world that has become one of the greatest epics of the twentieth century without its embodiment in another notion: sub-creation. Immediately, a question comes to mind: "What is sub-creation?" To continue our journey, we must answer this question. And we must find Tolkien's voice. As a fiction writer, Tolkien was by definition an artist, that is, someone who demonstrated artistic mastery and creation. Though Tolkien never pretended to be an artist, he became one through personal loves and interests. In his artistic endeavors, Tolkien was quite successful and tried to master different techniques in prose, poetry, and also drawing. He was truly an artistic man, someone who knows the nature and the essential character of art, and how to create it.

Even though he was interested in different forms of art, his main artistic expression was imaginative writing, mythopoetics. Tolkien had the ability to craft fairy-stories; he was someone who knew from within the essential nature of fairy-stories. As both artist and Roman Catholic, Tolkien naturally came to ponder the relation between the artist and his God. Of special concern to him were the themes of the relation between the Creator God and his creatures, as well as the nature and purpose of the imagination. The result of these intellectual, imaginative, and spiritual reflections was his characterization of the artist as a sub-creator.

Tolkien's initial observation regarding fairy-stories concerns their content. Opposing the contemporary definition of fairy-stories as tales about fairies, those little airy, tricky, flying creatures, Tolkien argued that fairy-stories were more about the land of Faërie. Tolkien's constant reference to fairy-stories as stories about the *land* of Faërie points towards the priority of the *created order* of Faërie. For him, Faërie is primarily a place and not a state of being; and fairy-stories are not about small creatures called fairies, but about a land called Faërie. They are about the Perilous Realm, the place of Faërie, a place where beings of all sorts stay and wander, enter and trespass, live and die. Tolkien's stress on the "spatial" and physical nature of Faërie leads to questions about the origin and nature of Faerie as a created order; andfor a Roman Catholic like Tolkien, a created order implies the existence of a creator.

The Source of Being: The Neoplatonic Eru

The first lines of the Ainulindalë, which most readers will remember quite well, are telling: "There was Eru, the One, who in Arda is called Ilúvatar; and he made first the Ainur, the Holy Ones, that were the offspring of his thought, and they were with him before aught else was made."[1] This is of course reminiscent of the creation account found in the book of Genesis, and is in line with the Thomist understanding of the Creator and of the creative act. Indeed, Thomas Aquinas stresses the inescapable fact that there is nothing that *is*, or *could be*, that is not itself under the Creator-God's sovereignty. Consistent with this, Tolkien also referred to God as the "supreme Artist and the Author of Reality."[2] At first then, it would seem that there is nothing much to be said about the origin and nature of the natural creation: there is a creator, there is a creation. There is no more to it. However, this would certainly be over-simplistic. For, if creation comes from a creator, there is little doubt that the nature of the creation will entertain a profound relationship with its creator—it will, in an analogical way, resemble it. Such a superficial interpretation of the beginning of the Ainulindalë would also be blind to the debate regarding the nature of Tolkien's sub-creation. The general framework used to interpret these Genesis-like lines is often a sort of Neoplatonic philosophy. Many scholars have defended that position.

1. S, 3.
2. L, 101.

Noting that Eru is described by Tolkien himself as "immensely remote,"[3] many commentators have concluded that Tolkien's creation is a "perfectly good Neoplatonist Christian cosmos" even resulting in a "full-blown *pagan* Neoplatonism."[4] And because Eru is "The One," other Tolkien scholars have hastily identified him with a Neoplatonic god. One of the greatest Tolkien scholar, Verlyn Flieger, has for example associated Eru with classic Neoplatonic metaphysical thought.[5] In fact, Flieger described the creation act along the lines of an emanationist theory that has profound implications for the rest of Arda's unfolding history. According to this perspective, emanation implies diminution, falling away from Eru's perfection and light. In fact, the whole concept of emanation as diminution, as splintered light, lies at the heart of Flieger's impressive work in which she makes use of this emanationist motif through the examples of the Lamp and the Trees of Valinor.

After reminding us that Eru is a remote figure, the Neoplatonic account of creation by the Ainur is presented as a *mediatory* act between Iluvatar's creative act and the actualized creation. This leads Flieger to conclude: "The concept of the Valar is especially important to the cosmology. While their position in the hierarchy suggests angelic beings, their role in the scheme of things is, from a strictly Christian point of view, eccentric."[6] This conclusion is shared by other scholars noting that creation by the Ainur represents a "divine distance" clearly not characteristic of the biblical God. If we follow that interpretation, we have to conclude that the Ainulindalë presents us with a deist account of creation in which the Ainur are closer to being creators than sub-creators. This would, supposedly, be further supported by Eru's approbative declaration: "Behold your Music!" This confirmation addressed to the Ainur might well validate the interpretation of creation as primarily an act of the Ainur. Flieger thus affirms that "the Music is not the physical act of creation, but only its blueprint. It is the pattern for the world *inpotentia*."[7]

While she forcefully argues in favor of the Neoplatonic Eru, Flieger also rightly maintains that "there is only one Prime Mover—Eru, the One. The Ainur, and more particularly the Valar, are sub-creators. They

---

3. L, 104.

4. Hutton, "The Pagan Tolkien," 63.

5. McIntosh, *The Flame Imperishable*, 50.

6. Flieger, *Splintered Light*, 54.

7. Flieger, *Splintered Light*, 58.

participate in the physical making of the world but could not have done so had not Eru first given them the theme."[8] Of course, the implication of a strong Neoplatonic association is to make Eru a merely functional creator, not an actual one. Thus, John Cox takes this interpretation to its logical conclusion when he suggests that the Ainulindalë, siding with the Neo-platonician philosopher Plotinus over against the "Hebrew tradition," reflects a radical dualism between the supreme simplicity and eternality of Eru and the temporal plurality of the created order represented by the Ainur.[9]

Certainly, the Neoplatonic interpretation of the Ainulindalë is a powerful one and should not be underestimated. St. Thomas himself was in fact well aware that emanationism was a *real* creational option. In his *De potentia dei*, dealing with the question of whether a creation "out of nothing" is even philosophically possible, St. Thomas considers the objection that "the same thing cannot be the principle of both perfection and imperfection."[10] Even if St. Thomas does not here explicitly debate Neoplatonic emanationism, it is quite obvious that it is what he had in mind in the passage just quoted. This would seem to argue for a dual principle in creation: one of perfection and another one of imperfection (or limitation), as the previous picture of creation would present the dual role of Eru and the Ainur, the latter being, of course, a "principle" of imperfection. In fact, if Eru is not the principle of perfection and imperfection, he must be, even though perfect himself, the origin of an imperfect and mediated world. Aquinas himself takes another road and implies that this objection would require the identification of another source or origin, which cannot be the case. The result of the emanationist account is that Eru creates a world which perfection is continually fragmented. Far from being the "source of being," Eru ends up being only the source of diminished life.

The Source of Being: The Thomist Creator

It is important to remember that the mere name of Eru, "The One," is not enough to argue for a Neo-platonist reading. The same is seen in most theological traditions, including Thomism. In fact, if we pay close

---

8. Flieger, *Splintered Light*, 55.

9. Cox, "Tolkien's Platonic Fantasy," 58.

10. Aquinas, *On Creation*, 6.

attention to Tolkien's account of creation, we come to see that Tolkien's Eru is actually much more than the distant, remote creator that Flieger envisions. Eru has consciously and out of his own power designed the world and all that is to happen, though that never precludes the real action of his creatures. As McIntosh points out, "Eru is no mere emanative source of all existence, but, more like Aquinas's First Being, is a personal agent who has self-consciously designed and created the world in such a was as to enable his creatures to learn something of his own mind through the study of his effects."[11] The Ainulindalë recounts Eru talking to the Ainur, saying:

> "And I will send forth into the Void the Flame Imperishable, and it shall be at the heart of the World, and the World shall Be; and those of you that will may go down into it." And suddenly the Ainur saw afar off a light, as it were a cloud with a living heart of flame; and they knew that this was no vision only, but that Iluvatar had made a new thing: Ea, the World that Is.[12]

In creating the world, Eru became its origin, also remaining its essential foundation through the presence of the Secret Fire. This means that understanding Middle-earth demands a grasp of the creative act that gave it existence. In most of the Christian tradition, understanding God entails understanding his nature, that is, his moral and eternal character. It also requires an investigation of the relationship between the Creator and his creatures, including their differences. This is best understood in the light of the specific and unique nature of the Creator-God. St. Thomas's theology of creation is both complex and broad in its implications. One of its main features is a consistent reference to the Creator of all things as the *source* of all being, as St. Thomas says: "Not only is it not impossible for God to create something, but from what has been established we cannot but hold that all things are created by him."[13] St. Thomas refers to the term "source" quite explicitly, often referring to it with terms such as "cause," or "mover," as seen in his philosophical construction of the cosmological arguments. For example, in the second book of the *Summa Contra Gentiles*, he affirms that "it belongs to God to be the principle and cause of being to other things."[14]

---

11. McIntosh, *The Flame Imperishable*, 51.

12. S, 20.

13. ST, Ia.45.ii.

14. SCG, II.vi.1. See also SCG, II.vi.3; ST, Ia.8.iii; Ia.8.iv.

However, St. Thomas is not satisfied with saying that God is the source of all that exists. Starting with the observation that that which is *actual* is closely related to that which was formerly only *potential*, St. Thomas affirms that God is the source of all for which being can be predicated. As he similarly argues in his *Quaestiones Disputatae de Potentia*, "whatever is made was possible before it was made for if it could not be, it could not be made, since the impossible cannot be the term of a change."[15] Therefore whatever is made, is produced from matter or a subject. Therefore nothing can be made out of nothing. Hence, nothing that exists, whether in actuality or potentiality, does so apart from the creating activity of God, the Source of all beings. To say the contrary would be to support the opinion that some *potential* things exist independently from God. Actual and potential things alike have their source in the originator of beings, the one in whom potentiality and actuality are coextensive.

Tolkien himself echoes St. Thomas in his use of the expression "Prime Being," even if it is in a rather loose reference to the Creator-God.[16] Moreover, Tolkien stresses in quite Chestertonian terms the ultimate sovereignty of God over all creations—whether "real" or "imaginary," whether "actual" or "potential." For example, he once stated that "in every world on every plane all must ultimately be under the Will of God," thus affirming with St. Thomas that all that exists has its source in God, the Divine Mind, source of our own minds.[17] And further, if God is the source of our minds, the implication is that this Creator is an intelligible being. Tolkien, in one of the devotional letters he was accustomed to send, wrote to his publisher's daughter that there is a "Creator-Designer, a Mind to which our minds are akin (being derived from it) so that It is intelligent to us in part."[18] The reference to God as the Designer leads us to investigate the relation between God and his creation. It is noticeable that Tolkien, throughout his legendarium, stresses the importance of recognizing the God of his mythology, Ilúvatar, as the Creator of Arda and of all things.

The problem Tolkien points to is that of the relation between creation and sub-creation. The question we actually face is whether or not the human artist can create a work of art, *a work of its own*. Given the

15. Aquinas, *On the Power of God*, 79.

16. L, 192.

17. L, 191.

18. L, 399. The importance of this allusion to the analogical spirit of Thomism cannot be underestimated.

nature of God as Creator, it would seem impossible to speak of the human artist as a creator. This might be one of the theological reasons for Tolkien's characterization of the human artist as a "sub-creator," thus emphasizing the submission of the artist to God, and consequently the submission of the sub-created reality to the created order. Further, to affirm that God is Creator of everything has important implications for determining the nature of human creativity.

The second important notion found in St. Thomas's doctrine of creation is the distinction established between the Creator and the creatures. It is usually understood that St. Thomas, and with him much of the Roman Catholic tradition, defends a transcendental and unified concept of being, itself the ground of all existent beings. In other words, St. Thomas's concept of analogy is most properly connected to God's being itself, thus creating a potential confusion between God's being and man's being. However, this is probably an overstatement, since St. Thomas repeatedly protested that he was trying to avoid the two opposing dangers of theological language, that is, univocity and equivocity. St. Thomas's concern is to provide a theological explanation of the relationship between the Creator and his creatures while at the same time maintaining the simplicity and uniqueness of the Creator.

Further, St. Thomas deals with the relationship between the Creator and his creatures using a specific notion taken from Aristotle and re-adapted through Christian philosophy. When it comes to the doctrine of creation, the most important general rule learned from St. Thomas is that "whatever is found in anything by participation must be caused in it by that to which it belongs essentially."[19] In St. Thomas, the language of participation is almost synonymous with the language of analogy. In fact, the concept of analogy in St. Thomas cannot be overestimated because it is the foundation of Thomist metaphysics. As Thomist scholar Gerald Phelan affirms, there is no understanding of metaphysics without an understanding of analogy because it is "axiomatic in metaphysics."[20]

However, before focusing on this concept, it is necessary to realize that, without disregarding the importance of the concept of analogy, it is subordinated to an all-encompassing principle, the "dominating principle" of Thomist philosophy, that is, the notion of *being*. As Phelan points out: "*being* become[s] the dominating concept in philosophy, the norm of

19. Velde, *Participation and Substantiality*, 5–8.
20. Phelan, *Saint Thomas and Analogy*, 2.

all reflection in the order of nature and the basis of all rational knowledge. And, being as such is intrinsically analogical."[21] The last sentence provides both the link between the concepts of being and analogy as well as the explanation for the problem of the relation between the Creator and his creation. "Being," in St. Thomas's thinking, belongs to all that exists, but neither univocally nor equivocally. It belongs to all analogically, that is to say, to each according to its own nature.

To focus on St. Thomas's concept of analogy itself is to realize that analogy is a complex principle and that it cannot be used without having been cautiously evaluated. The principle of analogy cannot be univocally applied to every problem. But once this cautionary statement has been heard, analogy becomes a governing principle in theological and philosophical reflection. In its simplest form, "the doctrine of Thomistic analogy, in its strict and proper meaning, is that whatever perfection is analogically common to two or more beings is intrinsically (formally) possessed by each, not, however, by any two in the same way or mode, but by each in proportion to its being."[22] The application of the concept of analogy to the relation and character of the Creator-God and human beings is based on the natural order. As Thomist scholar Ralph McInerny asserts about the realm of epistemology: "Our knowledge of God is gained from knowledge of creatures."[23] Since we know that human beings are creative and imaginative beings, we can analogically predicate God's creative and imaginative nature.

The creative analogical relationship between God and human beings fits St. Thomas's explanation of the relation between *essentia* and *esse*. The proportion between creation's *essentia* and its *esse* is the same as that of God's *essentia* and his *esse*. The proportion *essentia/esse* is a constant principle. Moreover, the proportion of God's *essentia* to his *esse* is analogical to the proportion of the *essentia* of creation to its *esse*. As a consequence, we can analogically predicate all perfections and characteristics present in man in the following proportional equation. The proportion of God's perfections to his *esse* is analogical to the proportion of humanity's perfections to its *esse*.[24] Thus, in terms of creativity, the proportion of God's creativity to his *esse* is analogical to the proportion

21. Phelan, *Saint Thomas and Analogy*, 7.

22. Phelan, *Saint Thomas and Analogy*, 23.

23. McInerny, *Rhyme and Reason*, 36.

24. Adapted from Lyttkens, *The Analogy between God and the World*, 474.

of humanity's creativity to its *esse*. At this point it is possible to equate this Thomist approach to Tolkien's expression "sub-creation." His statement that there is a Mind "to which our minds are akin (being derived from it)" is a Thomist application of the metaphysical concept of analogy. Reading Tolkien as Thomist myth-maker is to realize fully that "Creator" ascribed to God is an essential predication, while "creator" ascribed to human beings is a participative and analogical predication.

Another way to express the relation between the Creator and his creatures is to re-affirm that God is the self-subsisting primary Creator, while we are analogical, dependent sub-creators. This is the reason for Tolkien's use of the term sub-creation: man is an *analogical* creator, properly speaking, a *sub*-creator. Tolkien's concept is implicit in many passages of St. Thomas's *Summa Theologiae* where God is repeatedly referred to as "the first exemplar cause of all things."[25] St. Thomas also compares our sub-creative activities to that of an artist that "gives a definite shape to his material because of an exemplar before him, whether this be a model he looks at from outside or a pattern interiorly conceived in his mind."[26] God is thus the exemplar of all our abilities, including the capacity for invention, creation, and artistic sensitivity. Of this, Tolkien was particularly conscious because he was an artist, but also, or particularly so, because he was a Thomist. We could even go so far as to label Tolkien a Thomist myth-maker. Unfortunately, most Tolkienians would find this appreciation farfetched.

The Nature of Sub-creation

God the creator brought into being sub-creators. You, me, human beings. But exploring our nature as sub-creators raisons other questions. Among these, the relation between the two worlds, that of God and that of the human imagination. Tolkien himself was well aware of the necessity of thinking about the relation between what he calls the primary and the secondary worlds. About his own legendarium he wrote to Milton Waldman: "It is, I suppose, fundamentally concerned with the problem of the relation of Art (and Sub-creation) and Primary Reality."[27] For the artist who inhabits the primary world, it is indeed a fundamental problem to

25. ST, Ia.44.iii.
26. ST, Ia.44.iii.
27. L, 145n.

think about the nature of his own sub-creation. Tolkien reinforces this when he writes that "from beginning to end [his corpus is] mainly concerned with the relation of Creation to making and sub-creation," and therefore "references to these things are not casual, but fundamental."[28]

Approaching this question, and facing the dilemma of the power of human imagination, Tolkien did not adopt either of the following two extremes: either Faërie originates *only* in God's mind, or it originates *only* in the human mind. If these were our only two options, and if we applied these categories to Tolkien's mythology, it would entail that either Ilúvatar is the sole creator, or that the Ainur are themselves creators. If the second extreme exaggerates the creative autonomy of the Ainur, the opposite extreme tends to deny their relative sub-creative freedom. As far as this latter option is concerned, the answer is easy. Faërie cannot originate in the human mind only, because this would create an impossible Thomist metaphysical situation: an unprecedented total independence of a creaturely being from its Creator. In other words, it would entail a sovereign independence of the human mind from God and Faërie would lose its metaphysical foundation. As a consequence, there would be independence of a substance from the principle of existence in which all is supposed to participate.

In other words, it is necessary to ask about the origin of the Faërie realm. In fact, the human power of imagination gives rise to an interesting dilemma. It would seem that if God is the Author and Creator of all things, he should also be the Author of things that exist only in the realm of human creativity. On the other hand, it seems impossible for God to be the Author of anything to which he did not give actual existence and reality. St. Thomas also addressed this dilemma in his own time. For him it took the following form. To maintain that God did not actualize possible worlds and existences would seem to entail potentiality in God, that is, the presence of accidents in God. However, for St. Thomas, God is not potentiality but pure actuality. To assert the opposite would go directly against the doctrine of God's simplicity and aseity. St. Thomas resolved this dilemma by demonstrating that God creates the accidents themselves *within* substances and existences. God is pure actuality, and therefore, both actual and potential accidents derive from God himself.

It is difficult to understand how the fruit of human imagination could have its origin only in the Divine mind without existing in the human

28. L, 188.

mind. Moreover, it is a fact that Faërie does not have an individual *substance*, a real *existence*, thus leading to the necessity of locating the *proximate* origin of Faërie in the human mind. As Faërie has no actuality this would suggest it is mere, pure, potentiality. However, this is not possible: things that exist have some actuality in our world. In St. Thomas's terms, pure potentiality is the definition of prime matter (*materia prima*).[29] To argue the contrary would be to subvert completely both metaphysics and epistemology as we know them. But since Faërie does not originate in the human mind independently from God, it ultimately originates in God, through analogical participation. Several arguments support this view. First, God is the cause of all that exists, which means that Faërie, the fruit of the human imagination—Faërie's *proximate* cause—has as its *final* cause the God of St. Thomas's First Way. As St. Thomas affirms, "Since God is the efficient, exemplary, and final cause of everything, and since primary matter is from him, we infer that the origin of all things in reality is single."[30] Therefore, since God is the ultimate, final, and exemplar cause of all that exists, everything in reality and in the mind participates in God as do all essences (*essentia*).

Here again, the resolving principle is the concept of analogy. To resolve the tension about the origin of the sub-created world, it is first necessary to notice that this second order cannot be pure potentiality or pure actuality. As to the former, it would be equating the fruit of the human imagination with what St. Thomas calls *materia prima*, prime matter, but this, again, is clearly not an option.[31] Regarding the latter, there is only one thing, one being, of which "pure actuality" can be predicated, and it is God. If sub-creation is neither *pure* potentiality nor *pure* actuality, it must be *both* potentiality and actuality; and we can go further in saying that the potentiality of sub-creation comes from God's creative act and its actual nature from the actualization in the human mind. God is the author of all conceivable worlds, and we actualize some of them through our imaginative power given by God in the creative act. Finally, in paraphrasing Gilson's comment on the rational intellect, we can say that God knows all imaginary beings and worlds, not only distinct from each other, but also in their very individuality, with the accidents and the matter (*worlds*) which make them into particular beings.

29. See Kretzmann, *The Metaphysics of Creation*, 78n16.

30. ST, Ia.44.iv.

31. Kretzmann, *The Metaphysics of Creation*, 79. See ST, Ia.44.iii. See also SCG, II.16.i–iv.

This particular point also relates to the question of the freedom of the sub-creator. Two extremes are possible: we can make sub-creators mere shadows of the Creator's action, or we can shape them into autonomous creators. Both are mistaken. This is well-illustrated in Tolkien's mythology. Here again Tolkien probably found in Thomas a balanced approach to this metaphysical conundrum. The point of origin of a Thomistic resolution is found in the Ainulindalë, in which we find three examples of sub-creation.

The first example is the sub-creation of the Ainur themselves. After the episode of the discord of the Music by Melkor, Ilúvatar shows the Ainur a vision of their sub-creative activity.[32] We have seen that the Music of the Ainur has often been considered to be an example of strict creation on their part, and this passage could support that opinion. Read in Tolkien's Thomist context, however, the same account takes on a different meaning. It is not necessary to go into intricate discussion here since the foundational Thomistic account of creation has already been established. The question is, as Thomas writes, "whether it pertains to God *alone* to create."[33] Regarding this very question, we could summarize Thomas's answer, as well as that of Tolkien, stating simply that while Eru *creates*, the Valar only *make*. Thus "to make" is synonymous with "to sub-create." This distinction, McIntosh reminds us, goes back to a distinction the early church Fathers had already made between God's divine act of creation and the shaping or reorganizing sub-creative power of creatures.

It would thus seem that all sub-creative acts are not independent actions from Eru but exemplify his sovereignty. However, this should not be taken as a negation of the Ainur's own participation in the activity creation. At this point, we should always remember that affirming that creation itself is always the *proper act* of God only is by no means an affirmation of his *exclusive action*. The Ainur sub-create, playing an instrumental role by participating in the proper action of another. This participative activity is sustained by the Flame Imperishable that has kindled the existence of all creation. As McIntosh concludes, "Eru is . . . depicted as sending his own self, under the guise of the Flame Imperishable, to kindle the world, including its matter, in its very being."[34] Tolkien himself made this very point in *Morgoth's Ring*: "It refers rather to the

32. S, 17.

33. ST, Ia.45.v.

34. McIntosh, *The Flame Imperishable*, 93.

mystery of 'authorship', by which the author, while remaining 'outside' and independent of his work, also 'indwells' in it, on its derivate plane, below that of his own being, as the source and guarantee of its being."[35] The sub-creative ability of the Ainur is thus directly the fruit of this Secret Fire. This also will distinguish Melkor's sub-creative attempts.

The second example of sub-creative manifestation is that of Aulë, and of the sub-creation of the dwarves. After the first creation of Arda, the Ainur are promised the coming of the Children of Eru, Elves and Men. However, one of them, Aulë, is impatient, "for so greatly did Aulë desire the coming of the Children, to have learners to whom he could teach his lore and crafts, that he was unwilling to await the fulfillment of the designs of Ilúvatar."[36] Thus he decided to "make" another race, the dwarves whose form was not "complete" because it was not "clear to his mind." Ilúvatar then came to Aulë reproaching him, pointing out that given Aulë's limited sub-creating abilities, his creation could only live through his (Aulë's) being, drastically limiting the freedom of this new creation. Ilúvatar then commanded Aulë to bring an end to his making. Acknowledging his fault, Aulë repeatedly uses the verb "make" to refer to his sub-creation saying, "yet the making of things is in my heart from my own making by thee."[37] However, that alone is not indicative enough, since it is the same term used by Tolkien to refer to Ilúvatar's creation. What is more significant is his relating his own sub-creation to Ilúvatar's. It is because Aulë was created that he could sub-create.

The third example of sub-creation is that of the orcs by Melkor. The debated passage is Treebeard's statement that "the Dark Lord created the Trolls and the Orcs." Soon Tolkien received a letter from one Peter Hastings, manager of the Newman Bookshop, expressing profound enthusiasm at the reading of *The Lord of the Rings*, but also questioning some of Tolkien's seemingly theologically contradictory statements. One of his concerns was Treebeard's implication that the Dark Lord had made (or subcreated) Trolls and Orcs."[38] In fact, as the introduction to this letter reports: "Hastings suggested that evil was incapable of creating anything, and argued that even if it could create, its creatures 'could not have a tendency to good, even a very small one'; whereas, he argued, one of the

---

35. MR, 345.

36. S, 43.

37. S, 43.

38. L, 187.

Trolls in *The Hobbit*, William, does have a feeling of pity for Bilbo."[39] Tolkien's answer follows closely what we have just said. In his letter back to Hastings he noted a difference between creating and making, the latter referring to a counterfeiting of already existing realities. Evil does not create, and can only make, and that only in the sense of perverting.[40]

While Tolkien never sent the letter, he showed a fundamental agreement with Hastings' implied response. Evil is indeed completely incapable of creating anything; it merely makes by corruption or imitation. As Tolkien later remarks about orcs in his letter to Naomi Mitchison, "since they are servants of the Dark Power, and later of Sauron, neither of whom could, or would, produce living things, they must be 'corruptions.'"[41] Such an opinion is shared by Frodo who, because of his sufferings and experiences, as well perhaps because of his connection to the Ring, gained more insight into this question. And, as Tolkien advised Peter Hastings to remember that evil can only mock, not make completely new things. We do not know what was the basis of Hastings's own conviction that evil could not create, but Tolkien's is clear enough and exhibits the Thomistic position that no created being, whether in the primary or secondary world, whether evil or not, can demonstrate creative powers—merely sub-creative ones.

There is a further particularity about evil's impossibility to create, one that is seen in the nature of sub-creation, especially as far as evil is concerned. In a collection of short texts, "Myths Transformed," Tolkien pointed out a main difference between Morgoth and Sauron. Surprisingly, given the Ainulindalë's cosmology, the latter, at the end of the Third Age was more powerful than the former at the end of the First Age. To explain this incongruity—Sauron, after all, is only Morgoth's lieutenant—Tolkien stressed that Morgoth objected to the existence of the world and other creatures themselves. He was devoted to destruction.[42] The contrast here is between destruction and domination, for domination implies that something does exist to be dominated. Because of his will for complete destruction, Morgoth was unable to endue his "creatures" with a true will of their own. Because Sauron used his minions' enslaved will to obey his commands, his power could outgrow that of his master.

39. L, 187.
40. L, 190.
41. L, 178.
42. MR, 395.

This contrast is all the more striking when compared to Eru's creation or even Aulë's sub-creation of the dwarves. Writes Tolkien: "As the case of Aulë and the Dwarves shows, only Eru could make creatures with independent wills, and with reasoning powers. But Orcs seem to have both: they can try to cheat Morgoth/Sauron, rebel against him, or criticize him."[43] There must be preexisting matter or creation for corruption to happen, implies Tolkien. More importantly, in both the attitude of Eru and Aulë we witness a refusal of annihilating control over the creatures. Eru lovingly and willingly lets his creatures (the Ainur) be part of his developing creation while Aulë gives away control of his sub-creation (the dwarves) to the merciful judgment of Eru. What thus could characterize the difference between Eru and Morgoth's pretense to be creator is the gift of freedom and personal choice.

Beyond the mere metaphysical impossibility of evil having creating powers, another difference lies at the heart of sub-creation. Here lies the difference between true sub-creation and mere perverted imitation. Going back to the Ainur's discovery of their sub-creative abilities, a distinguishing feature is their love for things "other than themselves, strange and free."[44] Aulë expresses this very thought about the dwarves, his own sub-creation as beings he desired, beings *other* than him in order to *love* them.[45] The otherness and the love of sub-creation is characteristic of the Ainur's analogical power. This also is congruent with the baseline of Thomist theology. As McIntosh writes, "In the Ainulindalë, then, the sub-creative activity of the Ainur presupposes a recognizably Thomistic understanding of sub-creative possibility in terms of imitability of the divine mind or essence, yet the question remains as to how this theoretical outlook might practically inform the sub-creative act."[46] Ilúvatar's creative act is characterized by his goodness and the gift of freedom to his creation. He does indeed love his creation because it is "other," and so do the Ainur, except Melkor who made only servants to his will. Freedom and love of one's making is the most fundamental expression of true sub-creative stewardship.

43. MR, 409.

44. S, 18.

45. S, 43.

46. McIntosh, *The Flame Imperishable*, 114.

The Relation between Primary and Secondary Worlds

In order to understand the nature and origin of Faërie, it is also necessary to consider the relation between the artist, crafter, and sub-creator of the realm of Faërie, and God, the author of our created order. In the same significant draft letter to Peter Hastings, Tolkien answered one important question relating to our current topic. We do not have the copy of Hastings's original letter, but from Tolkien's answer we understand that one of his concerns was whether there were any bounds to a writer's sub-creative production—apart from the limits of human finitude. Tolkien responded: "No bounds, but the laws of contradiction, I should think. But, of course, humility and an awareness of peril is required."[47] What unites the laws of the primary and secondary worlds are precisely the laws of non-contradiction. Here, Thomism would imply that the sub-creator's freedom from necessity will still be conditioned by his "finiteness" most clearly expressed by his subjugation to the law of non-contradiction. Of course, this "non-contradiction" principle must not be taken as implying a non-contradiction between the primary and the secondary worlds. As Tolkien reminds us, "inside this mythical history (as its metaphysic is, not necessarily as a metaphysic of the real World) Creation, the act of Will of Eru the One that gives Reality to conceptions, is distinguished from Making, which is permissive."[48] The primary non-contradiction is an internal one. As Tolkien continuously asserted, a secondary World must be consistent, that is, internally non-contradictory. Indeed, "new forms" are brought to life by mere command of the sub-creator's "will." In his lecture "On Fairy Stories," Tolkien reminds us that one distinct characteristic of fairy-stories is that they are founded on reality but not enslaved to it.[49] There is indeed a sub-creative freedom. The primary world is what it is, but the secondary world is not out of necessity its exact reflection. This can be labelled "primary non-contradiction."

Another principle of non-contradiction is also at work, one we could label "secondary non-contradiction." While the primary focus of the sub-creator should be the internal non-contradiction of his world, any relation between primary and secondary worlds should not be obliterated. If, with respect to "primary non-contradiction," the most important category to consider is the metaphysical one, with respect to

47. L, 194.
48. L, 190n.
49. OFS, 65.

"secondary non-contradiction," the most important category to consider is the ethical one. This explains that while God is trinitarian, Eru is not shown as being so—thus demonstrating the metaphysical freedom exercised by the sub-creator. This is partially due to St. Thomas's concept of analogy; and by virtue of all things originating in the Mind of God, the ethical nature of both worlds will be identical. One example taken from Chesterton will make clear what is meant here. In the Father Brown story "The Blue Cross," the detective-priest makes a rather puzzling and striking statement. Contesting the false priest's remark about the absolute reach of human reason, he concludes: "Well, you can imagine any mad botany or geology you please. . . . But don't fancy all that frantic astronomy would make the smallest difference to the reason and justice of conduct. On plains of opal, under cliffs cut out of pearl, you would still find a notice-board, 'Thou shalt not steal.'"[50] Here we find an interesting presentation of the relation between the two worlds in the merging of the moral and metaphysical categories.

Here, Chesterton affirms, and Tolkien will follow him, that in any possible world, God's will—which reflects his nature, goodness, holiness, etc.—remains identical to the one we know in the actual world. Tolkien's dependence on Chesterton is obvious in a passage of manuscript "B," contained in the miscellaneous pages of "On Fairy Stories." In this unpublished passage, Tolkien concludes that even if Fairies existed, they would be bound by Moral Law, which is also binding in the created universe.[51] This is evidenced in Tolkien's mythology. One rider of Rohan puts it bluntly: "Good and evil haven't changed since yesteryear."[52] Certainly, moral values have not changed since the beginning of Arda. Nor have they changed in the primary world in which Tolkien thought moral values applied in a rather universal manner.

However, it is not only that the values of Arda are internally consistent, but that they are consistent with the moral values of the primary world. Talking about virtues is always complicated. To begin with, as Tom Shippey says, "Wickedness is always . . . the pursuit of some good in the wrong way."[53] But certainly goodness and wickedness are not a question of perspective. Rather, it is a matter of moral foundation, or of discerning

---

50. Chesterton, *The Complete Father Brown*, 1:17–18.

51. OFS, 254.

52. LoTR, II.3.ii, 428.

53. Shippey, "Orcs, Wraiths, Wights," 185.

the values of Tolkien's world. These values, or virtues, are essentially manifested in the hobbits: shrewdness, generosity, but also patience.[54] Pity, as well as self-sacrifice, is an integrative part of Tolkien's story, and this closely resembles the primary world.

Never, for example, do we witness the orcs, or the Uruk-Hai, displaying true moral values. Of course, some have noted that while orcs, goblins, and other servants of Sauron (and Melkor) do not exhibit certain values, they are however not without a frame of reference. It is not so much that they are amoral but that their values are perverted, as is their nature. For example, they respect their leaders, as we see from the interaction between the goblins and their Great Goblin in *The Hobbit*.[55] In fact, we could almost conclude that orcs probably live up to the standard of their society. Of course, we do not have much knowledge of the orcs' social values. In an unpublished letter sent in October 1963 to one Mrs. Munby, Tolkien wrote about the orcs that "in stories that seldom if ever see the Orcs except as soldiers of armies in the service of the evil lords we naturally would not learn much about their lives. Not much was known."[56] This, however, does not make them "moral." Certainly, orcs are responsible moral beings, though this does not necessarily mean they are "moral beings" in the sense of displaying true and good moral values. Orcs, more than any other race, are characterized by perversion, destruction, and treachery.

The description of the orcs in "Myths Transformed," is telling. The orcs, Tolkien tells us, were pitiless and cruel, drawn to wickedness.[57] During their captivity at the hands of Saruman's Uruk-hai, Merry and Pippin witnessed directly the orcs' doubtful morality. When the orcs and the Uruk-hai begin to dispute the possession of their captives, they both manifest obedience to their respective masters. Certainly, Uglúk and his armed band are able to make decisions, and manifest absolute obedience to Saruman—at the expense of the orcs led by Grishnákh. But they also display typical orcish morality in finding amusement in their prisoners' torment. Hence the question: "'What are they wanted for?' . . . Why alive? Do they give good sport?'"[58] Uruk-hai and orcs are able to act of their

54. L, 365.

55. H, 63–64.

56. Martinez, "What Is the Munby Letter?"

57. MR, 417.

58. LoTR, II.3.iii.

own wills, but it seems only for evil, "for their own sport," reports Tolkien in "Myths Transformed," thus echoing the previously quoted passage.[59]

It seems, then, that the orcs are moral beings displaying amoral values, a rather contradictory statement. This, however, should not strike us as very surprising. The previous discussion regarding sub-creation stressed that Ilúvatar was the source of all creation, properly creating all existing beings. That they are responsible beings is mere demonstration of that creative act. This, coupled with Tolkien's conviction that evil does not create but only makes through perversion, explains how orcs can display perverted moral values instead of merely being "immoral beings." Congruent with this is Tolkien's own statement, in his already cited famous letter to Milton Waldman, that "myth and fairy-story must, as all art, reflect and contain in solution elements of moral and religious truth (or error), but not explicit, not in the known form of the primary 'real' world."[60]

This relates to one of St. Thomas's arguments about the structure of possible worlds. To him, the question was not so much about the nature of possible worlds but about the nature of God "throughout" possible worlds. He approached this problem through the doctrine of the nature of God, especially his will and goodness. St. Thomas argued that God could be different in what he reveals of himself but that he would not, and does not, will goodness in different terms. In other words, God could only will an accident that is in direct relation with his moral character. God's goodness would remain identical even if God would not be to us identical to what we know in this precise world.[61] It is clear that Chesterton makes the same point. In any imagined world, God's revelation of his goodness would be the same, and in all worlds we would find a notice-board: "Thou shalt not steal." Whatever other worlds might have been, or could be in the human mind, they are subjugated to the moral character of God, which is reflected in his immutability.

Some could be surprised at the possibility, expressed by Tolkien, of finding a metaphysical difference between primary and secondary worlds. After all, metaphysics should be foundational. However, we should not forget that Tolkien should be read as a Thomist sub-creator. McIntosh is here again very helpful. Beginning with the observation that the aim of creating secondary worlds indeed is to sub-create by imitation the

59. MR, 418.

60. L, 144.

61. See Stump, *Aquinas*, 111.

consistency of the primary world, he writes, "However, for Tolkien this is because it also has the higher aim of reflecting or revealing something of the truth of that reality. An alternative, secondary reality, after all, is still part of our own world and as such has the duty of 'recovering' the truth of that reality."[62] The relationship between the two worlds, the primary and the secondary worlds, is ruled by a theological conviction: all worlds, created or sub-created, owe their origin and their inner consistency to the nature of the Creator of the primary world. This act of primary creation gave human beings their capacity for sub-creation which in turn reflects upon the secondary world values of the original creation.

Conclusion

When it comes to his notion of sub-creation, Tolkien reveals, both in concepts and in wordings, his Thomist conviction. While the Source of all being—both creator of created and sub-created universes—shares linguistic similarities with the god of a typically Neoplatonic brand, he is more aptly identified with the Thomist description of the Godhead. To this description, Tolkien consciously subscribes, even though, not being a philosopher or a theologian, we should not look for a Tolkienian theoretical account of sub-creation. Rather, in Tolkien, we should look at a concrete example of the human ability to create. Properly understood, in its theological context, sub-creation is the material embodiment of the God-given capacity for "creating," one of the most intimate qualities of the Creator. Analogically incarnated in human beings, the capacity for creating distinguishes us as rational and imaginative beings.

As such, sub-creation functions as a creative hyphen between the Primary and Secondary worlds. Because God is the Creator of both the actual world and the imaginative human beings that inhabit it, in him is found the meaning of all worlds. Every aspect of the subcreated reality finds its source in him, including morality. However, sub-creation is not, in and of itself, sufficient to explain the imaginative nature of Tolkien's creation. Or rather, there is a more fundamental notion that needs to be explored. sub-creation can only be exercised because it is nourished by one of the two most basic human powers: imagination.

62. McIntosh, *The Flame Imperishable*, 6.

Conclusion

—————— *Part Three* ——————

THE PERILOUS REALM IS Tolkien's great sub-creative accomplishment. In he creation of Middle-earth, however, it is not only Tolkien that we meet, but through him, the figures of Thomas, Chesterton, and Barfield remain ever present. It would be a great mistake, though, to think Tolkien had merely synthesized what these three major authors had already said about the imagination. Tolkien went further than Thomas in embodying his Thomist imagination in a sub-created world. He also went further than Chesterton in creating a mythology for a people, and for a language. And further again than Barfield did Tolkien go in valuing language and mythology in a more radical way than Barfield could have accomplished.

Tolkien was dependent on the influences of the three authors we have become acquainted with. Barfield provided a vision for the initial nature of the power of the imagination, following Coleridge's classic description. However, Tolkien was not satisfied with merely following Barfield. He needed a clear theological foundation which, if Barfield had his own, was more distinctly Catholic and Thomist. Then, in turn, Tolkien relied on Chesterton who, more than others, embodied his own Thomist theology in his own fields of Faërie.

Certainly then, Tolkien's theory of the imagination is a complex tapestry of influences woven together by an unseen thread, a holistic artistic nature: his Thomist outlook. Analogous to Niggle's Tree, Tolkien's Faërie was created only because there was something larger at play. And in the same manner, because of his Thomist approach to myth and imagination, we enter a realm that, like Niggle's Tree, is in full blossom.[1] Here, Tolkien's Thomism is more apparent for it is built and nourished by his view of the imagination, a distinctively Thomist one. This specific Christian understanding of the nature and power of the imagination is the unifying force of Tolkien's creative success.

Tolkien's lasting influence within the fantasy genre is largely due to the embodiment of his Thomist imagination. At the close of this third part, we are now ready to proceed further, and to Tolkien's fantasy we now turn our minds, and steps. This will be the last stage of our journey and, if we have not taken wrong turns, we should reach the legendary summit of Faërie.

---

1. Tolkien, *Tales from the Perilous Realm*, 139.

Part Four

The Beatitudes of Faërie

And this is the last end of the tales of the days before the days, in the Northern regions of the Western World. . . . They have been told by Elves to Men of the race of Eärendel, and most to Eriol who alone of mortals of later days sailed to the Lonely Isle, and yet came back to Lúthien, and remembered things he had heard in Cortirion, the town of the Elves in Tol Eressëa.

—J. R. R. TOLKIEN, *The Shaping of Middle-earth*

WORDS, GODS, AND SUB-CREATION are now behind us, and what is left? Maybe the journey should end here. After all, Tolkien's love was language, and his desire was for a mythology for England. We have rested at both, we have drank at both. Greater beauty awaits, though. For words and legends could not be discovered by we who walk these human fields, these fields we know, unless they were embodied. Tolkien's language was embodied in a distinctive English mythology. And his mythology, in turn, had to be embodied. A language, a myth; A myth, a culture, a kingdom, a realm. So was born Faërie, the Perilous Realm of fairy-stories. In a way, the invention of language and of mythology in turn gave birth to his theory and literary practice of fairy-stories.

This fourth part will be concerned with establishing and explaining Tolkien's theory of *Faërie*. Talking about Tolkien's theory of fairy-story is a difficult matter. The first problem we encounter is the definition of terms. The choice between the expressions fairy-story, fantasy, and Faërie is not an easy one. Tolkien used the terms *fairy-stories* and *Faërie* quite interchangeably, based on the argument that the former are merely accounts of adventures that happen in the latter.[1] Surprisingly for modern readers, Tolkien rarely used the term "fantasy" to refer to his works or to the nature of fairy-stories. Therefore, this latter term will be avoided in the following chapters. Rather, the terms Faërie and fairy-stories will be used.

In 1939, Tolkien was invited to give the Andrew Lang Lecture at the University of St. Andrews. With the possible exception of Chesterton's chapter "The Ethics of Elfland" in his *Orthodoxy*, "On Fairy-Stories" represents the most clearly articulated theological theory of Faërie and thus will be an essential part of our argument. In this essay, Tolkien addresses questions of the nature, origin, and function of fairy-stories, thus giving the essay a significant scholarly and theological content. Our discussion of Tolkien's theory of Faërie will first take place within the context of his theory of sub-creation, in which he discusses the nature of the human creative power.

If Faërie is described by Tolkien as entering a Perilous Realm, approaching Tolkien's definition is a similar entrance into a perilous realm. Not without reason does Flieger conclude, in her edition of *Smith of Wootton Major*, that Tolkien's concept of Faërie is difficult to define while at the same time remaining consistent throughout his career.[2] In fact, Tolkien's definition of Faërie, what we call now *fantasy*, is not the type of definition we might have expected. Tolkien does not deliver a precise, one-sentence definition. Instead, he wrote an essay, "On Fairy-Stories," and a story, "Smith of Wootton Major."[3] The closest Tolkien comes to defining precisely the essence of fairy-stories is in the last pages of the essay, when he describes Faërie through the four interwoven terms of Recovery, Escape, Consolation, and Eucatastrophe. As we will see in the following chapters, Tolkien's Faërie is *enlightened* by his understanding of the relation between the nature of mythology and his Thomist faith. In these three coming and final chapters, we will take the last, but most arduous, step towards the panoramic view of Tolkien's realm and explore the three functions of fairy-stories. To do so, chapters 11, 12, and 13 will, respectively, explore the importance of Recovery, Escape, and Consolation. Finally, chapter 14 will define Faërie.

1. OFS, 32.
2. Tolkien, *Smith of Wootton Major*, 60.
3. Tolkien, *Smith of Wootton Major*, 60.

11

Recovery

After commenting at length on the current academic view of the nature of "fairy-stories," Tolkien prepared to launch his full-blown assault against the fortress of contemporary academia. His opening salvo cannot be clearer: "The analytic study of fairy-story is as bad a preparation for the enjoying or the writing of them as would be the historical study of the drama of all lands and times for the enjoyment or writing of stage-plays."[1] To do so would be an abstraction, a complete loss of the inner life of stories, a loss of their particular embodiments. The essence of fairy-stories is not found in their analytic understanding. It would be a mistake to think that what Tolkien had in mind was merely the enjoyment of stories. It is much more than that, even thought that certainly is the necessary beginning. However, such a beginning cannot happen if, opening our fairy-stories, we find ourselves unable to see colors again, "and be startled anew." Something that was, must be again. Thus Tolkien famously begins exploring the deeper meaning of the term "Faërie" through a first function: Recovery.

---

1. OFS, 66.

Hidden Recovery

Tolkien initially defines Recovery very simply, as the "regaining of a clear view."[2] Here again we are confronted with a recurrent problem. Tolkien's definition seems, at first, to be too general to be helpful. "Regaining of a clear view," what is the precise meaning of this? What is it, that Faërie helps us regain a clear view of? For, clearly, the mere mention of the term "recovery" implies that something has been lost. Tolkien actually referred, in the course of his essay "On Fairy Stories," to the fantasy of "fallen man" and the necessity of a "return and renewal of health," both conveying an obvious religious dimension. But we should not decide too quickly to use theological language to explain what this Recovery is.

What does Faërie recover? It appears that two dimensions are included in the restoring quality of fantasy. The first one is the logical outcome of the workings of the imagination. We recall that for Tolkien, as for Chesterton, imagination helps "make" visible what is not seen. By making unseen things visible, imagination demonstrates the divinely created nature of man. In fairy-stories we witness the re-creation, the sub-creation, of an unseen dimension of the world. To explain further the term Recovery, Tolkien relies on Chesterton's fantasy. In his study on Dickens, Chesterton had argued that the quality of Dicken's writing was found in making the familiar unfamiliar, a process through which even such a common word as coffee-room could be transformed into the more fantastic "mooreeffoc." Chesterton remarks, "That wild word, 'Moor Eeffoc,' is the motto of all effective realism!—it is the masterpiece of the good realistic principle—the principle that the most fantastic thing of all is often the precise fact. And that elfish kind of realism Dickens adopted everywhere. His world was alive with inanimate object."[3]

Tolkien comments that "the word *Mooreeffoc* may cause you suddenly to realize that England is an utterly alien land, lost either in some remote past age glimpsed by history, or in some strange dim future to be reached only by a time-machine."[4] All creation, even the most familiar, is infused with fantastic elements, not because of an internal or essential transformation of *things* (things *per se* do not change) but because of a transformation of our *perception*, a transformation of the way we look at them. This is the first aspect of Tolkien's recovery, and through it, things

2. OFS, 67.

3. Chesterton, *Charles Dickens*, 47–48.

4. OFS, 68.

are recovered, empowered, elevated, and glorified. A poem could be made out of this sentence: "By the forging of Gram cold iron was revealed; by the making of Pegasus horses were ennobled; in the Trees of the Sun and Moon root and stock, flower and fruit are manifested in glory."[5] Iron did not reveal Gram, Sigurd's heroic sword, as we could have scientifically expected. What happens is precisely the opposite. Because we encounter Gram, or in Tolkien's story of Turin Turambar, the sword Gurthang, we come to know what cold iron is. Gram is not forged out of iron. Gram is but an exemplar of what iron can be. Ordinary things take on an extraordinary meaning through recovery. Even horses become more than they are. Here Tolkien is fully Chestertonian and points to the transformative power of fairy-stories, transforming our perception of the world into a truer and more fantastic one. Rightly, then, did Maisie Ward conclude that Chestertonian fantasy is an "extension of reality."[6]

Commenting on Chesterton, Tolkien uses, in "Manuscript A" of OFS, an expression that completely disappears in later versions: "cheerful fantasy." In fairy-story, the normal is seen from a different perspective, and man becomes sub-creator. The essential nature of human beings, being "sub-creators," is intimately tied to the cheerful nature of Recovery. Recovery as the regaining of a clear view, is the quality that Tolkien mostly associates with Chesterton. However, Tolkien himself noted that Chesterton's theory was good but too limited: the recovery of a "fresh vision" is its only quality.

True fairy-story, and so in turn, true Recovery, must reach farther. In fact, Tolkien adds, that "fairy-stories deal largely with simple or fundamental things, untouched by Fantasy."[7] Tolkien's comment has often been overlooked. This is rather unfortunate because Tolkien's second dimension of Recovery is essential. Recovery cannot work only in the context of abstract Fantasy, disembodied imagination. There can only be true fairy-story if there is a harmonious intermingling of the simplicities found in the world (cold iron, horses, roots) *and* their fantasy-setting. There can only be "freedom from Nature" if there is Nature. That is how fairy-story can manifest "flower and fruit" in glory. Fairy-story makes Nature luminous.

5. OFS, 68.

6. Ward, Introduction to *The Coloured Lands*, 9.

7. OFS, 68.

This second quality of Recovery complements the first one. It brings to a glorious plenitude what Chesterton's humble fantasy had only initiated. The renewal of vision is not an artificial construction of reality. It must transform and bring to full life the things of the Primary world. This dimension of Recovery is what Tolkien referred to as "creative" in "Manuscript B" of OFS,[8] a term he uses as a contrast to Chestertonian fantasy. For in fact, Recovery does not necessarily stop at the recovery of a clear view, it extends beyond it to offer a sub-creative manifestation of the full meaning of Nature. In doing so, creative fantasy becomes Nature's lover, and avoids both becoming its slave and destroying it. Creative fantasy, and maybe we should say *creative Recovery*, is a living testimony to the potency of the wonder of the created world.

While these two dimensions of Recovery are essential to an understanding of Tolkien's definition of Faërie, they are not enough to paint a clear picture of the *function* of Recovery. To do so, we need to explore how Recovery functions within the three Tolkienian realms of language and mythology.

Recovery and Language

The first part of our study in this book was concerned with Tolkien's view of language. We started with language for an obvious reason: it was Tolkien's first love, his first lifelong interest, his personal quest. As we approach the end of our investigation into Tolkien's Faërie, going back to language is our most obvious route. Recovery, as the first characteristic of Faërie, opens a window into the world, and for Tolkien, this world is made of language and stories. In fact, one of the most telling embodiments of Recovery in Tolkien's mythology is the Recovery of language and speech-rhythm. Of course, we are assuming here that something original to language has been lost. What could that be?

With Tolkien, we should always turn to stories. One particular side-comment made by the depository of the Red Book in *The Hobbit*, recounting Bilbo's adventures, is telling. As our pretend burglar finally makes his way into Smaug's lair, he for a moment gazes on Smaug and his wealth, "a wealth that could not be guessed," the narrator adds.[9] This is where the linguistic comment is found: "To say that Bilbo's breath was

8. OFS, 239.

9. H, XII, 194.

taken away is no description at all. There are no words left to express his staggerment, since Men changed the language that they learned of elves in the days when all the world was wonderful."[10] At first, second, and maybe even tenth reading, this reads rather as an innocuous statement about Bilbo's wonder. We could just read it off as simple metaphorical language and move along, which is probably what Tolkien himself thought most readers would, understandably, do.

In fact, Tolkien later referred to this three line description of Bilbo as a reference to Barfield's language theory. There is something intimate about words and meanings. "An odd mythological way of referring to linguistic philosophy, and a point that will (happily) be missed by any who have not read Barfield (few have), and probably by those who have."[11] Clearly for him there is more at stake than mere story-telling. Language changed. And now it has to be recovered. What is Tolkien trying to say, when noting that men changed the language they learned from the Elves? Verlyn Flieger has commented at length on the Barfieldean nature of this passage in her classic *Splintered Light*. The main thrust of the argument is that language was, at one time in its history, not divided between metaphorical and literal language. The nature of language was, so to speak, "premetaphoric."[12] Of course this does not clarify for us what Tolkien actually meant by this observation.

Anderson's annotation concludes that "Bilbo's breath was actually taken away,"[13] though this seems unlikely given the narrator's remark, quoted above, that "to say that Bilbo's breath was taken away is no description at all." The issue here is thus not the mere presence of a literal (descriptive, concrete) language. Indeed, the primary point is not whether or not "his breath was taken away" is a description or a metaphor. Rather, the point has more to do with the impossibility of describing, with words, a reality that is now broken. The "ancient semantic unity" is no longer the way words can be used, even though we might try to Recover a certain dimension.

This understanding of "the only philological remark" of *The Hobbit* is consistent with the evolution of its manuscripts, as John Rateliff has shown in his *The History of the Hobbit*. From the original manuscript to the final published version this comment reads as follows:

10. H, xii.

11. L 20–22, 435.

12. The reference to Barfield's theory of the "ancient semantic unity" as being metaphoric is not directly in Flieger but is used by Anderson, *The Annotated Hobbit*, 271.

13. Anderson, *The Annotated Hobbit*, 271.

> To say that Bilbo's breath was taken away *is to say too little*. There are no words to express his staggerment. (original manuscript, italics mine)

> To say that Bilbo's breath was taken away *is no description at all*. There are not words to express his staggerment, *not even in the language of the pithecanthropes which consisted (we are told) largely of exclamations*. (first typescript, italics mine)

> To say that Bilbo's breath was taken away is no description at all. There are no words left to express his staggerment, *since Men changed the language that they learned of elves in the days when all the world was wonderful*. (final typescript, italics mine)[14]

Note the evolution between the different versions (in italics). The first noticeable change is from "is to say too little" to "is no description at all," a change that will remain in the final edition. In the first typescript, the most puzzling change is the reference to an otherwise unknown people or race, the "pithecanthropes." At this point Tolkien's sub-creation breaks apart slightly, a rare exception to the consistency of his Secondary world. The term is in fact a technical anthropological one that the darwinist Ernst Haeckel used to describe "speechless ape-man."[15] The evolution conveys a clear meaning: *even* if language was only made of exclamations (that is, if it was not descriptive at all), no *words* (no matter their nature, literal or metaphoric) could express Bilbo's inner thoughts and emotions.

Finally, Tolkien's word-aesthetics comes in full force in the last significant change: "since Men changed the language that they learned of elves in the days when all the world was wonderful." Of course the replacement of the "pithecanthropes" with the "language learned of elves" is crucial. But it does not necessarily erases the point implied in the first typescript. What Tolkien adds in the final version is consistency. The appearance of the Elves in fact reinforces the very point he made in using "pithecanthropes." Language has been learned. Men, in Middle-earth, learned it from the Elves. Crucial to what Tolkien is referring to here are the first two words "since Men," implying also a dramatic break in the linguistic and philological relation between the two races.

"Bilbo's breath was taken away." What does that mean, at the end? As Christopher Gilson writes, "this originally poetic figure of speech

---

14. Rateliff, *The History of the Hobbit*, 2:534–35.

15. Rateliff, *The History of the Hobbit*, 2:537.

exemplifies Barfield's thesis that the fairly recent emergence of internalization in English diction led in turn to new metaphoric expressions
of feelings indirectly as the effects of external agency."[16] Barfield's thesis
was that originally several meanings could be indistinguishably carried
in one term. In the case of this sentence, Bilbo's breath was figuratively
taken away, and this can express both the fact that the sight of Smaug and
his treasure cut off Bilbo's breath (something *external*), and that his emotions (Gilson's *internalization*) could not be described. That could be the
simple meaning of the philological observation. At some point in history,
one word could describe both the external and the internal phenomenon.
But not anymore.

One of the most fascinating philological comments, however, is not
necessarily this part of the sentence, but the observation that language was
learned of the Elves—and language was one. The birth of Men's language
is narrated in *The Book of Lost Tales*. Among the Quendi, who received
speech directly from Ilúvatar, one named Nuin—of the Hisildi or twilight
people—reached Murmenalda, the Vale of Sleep, and there found Men,
still asleep. There, Nuin, the "Father of Speech," taught language to Er-
mon and Elmir the first two Men.[17] In "The Lhammas," Tolkien further
describes the influence Dark Elves and Green Elves had on the language
of Men. Elves loved "the making of words" and shared this pleasure with
Men, and so it happened that from the Lembi, "are come . . . the manifold
tongues of Men, save only the eldest Men of the West."[18]

At this point Men and Elves were close together, bound by a learned
language. Unfortunately, this did not remain. Tolkien's mythology presents a dramatic breaking away of language, myth, and culture between
Elves and Men, to the point of estrangement. However, all can be rediscovered. This Recovery, however, is not a magical process, but an historical one. Recovery of language is historical and needs mediators, or rather
Recoverers. These Recoverers are rare, but one of the most significant is
Bilbo, of course. Throughout *The Lord of the Rings*, Bilbo always discovers,
reclaims and reproduces for his own the specific syntax of other tongues.
In fact, we must remember that most of the songs and poems that reach
us throughout Middle-earth's history, in English, descend primarily from

16. Gilson, "His Breath Was Taken Away," 45.

17. HoME, I.262–69.

18. HoME, V.176.

Bilbo's Recovery of them in the Common tongue.[19] Without Bilbo's translation and adaptation, there would be no song in the tongues of Elves and Dwarves. Consider for example the "dwarf-song" below:

> Farewell we call to hearth and hall!
> Though wind may blow and rain may fall,
> We must away ere break of day
> Far over wood and mountain tall.[20]

The simple speech-rhythm, short syllables and hard vowels, is typical of a Dwarvish language—and that also translates in the Common tongue. Certainly Bilbo Recovered and reclaimed Dwarvish songs for the rest of us.

The same is true for Bilbo's Recovery of Elvish poetry. Turn first to this Elvish poem "Oilima Markirya" ("The Last Ark"), composed in Quenya:

> Man kiluva kirya ninqe
> oilima ailinello lute,
> nive qimari ringa ambar
> ve mainwin qaine?[21]

Ross Smith points out the abundance of sonorants and vowels in "The Last Ark," and that the "majority of [words] end in a vowel."[22] This translates thus in English:

> Who shall see a white ship
> leave the last shore,
> the pale phantoms
> in her cold bosom
> like gulls wailing?[23]

Of course, the pattern in Quenya is more regular than its translation in the Common tongue (which adds one line), but the general pattern still seems to hold. The same is true of Bilbo's many translations in the Common Tongue. He is striving to "recover" the poetic patterns of the Elvish language and thus tried to imitate Elvish in his rendering of the Song of Eärendil:

---

19. Most of the phonology comments below are taken from Smith, "Fitting Sense to Sound."

20. LoTR, I.i.5, 104.

21. MC, lines 1–4, 213.

22. Smith, *Inside Language*, 60.

23. MC, lines 1–5, 214.

Eärendil was a mariner
That tarried in Arvenien
He built a boat of timber felled
In Nimbrethil to journey in;
Her sails were wove of silver fair,
Of silver were her lanterns made,
Her prow was fashioned like a swan,
And light upon her banners laid.[24]

The first word of this song is the eponymous "Eärendil," poetic subject of this long poem. The name has a stress at the second syllable, and in iambic tetrameter, that is where the stress would fall. This seems to exemplify the Elvish flow of rhythm and sound, avoiding the typical strong association of consonants found for example in English. The composer, or Recoverer—whether Bilbo or Frodo—functioned as a mere discoverer and less as a creator.

As for Rohirrim poetry, the composer is aiming for each complete thought to be on one line, rather than in a complete stanza. Poetry and thought is thus much less self-contained than in Elvish, which is also quite consistent with the development of peoples and languages in Tolkien's mythology:

Where now the horse and the rider? Where is the horn that was blowing?
Where is the helm and the hauberk, and the bright hair flowing?
Where is the hand on the harpstring, and the red fire glowing?
Where is the spring and the harvest and the tall corn growing?[25]

Again here, the language itself tries to Recover the rhythm pattern of the language of the Rohirrim, and is most likely only partly successful. The simple but strong rhythm, associated with repetitive rhyming, flows in a manner not dissimilar to Elvish poetry. This part of the poem, one of the most famous ones now that it has been brought to the screen, is another example of applied Recovery, the reclamation of a poetic tradition for the enjoyment of others. Thus, the composer-translators of the Red Book of Westmarch are imaginative mythopoets: they rediscover and re-appropriate a linguistic and poetic tradition. The fascinating conclusion is that there is a mutual relationship between language and Recovery. "Language makes Recovery possible," but Recovery also makes language possible.[26]

24. LoTR, I.2.i, 227.

25. LoTR, II.3.vi, 497.

26. Jeffrey, "Tolkien as Philologist," in Chance, *Tolkien and the Invention of Myth*, 67.

Recovery is for Tolkien the first function of Faërie, and possibly one of the most important ones. This would explain why this function of Recovery stands so close to Tolkien's love of language.

Recovery and Mythology

Language, though, does not appear in the void. It is embodied in culture and history. If the function of Recovery has a place in Tolkien's created languages, it also has an important role to play in Tolkien's sub-created world. Though Tolkien's first function of Faërie is perfectly embodied in his own sub-created stories, Recovery also plays a significant part in the actual world. This observation, though, is not as evident as his fantasy use of Recovery. The bridge between the use of Recovery in Faërie and the actual world is, in one word, through rediscovered and applied "embedded mythology." This expression refers to the manner in which Tolkien, in his own mythological corpus, builds Middle-earth's very own mythology. There is a "mythology within the mythology," so to speak. A large part of *The Lord of the Rings* relates to this "mythology within the mythology." We gain a glimpse of Galadriel's place within the mythological past of Middle-earth. We know that Aragorn also relate to such a distance and "legendary" past. There is much that points us back towards a "tradition": that of the Elves, of Gondor, or even of the Ents. In a way this "mythology within the mythology" can be called "tradition," and most of what Tolkien has to say about Recovery and mythology can be framed as a recovery of the "traditional" past. However, the term "tradition" is very connoted and we must tread carefully. To do so, some background is needed.

Writing the first of the stories that would later form the legends published as *The Silmarillion* during World War I, Tolkien can be ranked among the great war authors of the first half of the twentieth-century, and as such, shares in great part their concerns. Among these, the complete reshaping of a world that has collapsed and taken down with it the very fabric of the Modern world. So not only is Tolkien's work informed by the War and thereby an answer to the traumatic horrors of the century, it is also an answer to the failures of the Enlightened civilization. Some went as far as saying that *The Lord of the Rings* was decidedly anti-Modernist.

Certainly the ravages of the War reached deeper than visible death and destruction. The "past" was questioned, social and philosophical

assumptions were crumbling, and the need for something new was beginning to rise. This entailed a strong rejection of traditional rules, expecta-
tions and attitudes. New "war writers" would redefine the world, and they
would turn their back on a world that did not fulfill its promises. Tolkien
enters our story here. He also is a "war writer," and wrestles with the same
challenges. What then is Tolkien's relation to the past, what is his relation
to previous traditions? The modern view of tradition already prevalent
in Tolkien's time was one of polite, but firm, rejection. As we saw in the
first chapter, the social establishment that had united society and religion
during centuries was slowly eroding, legitimating the rejection or passive
ignorance of the past. The new light was one of progress, and progress
meant a haughty superiority.[27] Of course Tolkien would take issue with
this view of progress, especially considering his acquaintance with Christopher Dawson. The famed English historian did not promote a simplistic
rejection of progress, and neither did he argue for a blind acceptance of
tradition. Instead, his history of change is one of growth through change,
of cyclic transformation. A fascinating element of Dawson's inquiry in
Progress and Religion, was his quasi prophetic belief that the "religion of
Progress" was declining.[28] Thus, neither the past nor progress could help
humankind face the challenges of a new society. Without any mediating
tool, there was no hope for moving forward.

Here, we turn back to Tolkien's Catholic imagination, nourished by
Dawson's historical philosophy and Newman's theology. For Tolkien, like
for these other two Catholic thinkers, the mediating elements between
Man, on one hand, and the apparent paradox of past-progress, was tradition. But here we must clarify what Tolkien understood by "tradition."
The image that best describes tradition for him is not that of a stone
sculpture, magnificent and fixed for the ages to come. The best image was
rather one of the tree, Tolkien's beloved tree. Tradition is akin to a living
organism, that develops and changes, and should both be apprehended
and received personally. In other words, Tolkien offered an argued rejection of Modernism's rejection of tradition.[29]

While Tolkien never formulated a philosophical construal of tradition, he used it to give force and direction to his writing. In fact, many of
the central characters of *The Lord of the Rings* display one of two attitudes

27. Smith, "Tolkien's Catholic Imagination," 80.

28. Dawson, *Progress and Religion*, 3.

29. Smith, "Tolkien's Catholic Imagination," 78.

towards tradition: rejection or recovery. In Thomas Smith's reading of tradition in *The Lord of the Rings*, the wisest characters Tolkien created are deeply in tune with their own tradition, without any sign of debilitating sclerosis. These are Gandalf, Galadriel, Faramir, and, of course, Aragorn, whose contrast with Denethor best illustrates the difference between the Recovery and the rejection of tradition.

Rejection is the most obvious attitude towards tradition and clearly voiced by Denethor in his dialogue with Gandalf when the White Rider arrives in the great city of Minas Tirith. The Steward's tradition goes back to the remote history of Gondor, when the last king Eärnur disappeared, challenged by the Witch-king of Minas Morgul. The line of the kings was broken and Gondor was then ruled by the Line of the Stewards.[30] While they exercised all the powers of the kings, the Stewards, notes Tolkien, "never sat on the ancient throne; and they wore no crown, and held no scepter," anticipating a return of the king.[31] However, when Denethor sees through Gandalf's arrival in Minas Tirith that the time of the Stewards was drawing to an end, he could only manifest doubts about his role as Steward, reclaiming for himself the rule of Gondor, without consideration to the prospect of the return of the king.[32] Denethor's doubt leaves no room for the tradition of the King to become true again. Tradition lies in the past. It is a tale that Denethor passively holds up to: "Tradition for Denethor has become sclerotic, a vehicle for self-aggrandizement, rather than service in humble recognition of one's own vulnerability and contingency."[33] This rejection of tradition leads Denethor to rely only on his own present, and then to despair. The tragic consequence of this disillusioned rejection of tradition is the burning alive, or attempt at, of his own son Faramir. For Denethor, the tradition of Kings and Stewards was merely one of possession, power, and rule.

By contrast, Aragorn's appropriation of tradition is an example of Recovery. In the Tale of "Aragorn and Arwen," this process of personal Recovery starts when Aragorn receives and claims for himself the ring of Barahir, the symbol of Man's pledge to the Elves. Up to this point, Aragorn is merely a receiver of tradition, not a Recoverer. This is achieved only when, after having first gazed on Arwen, he fully recognizes the fate

---

30. LoTR, III, Appendix A, 1027.

31. LoTR, III, Appendix A, 1028.

32. LoTR, III.5.i, 741.

33. Smith, "Tolkien's Catholic Imagination," 93.

attached to his lineage. In reclaiming the line of the Kings, and the destiny, Aragorn willingly accepted the challenges, becoming the chief of the Rangers, unceasingly laboring against Sauron. And so Aragorn holds to the renewed tradition of Men, and of the kings of Arnor and Gondor, and through this Recovery, revived the lines of the kings of old and restored the White Tree of Minas Tirith, while uniting for the third time Men and Elves. Aragorn's Recovery is complete when seen as a restoration of the tradition, not only of the Kings of Gondor, but of the tradition of Valinor. This, again, is the symbol of the ring Barahir, ancestor of Gondor, received from Finrod, chief of the Noldor during the battle of Dagor Bragollach.[34]

This contrast between rejection and embrace of tradition (in a manner of speaking, *mythology*), between Denethor and Aragorn permeates their characters and decisions. Even the Steward's loss of hope at the despairingly late arrival of the Rohhirim is telling. This, despite an almost mythological past sealed by oath between the Steward of Gondor, Cirion, and Eorl, illustrious ancestor of Rohan: "This oath shall stand in memory of the glory of the Land of the Star, and of the faith of Elendil the Faithful, in the keeping of those who sit upon the thrones of the West and of the One who is above all thrones for ever."[35] In a way, Denethor's identity is intimately tied to his rejection of the past, of a mythological tradition. In fact, Denethor reads Gondor's mythological past as nothing more than made-up stories. His definition of "mythology," if we asked him for one, could come very close to the cliché definition of false, invented, or distorted beliefs.

Of course Denethor is not alone in such a negative view of tradition and mythology. During Aragorn, Legolas and Gimli's encounter with Éomer, one of the riders comments on hearing the word *halflings*: "Do we walk in legends or on the green earth in the daylight?" To which Aragorn, steward of Middle-earth history, answers: "For not we but those who come after will make the legend of our time. The green earth, say you? That is a mightier matter of legend, though you tread it under the light of day!"[36] For Aragorn, not only the halflings, but the earth itself, all of Middle-earth, is the stuff of legend. But that is not opposed to their historical and concrete reality. Aragorn is a true Recoverer of tradition, of legend, of mythology. In doing so, Aragorn acknowledges the limits of

34. S, 147.

35. Tolkien, *Unfinished Tales*, 305.

36. LoTR, II.2.ii, 424.

his own understanding and existence, in contrast to all those who reject their mythological past and assert their own independent interpretation of history.

In this way, Tolkien's appropriation of Recovery, especially of tradition and mythology, is reminiscent of Newman's seven notes in *Essay on the Development of Christian Doctrine*. The third note, "the power of assimilation," is particularly telling. For the great Catholic convert, the third character of "development" is, in essence its *uniting* power, the union of faithful respect and growth of a tradition. This phenomenon is the image of Recovery. Thus Newman writes: "In the physical world, whatever has life is characterized by growth, so that in no respect to grow is to cease to live."[37] Thus tradition grows and, ever growing, remains itself, awaiting the fullness of Recovery.

Further, as Thomas Smith argues, "the characters who break with tradition in Tolkien's work do so in part because they seek the 'freedom' of being released from the fact of their neediness and vulnerability."[38] This is typically what happens to those who rejected tradition. For example "modernizers," like Saruman and Sauron with their machines and slaves and bureaucracies, are not imagined by Tolkien to denounce the abuses of technology. Or rather, not primarily. If Tolkien's depiction of technological abuses applies especially to Sauron and Saruman, it is essentially because this technological use is the image of the rejected religion of Progress—itself rejection of tradition—and an attachment to one's own independence. This Progress is a plunge forward into an unknown that Sauron and Saruman have to create for themselves. The same applies to the Numrenoreans who will reject their tradition of worship, reject their link to the Elves, Valinor, the Valar, and claim total autonomy. Aragorn, stands again in opposition to independence while typifying service in humility. Here, Recovery of tradition is only possible through abandonment of oneself, to the service of others, which is exactly what Aragorn learns during his years of Exile. It is also what the Ainur learn when joining in the Great Music.

The embodiment of Recovery within and through the rediscovery of tradition is an essential element in Tolkien's worldview, not only in his sub-created world, but also in the actual world. It is not the place here to talk extensively about this aspect of Tolkien's thought, but certainly his

37. Newman, *An Essay on the Development of Christian Doctrine*, 185.

38. Smith, "Tolkien's Catholic Imagination," 87.

view of Recovery and tradition is consistent with his Roman Catholic view of the church, something that comes across throughout his letters, notably those written to his sons Christopher and Michael.[39]

Conclusion

Tolkien's first function of Faërie appears at first to be merely defined by its sub-creative dimension. However, Tolkien gradually shifts his argument from a mere creative one towards a more theologically oriented one. Thomas Smith's comment here is perceptive: "I suggest Tolkien turned toward fantasy as a way of recovering tradition—in contrast to the rejection of tradition—because his Catholic imagination led him to think about tradition in a mediating way."[40] While Tolkien defined Recovery as the regaining of a "clear view," he did not anchor this concept in a theoretical vacuum but in a theological one.

In fact, Tolkien's Recovery is essentially a commentary on the creative power of imagination embodied in a lost world, a world to be recovered. Both notions, that of the imagination and of something "being lost," have a clear theological coloration. More specifically, Tolkien is grounding this first function of Faërie in his Thomist convictions about the nature of the sub-creative ability and of the inescapable presence of the "Fall" in the Primary, and even the Secondary, world. Because of this primordial loss, Tolkien's sub-creation can only require something like Recovery, through which the original world is recovered.

But what happens if this "amputated" world is accepted as the only possible reality? What happens if the lost world disappears completely from our human longing? This Tolkien addresses in his discussion of the second function of Faërie: Escape.

39. See for example L, 394.
40. Smith, "Tolkien's Catholic Imagination," 83.

12

Escape

RECOVERY MIGHT BE THE first function encountered in Faërie, and as such deserved an extensive treatment. But it is certainly not the only function of fairy-stories, nor the most controversial one. This privilege belongs to the second function of fairy-stories: Escape. Ironically, this very term is, still now, used to disparage fantasy. In fact, fantasy cannot escape being associated with "an inability to face facts," hiding away from the real world.[1] It is rather telling that Tolkien, conscious of this negative connotation, still chose it to define Faërie. To explore the significance of Escape as a defining dimension of Faërie, we will begin by presenting the two negative and perverted forms of escape in Tolkien's works—Despair and Denial—before turning to his discussion of true Escape. Finally, we will explore the concrete manifestation of Escape in the two areas of language and myth.

Escape as Despair and Denial

The main common charge brought again fairy-stories is their "escapist" nature. Tolkien was well aware of this common misconception and respond at length in *On Fairy-Stories*. To present the true nature of Escape, Tolkien contrasts it with the two negative visions of an escape: Desertion and

1. Tuan, *Escapism*, 5.

Denial. Only if we understand how these two perverted escapes twist the true goal of the Escape, will we see the force of Tolkien's vision of Escape as a mark of fairy-stories. Tolkien's initial observation is that Denial and Desertion, as well as true Escape, both relate to a world in which suffering and evil are at work. The difference between Denial and Desertion, on the one hand, and Escape on the other, concerns the attitude we will adopt.

For Tolkien, the flight of the deserter is characterized by a delusion. It forgets and turns its back on sorrow, it is a "failure to recognize sorrow and death as human agony."[2] Desertion is thus not only seen in the inability to recognize that there is hope beyond the walls of the prison. Desertion is also the inability, or rejection, of *dyscatastrophe*—the supposedly final word of evil and destruction. Two forms of Desertion thus appear in Tolkien's work. One is based on the absence of hope, the other on the absence of tragedy. While the first form of Desertion is easy to understand, the second one is not. But to Tolkien, both are equally problematic.

To begin with, the absence of hope is key to understanding Denethor's attitude throughout the events that lead towards the siege of Minas Tirith. Despair is ever growing on Denethor, not least because of his use of the Palantir. His glimpse of Sauron's plan, though partial, only serves to deepen his despair for Sauron cannot make the Palantir stones lie, remarks Gandalf. What Denethor has seen is real. But Sauron can "by his will choose what things shall be seen by weaker minds."[3] Because Denethor is indeed of a weaker mind, his visions of the Palantir could only fuel a sense of desperation that had been for a long time, growing on him. Denethor's paranoid attitude was evidently fueled by his Despair. Surrendering to despair, he chose, in his suicide, Desertion instead of Escape.

The striking opposition between Aragorn and Denethor is also clearly seen in the manner in which they relate to Gondor's history. We could revisit our comparison of Aragorn and Denethor in the light of the mythological history of the realms of Gondor and Arnor. Thus for example, towards the end of *The Lord of the Rings*, as Rohan prepares to come to Gondor's aid, Aragorn chooses to take for himself the Path of the Dead. Coming through Rohan's stronghold of Dunharrow, he was greeted by Éowyn who, hearing of his chosen road, can only show her distress: "'But, Aragorn' she said at last, 'is it then your errand to seek

---

2. Timmerman, *Other Worlds*, 56.
3. LoTR, III.5.ix, 860.

death? For that is all that you will find on that road.'"[4] But no matter Aragorn's explanation, Éowyn can only believe that Aragorn is deserting the fight, that he capitulated to the call of despair. To the Lady of Rohan, Aragorn should go to war, even if all else failed, he should seek glory in battle, if not victory.

Of course Éowyn assumes that the Path of the Dead is but an instance of the Path of the Deserter. Maybe this is even what fueled her own despair, leading her to face the king of the Ringwraiths under the walls of Minas Tirith. Éomer's reaction is not as direct and obvious but implies the same conclusion: Aragorn is lost to them.[5] For both of them Aragorn has deserted their world. He has deserted the Perilous Realm. How could Éowyn and Éomer have thought differently about Aragorn's choice? After all, their attitude seems quite natural! Both can only conclude of Aragorn's possibly unconscious desertion because they base their thinking on what they know, or rather believe of Aragorn. If he is a "mere ranger," then of course Éowyn is right, and Aragorn is doomed, and every member of the Grey Company with him. However, what if Aragorn is in fact "Elessar, Isildur's heir of Gondor"? Then the Shadow Host obeys his command; then Aragorn can release them of their oath, holding it fulfilled.[6] Then the Path of the Dead becomes providential and becomes the path of unexpected victory.

In this example, we gaze upon Escape in the light of Recovery. The Recovery of mythological history (what we called *tradition*) gives meaning to Aragorn's Escape. Following the Path of the Dead is not Desertion, it is Recovery of tradition and as such, is true Escape to the world as it should be, a world where Sauron is defeated, where he reclaims the throne of Arnor and Gondor, and where Elves and Men are again bound through his union with Arwen. Thus, Aragorn's Escape is not a Desertion, but a *reclamation* of his own history and place within the mythology.

There is another form of Despair described in Tolkien's work, a more subtle and dangerous one. It is Denial, despair as flight and negation of human tragedy. For example, Gandalf recounts his fight with the Balrog, saying:

> I was alone, forgotten, without escape upon the hard horn of the world. There I lay staring upward, while the stars wheeled over,

---

4. LoTR, III.5.ii, 766.

5. LoTR, III.5.iii, 778.

6. LoTR, III.5.ix, 858.

and each day was as long as a life-age of the earth. Faint to my
ears came the gathered rumour of all lands: the springing and
the dying, the song and the weeping, and the slow everlasting
groan of overburdened stone.[7]

Gandalf cannot evade the reality of the world around him. He cannot
deny the tragedy of the world around him. While for Gandalf, there can
be no room for this kind of Desertion, this attitude of Denial is seen
in others. It is for example clear in the Ent's attitudes towards the wars
of Men. In fact, Treebeard himself has "not troubled about the Great
Wars . . . they most mostly concern Elves and Men." He later adds: "I am
not altogether on anybody's *side*, because nobody is altogether on my
side, if you understand me."[8] Treebeard displays here a kind of ethno-
centricity that could easily lead to Denial. However that is not the case
and the Ents finally—quickly, by Entish standards—decide to participate
in the war against Saruman. Of course, their decision is mainly due to the
great danger they face.[9] The fact remains: the Ents have to face the plight
of the free races. They cannot overlook the developing tragedy affecting
all living beings

A stranger case is that of Tom Bombadil, who also shows signs of
Denial. When suggesting that the Ring be taken to Tom for safe-keeping,
Gandalf counters: "If he were given the Ring, he would soon forget it, or
most likely throw it away. Such things have no hold on his mind."[10] Tom,
continues Gandalf, has retreated to his own little land and he cannot
grasp the condition of the other races of Middle-earth. Strictly speaking then, Tom is not denying the plight of the Free folks. He is merely
impermeable to it—he has no understanding of it. The reasons are manifold, but they all have to do with Tom's identity which is, and likely will
remain, enigmatic.

There is nothing more difficult than avoiding Escape as Denial. It
is much easier to avoid Desertion itself. Avoiding Denial requires something closely akin to heroism. Resisting Denial requires a sort of humble
courage than sends someone into battle even though there might be nothing to be gained. Éomer displays such heroism after the fall of Théoden
when, while the armies of Mordor are closing in on the Rohhirim, the

7. LoTR, II.3.v, 491.
8. LoTR, II.3.iv, 461.
9. LoTR, II.3.iv, 474.
10. LoTR, I.2.ii, 259.

lust of battle comes on him and he prepares to take his last stand.[11] Éomer is worthy of Théoden's "resistance" to Denial. After Gandalf cured him from the hold of Saruman, Théoden refuses to take refuge in the stronghold of Dunharrow: "You do not know your own skill in healing. . . . I myself will go to war, to fall in the front of battle, if it must be."[12] Humility and courage are the primary ingredients of true Escape. Indeed, Escape towards the real world demands the humility and the courage to confront the world with all its sorrow and tragedy. Humility and courage sustain acceptance. Having explored the negative embodiment of the Escape of the deserter, let us now turn to the manifestation of Escape that can be found in language and myth.

True Escape: The Flight of the Prisoner

Despair and Denial are not the only two forms of escape. Quite the opposite: they are the perverted forms of the true nature of Escape. In *On Fairy-Stories*, Tolkien devotes to Escape almost three times the length allotted to Recovery, testifying to its essential importance as one of the most important functions of fairy-stories.[13] To explain the meaning and function of escape, Tolkien proceeds in two steps. First, he answers the challenge of those who claim that escapism, the essence of fantasy, is harmful. It is an interesting fact that Tolkien's co-parishioner at St. Aloysius, historian Christopher Dawson, saw religion being criticized, as he puts it, as "escapist," that is, as a "substitute for reality."[14] Faërie thus stands united with religion with respect to that criticism. Indeed, the main charge against Faërie was, and still is, that it is escapist. As Shippey reports, "The cry that 'fantasy is escapist' compared to the novel is only an echo of the older cry that novels are 'escapist' compared with biography."[15] To Tolkien, this charge was highly mistaken. The contrast between "Escape" and "Real Life" was an artificial one because neither term was defined properly.

To begin with, it seems that "real life" was mainly equated with technological and scientific progress. Tolkien, for example, scorned the "clerk

---

11. LoTR, III.5.vi, 829.

12. LoTR, II.3.vi, 507.

13. OFS, 69.

14. Dawson, *Christianity and European Culture*, 193.

15. Shippey, *The Road to Middle-earth*, 286.

of Oxenford," for welcoming urbanization, mass-production, and robot factories. When we accept the flight of the deserter, and adopt his world, we will gain only the Shire of Sharkey and Saruman. Desertion, a form of capitulation in the face of evil and adversity, will leave free rein to the ones who work destruction. There is, however, another attitude, one that does not reflect an attitude of Denial and passivity.

If we welcome the Escape of the prisoner, we will accept to sail to Tol Eressëa. Moreover, writes Tolkien, "I cannot convince myself that the roof of Bletchley station is more 'real' than the clouds."[16] The reason is simple. This form of Escape is a "reaction" against the world as it is, a reaction against nature through "improved means to deteriorated ends."[17] In fact, the elm-tree is more substantial than the Morlockian horror of the factory chimney.[18] It has more *life*.

Further, Escape is for Tolkien simply analogous to "escape from prison." Tolkien's example of the man in a prison is strangely reminiscent of Chesterton's example in the chapter "Fairy-tales" in *All Things Considered*. Suppose, writes Chesterton, that a man was born in prison, accustomed "to the deadly silence and the disgusting indifference; and suppose he were then suddenly turned loose upon the life and laughter of Fleet Street. He would, of course, think that the literary men in Fleet Street were a free and happy race; yet how sadly, how ironically, is this the reverse of the case!"[19] Even though the example here does not have the exact same content, and not the same purpose, the parallel remains striking. Tolkien continues by arguing that the rejection of the sane and true form of escape merely reflects the pessimism and cynicism of his age.[20]

Tolkien's critics present the world in all its evil and suffering as natural and unavoidable, without remission and without hope, without longing and without glory. Tolkien rhetorically asks: "Why should a man be scorned, if, finding himself in prison, he tries to get out and go home?"[21] The last sentence provides further understanding into the function of escape in Tolkien. We see that escape is closely related to recovery: it is

---

16. OFS, 71.
17. OFS, 94.
18. OFS, 94.
19. Chesterton, *All Things Considered*, 255.
20. OFS, 69–70.
21. OFS, 69.

the restoration of a healthier and more "visionary" past. Escape is the practical outcome of the first function of fairy-stories, recovery.

The Prisoner, longing for his former life and home, for his friends and family, cannot and should not be blamed. He is merely trying to "escape to life." That is where the contrast between Desertion and Escape becomes clearer. Escape has a positive relationship with the world as it should be. In other words, Escape reveals a deeper yearning, a deep-seated longing: estranged from the world, we need something else, we need to escape. Escape is not denial of the world, it is embrace of the true world in all its glory, tragedy, and heroism. But most of us do not accept the world as it is or should be and construe an artificial world often called "modern." This constructed world is founded on ordinary impressions and perceptions, but point to a deeper reality. This explains why to Tolkien it is desirable to escape from this modernized world.[22] The "modern world" can legitimately be escaped from, because it is an artificial world. It is neither the world as it should be, nor the world as it actually is. In fact, Escape demands true vision. Escape needs Recovery, the "regaining of a clear view."

Escape and Language

To do so, we will try to see how Escape is embodied into Tolkien's view of language. Of course, how Escape and language relate is not at first obvious. But that is partly due to our persistent misunderstanding of Tolkien's Escape. The matter becomes clearer if we associate Escape with "liberation." Barfield is helpful here. In a way, his theory of "ancient semantic unity," to which Tolkien partly associated himself, is a theory of the *liberation* of meaning. In that, Tolkien and Barfield stand together. The essential role of meaning is seen throughout Tolkien's works, but a particular instance can be found in Pippin and Merry's encounter with the Ent Treebeard. Upon learning the hobbits' *real* names and being asked in return his own name, Treebeard replies negatively: "For one thing it would take a long while: my name is growing all the time . . . so my name is like a story. Real names tell you the story of the things they belong to in my language."[23] Names are meaningful. Treebeard makes the same kind of comment about the Entish name for "Orc." Their name is "as long as

22. Purtill, *Lord of the Elves and Eldils*, 20.
23. LoTR, II.3.iv, 454.

years of torment, those vermin of orcs."[24] For Treebeard, language is much more than words used to describe the world. Words convey something real and true, even if the meaning in question is not at first obvious.

There is nothing magical about Treebeard's statement,[25] but there is something deeply relevant. Words and meaning are so united that one cannot be considered without the other. Thus, a name tells more about the person that one might think. There is more at play than mere words, for all names tell a story. This explains why Treebeards finds Pippin and Merry quite hasty to call *themselves* hobbits. As a matter of fact, that is how Gollum—and Sauron!—would actually track Bilbo and the Shire. After the part "the hobbit" played in the quest for Erebor, it was inevitable that the name "hobbit" would lead directly to the *Shire*. It is telling that the two words that send Gollum and Sauron on Bilbo's track are "Shire" and "Baggins," rather than the term "hobbit" itself. In *Unfinished Tales*, Christopher Tolkien notes that Gollum—or Sauron for that matter— could not know that "hobbit" was a local term by a local language and was not a universal description in Westron language.[26] Though both Gollum and Sauron did not know where the Shire precisely was, the conjunction of "Shire" and "Baggins" could only lead to Bag End and to the "thief Baggins." It is literally impossible to conceal the deep meaning of names.

But often the relationship between name and story is forgotten or rejected. A case of such disconnection happens with the hobbits and the Ents, whose existence is nearly forgotten, as are their names. First, hobbits have disappeared from the "old list" complains Merry: "We always seem to have got left out of the old lists, and the old stories." And Pippin to immediately re-introduce the name and the history of "hobbits" into the list of living beings: "Half-grown hobbits, the hole-dwellers."[27] Second, and interestingly, Ents are also a topic "out of the shadow of legend," but in Rohan. Upon his first sight of an Ent, king Théoden's first reaction is one of disbelief, to which Gandalf replies: "You have seen Ents, O King, Ents out of the Fangorn Forest, which in your tongue you call the Entwood. Did you think that the name was given only in idle fancy?"[28] No, of course. The name goes with the story, but the story has been forgotten.

24. LoTR, III.6.vi, 957.

25. Contra Zimmer, "Creating and Re-creating World with Words," in Chance, *Tolkien and the Invention of Myth*, 56.

26. Tolkien, *Unfinished Tales*, 342.

27. LoTR, II.3.iv, 454.

28. LoTR, II.3.viii, 536.

The name and the meaning were united: from Entwood, one should infer that the "wood of the Ents" belongs to Ents. Whatever they could possibly be, Ents must then be owners or guardians of the wood. Hence, maybe, the name "shepherds of the trees." The meaning should be clear, but it has become alienated from the reality of the world. But liberation, Escape, is possible. Escape provides "linguistic anamnesis," a recollection of language and its connection to the "old stories."

But there is more, still, to discover about the escapist nature of language. For it is not only that language provides a reconnection to the stories. Language is in itself the means through which Tolkien allows his sub-created world to live. A great part of the ongoing attraction to Tolkien's Middle-earth is the inner life he has succeeded in giving his mythological corpus. We do indeed enter a sub-created world, and not merely a story. At each turn of the page, the reader discovers that the world in which the story is embodied is much larger than the story itself. This lasting emotional effect is accomplished by Tolkien largely through language. Of course, the reader will encounter Tolkien's use of a mythological language throughout his Middle-earth corpus, especially in the *Silmarillion* where the reader discovers the depth of Tolkien's sub-created world. The constant reference to names in the mythological past serves to give a constant sense of both familiarity and strangeness.

In *The Lord of the Rings* also, such examples are numerous. One of the most memorable isFrodo's cry to Elbereth while surrounded by the Nazgûl on Weathertop (I.1.xi), or at the ford of Bruinen, where Frodo defies them with a reference to the Elvish mythological past: "By Elbereth and Lúthien the fair, you shall have neither the ring nor me!" (I.1.xii). Aragorn also makes constant reference to a world outside their immediate story as with his singing of the Lay of Lúthien on Weathertop (I.1.xi), or his reference to the cats of Queen Berúthiel talking about Gandalf in Moria (I.2.iv). Legolas when he shoots the winged Nazgûl over the river Anduin blesses his arrow with a sigh, "Elbereth, Gilthoniel!" (I.2.ix).

This, however, is not only the attitude of the main characters of Tolkien's epic tale. Even ordinary Gondorian soldiers display the same use of language. Damrod, a ranger of Ithilien for example invokes the Valar for protection during an attack of the Mûmak (II.4.v) and Sam, rescuing Frodo in Cirith Ungol, uses the safe word "Elbereth" before rejoining with his master (III.6.i). The narrator himself gives the reader glimpses of a world not described in the story. Théoden's charge is made alive through such a use of language: "he was borne up on Snowmane like a god of old, even as Oromë the Great in the Battle of the Valar when the world was young." (III.5.v) Reference to a world outside the actual story provides a richness and depth to the sub-created world that would not have been attained otherwise.

In fact, that is the great function of language: it provides an escape from the potential bondage of the story. Indeed, that is always the great force of sub-creation. Through imaginative creation, the Secondary world takes upon a life of its own, a life that goes beyond the story. This is Escape in its noblest form. Like the escape of the prisoner, it refers to a world outside the prison-walls. Thus, when a sub-created world does not acquire additional depth, when it is bound to the actual description of the author or narrator, an essential dimension of sub-creation is lost, and imagination becomes limited.

Of course Tolkien also embodies this through the "transmission conceit" of *The Silmarillion*.[29] The trans-generational transmission of the tradition, and of the Red Book of Westmarch, is essential to the mytho-logical depth Tolkien succeeds in creating. The history of the transmission of Middle-earth's history is central to many manuscripts left unfinished by Tolkien. In fact, an essential part of the multi-volume *History of Mid-dle-earth* is dedicated to this transmission. Many have connected this to the coherence of Middle-earth. But the transmission of Middle-earth's mythological history not only gives coherence to the sub-created world: it also gives it depth. Tolkien refers constantly to this phenomenon in his works. Thus, *The Book of Lost Tales* "are framed to form a sequence of linked tales *told* by a succession of narrators."[30] There, the Ainulindalë is narrated by Rúmil of Tírion.

As for the events of *The Lord of the Rings*, they reach beyond the events themselves and involve other part of history: Beren, Luthien, Nú-menor, Bandobras "Bullroarer" Took, and Eorl father of the Rohirrim, the Eorlingas. This is brought to light through translations, poems, and other reported legends. This is clearly seen in the tentative titles given to the Red Book, especially the final one given by Frodo:

> The Downfall of the Lord of the Rings
> and the Return of the King

---

29. In the words of Joosten, "Poetry in the Transmission Conceit," 153–62.

30. Flieger, *Interrupted Music*, 66.

(as seen by the Little People; being the memoirs of Bilbo and Frodo of the Shire, supplemented by the accounts of their friends and the learning of the Wise)
Together with extracts from Books of Lore translated by B. Baggins in Rivendell.[31]

This story of transmission also explains why the reader can find it difficult to answer the following question: "If the transmission of the story is connected to a mythological past, whose past is it?"[32] Elves, Men, Hobbits?—since they are after all the ones to put in writing this mythological history. All of them, Flieger answers. The story told belongs to the one who actually speaks, when he speaks.[33] In this way again we escape the bounds of the story and enter Middle-earth's long history.

Again, we find Escape through language. This is also connected to the meaning of the world found outside the story. The deep relationship between language and story is also seen in Tolkien's comments about the "modern world" in his essay "On Fairy-stories." His remarks against the world of top-hats and railway stations are not mere rhetoric. Tolkien's sarcastic anti-modernist comments find a rather surprising embodiment in his use of language.[34] To those who would argue for the sophistication and refinement of the city's way of life, Tolkien answers by giving the trolls of *The Hobbit* a distinct Cockney accent:

> "Mutton yesterday, mutton today, and blimey if I don't look like mutton again tomorrer," said one of the trolls.
> "Never a blinking bit of manflesh have we had for a long enough," said a second. "What the 'ell William was a-thinkin of to bring us into these parts at all, beats me—"[35]

Of course, we must not over interpret this observation. However, given Tolkien's suspicion of modern industrialized life, this might be indicative of his personal attitude.Escape is for Tolkien clearly not opposed to real-life but to an industrialist construction of what "real life" should be. The description of the modern world, "alive" with industries and technology, is not the essence of real life. Critics do not understand the nature and escapist function of fairy-stories because they do not know what real life is

31. LoTR, III.6.ix, 1004.

32. That is the same question Flieger addresses in her *Interrupted Music*, 45–54.

33. Flieger, *Interrupted Music*, 49.

34. King, "Recovery, Escape, Consolation," 45–46.

35. H, 33.

in the first place. Chesterton had made, or rather implied, the same point in many of his works. Moreover, these same critics, the monsters of Tolkien's Beowulf essay, are confused regarding the nature of escape itself. It is something quite different from the "flight of the deserter." Escape does not turn away from a world of sin, a world of "hunger, pain, sorrow."[36] Rather, escape looks at this world, intensely, and sees strangeness and unexpected glory in its midst. Escape can do so because it considers that this world is a mixed one: it is both "joy and sorrow," "hope and death," and there is no shame in wanting to escape from death. To those who argue that escape is an illusion because it is a flight out of reality, Tolkien counter-argued that escape is very real, and very legitimate.[37]

Escape and Myth

Escape is not only connected to language. It is also of primary importance in the nature of mythology, especially for Tolkien. We will not discuss mythologies in general here, but we will pay particular attention to Tolkien's own mythology and the manner in which Escape is one of its essential functions. As we have said before, Tolkien saw Escape as contrasting the real and the modern worlds. Actually, Tolkien himself does not use the word "real." Instead, he is content by noting that Escape provides freedom from the so-called "modern" world. But then, what is this Escape leading us to? Like the prisoner going home, it leads us to the reality that has always been waiting for us. For the prisoner, it is family and home. For the one who enters the Perilous Realm, it is a world freed from the inescapable limitations of modern progress.

That seems simple enough. But it is deceptively simple. After all, what does that mean, exactly? Why is Escape taking us away from the "modern" to a "real" world? Why is the modern world analogous to a prison? Key to answering the question is Tolkien's attitude towards the naive stance his contemporaries had adopted towards the modern and scientific view of the world. Thus can Tolkien exclaim in disbelief: "Not long ago—incredible as though it may seem—I heard a clerk of Oxenford declare that he 'welcomed' the proximity of mass-production robot factories, and the roar of self-obstructive mechanical traffic, because it brought

36. OFS, 69.
37. OFS, 69.

his university into contact with 'real life.'"[38] What Tolkien is reacting against here is not science in itself, but "the march of Science"—Tolkien here is quoting an advertisement published in the magazine *Punch*—denounced by Christopher Dawson and G. K. Chesterton. Escape from the modern scientific world is an escape out of the world where a certain kind of science, absolute in its rational tyranny, reigns. In a way, a key element of the "modern" world for Tolkien is that it is ruled "by the hypotheses (or dogmatic guesses) of scientific writers who classed Man not only as an 'animal'—that correct classification is ancient—but as 'only an animal.'"[39]

Tolkien further continues with his combination of lyricism and sarcasm: "The notion that motor-cars are more 'alive' than, say, centaurs or dragons is curious; that they are more 'real' than, say, horses is pathetically absurd. How real, how startlingly alive is a factory chimney compared with an elm tree: poor obsolete thing, insubstantial dream of an escapist!"[40] *Insubstantial* dream is an interesting expression under Tolkien's pen, and might recall some theological expressions. Other expressions used by Tolkien testify to this anti-modernist argument through fantasy escape. Among these expressions Tolkien used "March of Science,"[41] "improved means to deteriorated ends" or again "the rawness and ugliness of modern European life."[42] All three expressions are taken from Dawson's *Progress and Religion*, who himself was a perceptive critic of modern life and culture. The problem of the "modern," for Tolkien, is the utopia of a "Robot Age," an expression that is likely borrowed or adapted from Christopher Dawson.[43] This utopia is one of exclusive scientific rationality, thus becoming what Chesterton had famously described as real "madness": reason without imagination.

In Tolkien's created mythology, this lack of imagination—a lack of true reality—comes through in his shorter writings. In *Smith of Wootton Major* this lack of imagination, lack of insight, is most strongly symbolized by the character Nokes, "a solid sort of man with a wife and children,

---

38. OFS, 70.

39. OFS, 83.

40. OFS, 71.

41. OFS, 70.

42. The original quote of the latter expression reads: "The rawness and ugliness of modern European life is the sign of biological inferiority, of an insufficient or false relation to environment, which produces strain, wasted effort, revolt or failure." Dawson, *Progress and Religion*, 68.

43. Dawson uses the expression "robot utopia" in his *Understanding Europe*, 204.

and careful with money."[44] What is crucial here is the stress on Nokes' lack of imagination, his exclusive rationality, so to speak. Notice that Nokes is not the embodiment of evil as Morgoth or Sauron can be in the rest of Tolkien's mythological corpus. His "great fault" is not his wickedness, but his lack of imagination. Tolkien himself points this out in a small essay recently published in Verlyn Flieger's new edition of *Smith of Wootton Major*. There, Tolkien provides comments about the story and its characters, noting that Nokes "seems to have been generally fond of children," thus relativizing Noek's character failure.[45]

Of course, Nokes' major ethical fault in the story is his dishonesty. After all, he has few scruples in taking credit for Alf's work. But more than that, Nokes cannot see that the world might be larger than that of Wootton Major. Maybe even Faërie might lie nearby—"westward," Tolkien notes.[46] Nokes, the Master Cook, demonstrates this subtle rationalization in his attitude towards Prentice when preparing the Cake. Going over the ingredients that were supposed to go inside the Cake, Nokes discovers a star, the *fay-star* adds Prentice. But when his apprentice notes that the star "comes from Faery," Nokes' reaction is one of condescending rationality: "All right, all right. . . . It means much the same; but call it that if you like. You'll grow up some day."[47] To Nokes, Faery is impossible because it does not fit within the parameters of his reason-only approach to his position as Master Cook. The beauty of Faery, into which Smith later walks, plays not part in Nokes' world. Thus his reality is amputated of true beauty and a broader history. At the end, what is missing from Nokes' world is imagination and the stories in which it is embodied.

By contrast, the world of "Faery" offers Smith—the young boy who ate the star in the Cake—an escape, from the all too familiar world of Wootton Major. Because he has not lost his imagination, he can actually believe the stories, the children tale, and enter Faery. In doing so, he also escapes the "vulgarization" of Wootton symbolized by Nokes.[48] Nokes's life is the modern, "factory-like" one, the world the Oxford don had called the "real life." Discovering that the story of Faery is true, Smith escapes the constructed world offered by Nokes.

44. Tolkien, *Smith of Wootton Major*, 9–10.

45. Tolkien, *Smith of Wootton Major*, 97.

46. Tolkien, *Smith of Wootton Major*, 84.

47. Tolkien, *Smith of Wootton Major*, 13.

48. Tolkien, *Smith of Wootton Major*, 93.

When first aware of Faery, something begins to change in Smith and the star appears, bright on his forehead. The most noticeable change in Smith, though, is not the star he would wear for many years, but the change in his voice which became more beautiful.[49] Smith's Escape is no more a flight from the world than the escape of the prisoner. It is, here also, finding one's true home.

The change produces in Smith a deep change and love of music and song. While at his work in the Wootton smithy, he can only sing when working iron into beautiful creations. And, "that was all that most people knew about him."[50] We of course remember that for Tolkien, music and song are essentially the manner in which mythology is recalled to memory. Through song and poems mythologised history is brought to the present. It is the case, already mentioned, of the story of Beren and Lúthien sung by Aragorn on Weathertop. It is also Bilbo crafting the poem of Eärendil, Sam reciting part of "The Fall of Gil-galad," or Gandalf's words about Dwimordene, Lórien. Constantly, poems and songs are the vehicle of myth.

In a way, it is the case also with Smith, though not explicitly. But the fact that the fay-star leads Smith to adopt singing and journey to Faery encourages us to see the connection as determinant. However, discovering myth through songs and poems is not the last Escape for Smith. What goes hand in hand with Escape to myth, is the Escape to Faery.

Conclusion

Escape is thus not what the critics assume it is. There is no sense in Tolkien that Escape is a desertion from the world. Of course this is only true because the world is not as it should be. There is nothing wrong, in Tolkien's mind, in escaping a world that is deeply damaged in order to recover a clear view of the world. Thus, Escape leads to Recovery: they imply each other, and we cannot dispense with one of these if we want to correctly understand Faërie. There is of course a third term, Consolation, without which Faërie is not complete.

49. Tolkien, *Smith of Wootton Major*, 20.
50. Tolkien, *Smith of Wootton Major*, 22.

13

Consolation

RECOVERY LEADS TO ESCAPE. Escape introduces us to Consolation, the greatest mark of Faërie. In fact, if the two other functions are essential to fairy-stories, the happy ending, "the *eucatastrophic* tale is the true form of fairy-tale, and its highest function."[1] Certainly, this consolation is one of the most important characteristics of fairy-stories. If Recovery is the first logical dimension of fairy-stories, if Escape (or "escapism") is the most common charge, then Consolation is the most important mark around which everything else revolves. Consolation is the destination-point of Recovery and Escape. To explain how Consolation should be seen as the foremost dimension of fairy-stories, we will begin this chapter by identifying Consolation with a specific kind of "happy ending," what Tolkien calls the Eucatastrophe. Then we will try to see how Consolation is embodied by Tolkien in his view of language and myth.

Consolation and the "Happy Ending"

The joy of the happy ending is expressed by Tolkien through another term, the *eucatastrophe*, the good catastrophe that is the accomplishment of the story. Consolation is dependent upon a "sudden and joyous turn." Notice first the two characteristics of a true happy ending: it is sudden,

---

1. OFS, 75.

and it is, of course, joyous. It is not enough that the ending be "happy," but it must be sudden, it must come down on us like a "thief in the night," unexpected. Hence, Tolkien's use of the term "turn" is very pointed. Eucatastrophe is not just a slight change of direction, it is a turn; it is the world "turned upside down." The eucatastrophe is the conversion of all suffering and evil into the final and ultimate joyous denouement. As Shippey says: "Tolkien, of course, being a Christian, did in absolute fact believe that in the end all things would end happily, that in a sense they already had—a belief he shared with Dante, and a matter of faith beyond argument. It needs to be said, though, that he was capable of envisaging a different belief and even bringing it into his story."[2] However, this happy ending never effaced the two necessary elements of Consolation: dyscatastrophe and eucatastrophe, for the latter cannot be experienced without the former.

For Tolkien, the implication is clear. Far from being naively optimistic, eucatastrophe is *joy* in the face of pain and hardships. In *The Lord of the Ring*, the eucatastrophic nature of Faërie is clearly seen at, for example, the battle of Helm's Deep. At the precise moment when the defeat seems consummated, both the king and Gandalf make a sortie: "And with that shout the king came. His horse was white as snow, golden was his shield, and his spear was long. . . . Light sprang in the sky. Night departed. . . . There suddenly upon a ridge appeared a rider, clad in white, shining in the rising sun."[3] The catastrophe of the battle should have led to certain defeat, but at the most desperate point of the battle, suddenly appears Gandalf, and with him Erkenbrand, lord of the Westfold. Eucatastrophe is victory. Another example of eucatastrophe is found with Éomer during the battle of the fields of Pelennor when, all seemingly lost, Aragorn came from Pelargir.[4] Defeat vanishes with the night; victory is brought by the daylight.

However, we should immediately note that if Eucatastrophe is one element of Consolation, it requires, *at the very same time*, dyscatastrophe. This second element of Consolation, notes Flieger, "is what makes the joy at deliverance so piercing, and less to the denial of universal final defeat."[5] For in fact, there can never be a happy ending, true consola-

---

2. Shippey, *The Road to Middle-earth*, 174.

3. LoTR, II.3.vii, 528.

4. LoTR, III.5.vi, 829.

5. Flieger, *Splintered Light*, 27.

tion, if not for the "joyous turn." But this joyous turn cannot happen if the world is not legitimately and completely threatened. If the danger is not real, pressing, there can be no Eucatastrophe—merely an easy resolution, a placebo of joy.

Examples of dyscatastrophe also fill the pages of Tolkien's works. Frodo and Sam cannot avoid being hopelessly trapped by "rivers of fire [that] drew near."[6] Tolkien's chapter on the destruction of the Ring of Power could not have left us with Frodo just throwing the ring into the fire and turning away to go home. The world, *his* world, needed to be under threat—and so was he. Thus, Tolkien presents us with a Frodo overtaken by the Ring. When Sam joins his master in the chasm of Mount Doom, he finds Frodo claiming the Ring for himself.[7] The world is lost, Sauron has won. And because Sauron has just won, he also has lost. Gollum struggles for the Ring and tears it from Frodo's finger. Both Gollum and the Ring fall into the fire, and Sauron is vanquished through the evil he had wrought. Dyscatastrophe is a condition to Eucatastrophe. The joyous turn happened: Frodo and Sam are honored at the field of Cormallen, they witness the great end of the Third Age, the wedding of Aragorn and Arwen, and they restore the Shire.

The absolute need of dyscatastrophe is also manifest at the very end of *The Lord of the Rings*. Indeed, the "happy ending" is charged with melancholy. Preparing for his final journey to the Grey Havens, Frodo explains to a distraught Sam that happiness is not for everyone: "I have been too deeply hurt, Sam. I tried to save the Shire, and it has been saved, but not for me."[8] Some wounds cannot be easily healed, or forgotten. The Eucatastrophe of the end of the Third Age still does not erase Frodo's hurt and wounds. He has to leave the Shire and has been granted passage to Tol Eressëa, in view of Valinor.

Dyscatastrophe is thus equally crucial to a good fairy-story, but it not synonymous with a final defeat. The balance between hope and defeat is ever present in Tolkien, at times weighing down more towards the side of "defeat." In one of his letters, he can thus write: "Actually I am a Christian," Tolkien wrote of himself, "and indeed a Roman Catholic, so that I do not expect 'history' to be anything but a 'long defeat'—though it contains (and in legend may contain more clearly and movingly) some

6. LoTR, III.6.iv, 929.

7. LoTR, III.6.iii, 924.

8. LoTR, III.6.ix, 1006.

samples or glimpses of final victory."[9] Throughout the "long defeat" we can still see the glimpse of victory. Defeat and victory are not, therefore, antithetical to each other.

Consolation and Language

The tension between defeat and hope, Consolation, is partly experienced through language. This, of course, should not surprise us given how crucial songs and poems are to Tolkien's works. Consolation is subtly present in Frodo's remembrance of "Bilbo's song." There is, in Frodo's version of the song, a deep melancholy.[10] Frodo, who cannot remember if the song is one of Bilbo's or not, seems comforted by the words from the old familiar song, by the presence of Bilbo through these poetic words. Of course, consolation is often subtle. The consolation provided by this song is repeated when Frodo meets Bilbo again in Rivendell on his way back to the Shire.[11] Tolkien's description of Bilbo embodies a sense of comfort. Bilbo sits, cosy by the fire, comfortably in Rivendell. Bilbo is there, "at the end of all things," comforted. And he adds: "What more could one want."[12] Bilbo has finally found rest and sleep from the troubles of his adventures.

The same kind of consolation is experienced by Frodo on the way to the Grey Havens, softly singing to himself another of Bilbo's songs, "Upon the Hearth The Fire Is Red," that was first sung by Frodo, Sam, and Pippin, as they walked through the Shire on their way to Crickhollow.[13] The repetition of the song at the close of the book brings melancholic consolation of the same kind previously experienced by Bilbo.[14] It brings to Frodo an old sense, maybe almost forgotten, of the simple joys of the hobbit life, and of his friends. Maybe even there is consolation for their coming parting.

Consolation is also embodied in the stories through the names used. So for example "Elessar," the name chosen by Aragorn as his royal name, is charged with mythological reference and with consolation. The Elessar, the elf-stone, first appears in the tale of Galadriel and Celeborn,

9. L, 255.

10. LoTR, I.1.iii, 72.

11. LoTR, III.6.vi, 965.

12. LoTR, III.6.vi, 965.

13. LoTR, I.1.iii, 76.

14. LoTR, III.6.ix, 1005.

where the stone is described as being crafted by Enerdhil, jewel-smith of Gondolin who made it for Idril, wife of Tuor and mother of Eärendil. Consolation is first associated with the Elessar when Idril gives the stone to her son as a sign of hope.[15] Later on, a similar stone reappears in Middle-earth's history, when Galadriel gives Aragorn this very stone.[16] Whether the same—returned by Gandalf to Middle-earth—or a different one—made by Celebrimbor for Galadriel—even the Wise cannot decide. Later, in *The Lord of the Rings*, Bilbo writes the poem/song about Eärendil, to which Aragorn insists should be added "a green stone."[17] In any case, the fact that Aragorn chose the name Elessar as his reigning name brings consolation to the future story of the Fourth Age. This enduring Consolation is evidenced in Aragorn's renewal of Elendil's Oath.[18]

Sam, for his part, also finds consolation in songs and rhymes. As he tries to rescue Frodo from the tower of Cirith Ungol, Sam finds himself at a loss, close to despair. Reaching the top of the tower, he still has not found Frodo. Then "at last, weary and feeling finally defeated," Sam begins singing:

> In western lands beneath the Sun
> the flowers may rise in Spring,
> the trees may bud, the waters run,
> the merry finches sing.
> Or there maybe 'tis cloudless night
> and swaying beeches bear
> the Elven-stars as jewels white
> amid their branching hair.
> Though here at journey's end I lie
> in darkness buried deep,
> beyond all towers strong and high,
> beyond all mountains steep,
> above all shadows rides the Sun
> and Stars for ever dwell:
> I will not say the Day is done,
> nor bid the Stars farewell.[19]

15. Tolkien, *Unfinished Tales*, 249.
16. LoTR, I.2.viii, 366.
17. LoTR, I.2.i, 231.
18. LoTR, I.2.vii, 350.
19. LoTR, III.6.i, 888.

And while darkness had begun to "cover him like a tide," it is Frodo's voice that Sam hears responding to his song. Tolkien does not comment on Sam's feeling at that moment, but we should expect great consolation and relief to come upon him. In Sam's song, however, it is not only consolation through language that we witness. It is consolation through a language that brings us back to the mythological history of Middle-earth.

Consolation and Myth

The connection between language and myth should not surprise us. At this point, we have become quite familiar with Tolkien's way of uniting language and stories. It should not come as a surprise that Consolation is not only embodied in Tolkien's use of language but also in the relationship between his characters and mythological history. Of course, most of the examples already mentioned unite language and myth. When Sam sings the poem on the stairs of Cirth Ungol, it is—consciously or not—the mythology of Valinor, the "western lands," that are made alive to him. When Frodo laments in rhymes about Gandalf; it is of Olórin, Maiar of Manwë and Varda, that Frodo mourns over. There too, there is consolation for Olórin was ever the Maiar who "took pity on their [the Children of Iluvatar] sorrows; and those who listened to him awoke from despair and put away the imaginations of darkness."[20] In fact, when Consolation is found through a reference to mythology, it is mot often a reference to the mythology of Valinor.

The Consolation of the happy ending is also clearly referenced by the news of Aragorn's victory brought by the eagles to the city of Minas Tirith:

> Sing now, ye people of the Tower of Anor,
> for the Realm of Sauron is ended for ever,
> and the Dark Tower is thrown down.
> Sing and rejoice, ye people of the Tower of Guard,
> for your watch hath not been in vain,
> and the Black Gate is broken,
> and your King hath passed through,
> and he is victorious.
> Sing and be glad, all ye children of the West,
> for your King shall come again,
> and he shall dwell among you
> all the days of your life.

20. S, 18.

And the Tree that was withered shall be renewed,
and he shall plant it in the high places,
and the City shall be blessed.
Sing all ye people! [21]

Through the distinct biblical phraseology, despair vanishes, and Consolation can be fully spread throughout the land: "the days that followed were golden, and Spring and Summer joined and made revel together in the fields of Gondor." The realm itself seems to feel the effects of Consolation.

Of course, the greatest manifestation of Consolation in myth is at the end of *The Lord of the Rings*, when Galadriel, Elrond, Gandalf, and Frodo, among others, take the ship to Valinor.[22] As for Sam, Consolation awaits not in the form of Middle-earth's mythological history but his own personal history. Waiting for him are Rose and Elanor, the Shire and his mayorship. Together with Merry and Pippin, he also finds consolation in the simple things of hobbit-life, walking back to the Shire with his friends.[23] Sam, at the end of all things, closes the story with the epitome of all consolations: "Well, I'm back."[24]

Consolation, which comes through the "good catastrophe," is embodied in a mythological history, which also revolves around the two additional theological notions of truth and hope.

One such received tradition is that of the "Children of Húrin," the *Narn i Chîn Húrin*, particularly concerned with the deeds of Tuor and Túrin. Of particular relevance here is the story of Túrin Turambar, because it has acquired a reputation of hopelessness rarely seen in Tolkien's works. In *The Book of Lost Tales*, Tolkien thus summarizes the end of the story:

> Turambar indeed had followed [his sister] Nienori along the black pathways to the doors of Fui, but Fui would not open to them, neither would Vefántur. Yet now the prayers of Úrin and Mavwin came even to Manwë, and the Gods had mercy on their unhappy fate, so that those twain Turin and Nienori entered into Fôs' Almir, the bath of flame . . . and so were all their sorrows and stains washed away, and they dwelt as shining Valar among the blessed ones, and now the love of that brother and sister is very fair; but Turambar indeed shall stand beside Fionwë in the

21. LoTR, III.6.v, 942.
22. LoTR, III.6.ix, 1006.
23. LoTR, III.6.ix, 1008.
24. LoTR, III.6.ix, 1008.

Great Wrack [Last Battle], and Melko and his drakes shall curse
the sword of Mormakil [Túrin].[25]

When the reader first comes across the story of Túrin, there seems at
first to be no Consolation in the cycle of Túrin Turambar. It is the closest
Tolkien comes to painting an absolutely bleak world. Of course, given
Tolkien's definition of a "good" fairy-story, we can only wonder at the
presence of such a dark tale within Tolkien's *corpus*.

This, of course, is the case only if we dissociate the tale of Túrin
with the rest of the mythology. Consolation is present in the cycle of
Túrin in the "Sketch of the Mythology," an earlier draft of the Silmarillion
published in *The Shaping of Middle-earth* as "The Earliest 'Silmarillion.'"
There, Tolkien provides a view of the "end of history," in which Túrin
intervenes again. Then, at the end, the spirit of Morgoth will "creep back
over the Walls of the World" (this is known as "the prophecy"), and a
last battle will be fought. There and then, Eönwë [Fionwë in this earliest
draft], banner-bearer and herald of Manwë, will fight and vanquish Morgoth.[26] Then the light of the two Trees of Valinor, Laurelin and Silpion,
will be rekindled and the world be renewed.[27]

Of course, the "Sketch" is precisely only that, and it is impossible to
imagine the specific way Tolkien would actually have written the end of his
mythological corpus. Christopher Tolkien notes that this line of writing,
this prophecy, is "associated with other conceptions that had clearly been
abandoned."[28] Maybe then Tolkien would have written the last battle of
Valinor in a different way. However, it is highly probable that the place of
Túrin within this eschatological story would remain somewhat identical.
Thus, the projected end of this "early Silmarillion" is still relevant—and
in fact, quite telling. What is clearly at the heart of this last battle is the
eschatological hope, hope and joy at the restoration of the world.

There is then also Consolation at the end of the cycle of Túrin. But it
is a hope buried under the dyscatastrophe of the world. There is a deeper
hope, reaching beyond the immediate hope of a given story within the
mythology. This final hope is the ultimate embodiment of true Consolation—with its twin components of dyscatastrophe *and* eucatastrophe.

25. HoME, II.115.

26. HoME, IV.40. In "The Hiding of Valinor," it is Fionwë who will be the bane of
Morgoth (HoME, I.247).

27. HoME, IV.76.

28. HoME, IV.76.

The Eucatastrophe, the joyous turn, takes us back to the Consolation embedded in mythological history—something Tolkien identifies an essential dimension of fairy-stories. They are not children-tales. They are not even concerned about moralistic teaching—George McDonald's greatest temptation, according to Tolkien. Rather, they point back to the origin of all things where all answers are found. The Eucatastrophe can only lead us back to Faërie. In doing so, a deep yearning for the truth of home, Tolkien's "real world," is satisfied. A "primordial [human] desire" is finally fulfilled. And, in jointing together myth, hope, truth, and Consolation, Tolkien gives to his theory of fairy-stories a decidedly theological turn.

Conclusion

Consolation is the final and highest mark of fairy-stories: it is the fulfillment of everything a good fairy-story is. Consolation is the end of Recovery and Escape, it is the point at which everything has plenitude. For Tolkien, this uniting function of fairy-stories can only be ultimately grounded in the archetype of all fairy-stories, that of the incarnation. Concluding his essay "On Fairy-Stories" on such a note, Tolkien brings together his academic expertise and his Thomist theology. In doing so, Tolkien does not become primarily a theologian. He remains a mythmaker, though one in whom theological virtues like hope and truth, and essentially Consolation (or, "joy"), play a definite role.

14

Faërie

RECOVERY, ESCAPE AND CONSOLATION: these are the three essential ingredients of Faërie. They have helped us understand how Tolkien relied on language and myth to give form to his mythopoeic project. With these three dimensions of Faërie, it would seem that we have finally come to a clear and final understanding of Tolkien's view of fairy-story. However, is it really the case? With these three words, have we completely understood what a true fairy-story is? Is Faërie merely synonymous with fairy-stories? Is it a more of a way to look at the world? Or maybe is it closer to a manner of writing? Clearly, something still escapes our grasp. If language and myth are used by Tolkien to embody Recovery, Escape, and Consolation, how do these three key notions give form and substance to Faërie? In this last chapter, we can turn to a fuller and more comprehensive definition of Faërie. To achieve this goal, we will look again at these three fundamental words: Recovery, Escape, and Consolation.

Recovery and Faërie

Faërie, the Perilous Realm which path opens before us when we open the pages of *The Lord of the Rings* or *The Silmarillion*, is an unfamiliar land. We are pilgrims in this territory. This is constitutive of Tolkien's definition of Faërie. It is the Secondary, unfamiliar, World through which the

Primary World can often gain consistency and meaning. This sense of "strangeness" is evidently crucial to Chesterton, but also to Tolkien. But why is that the case? The best explanation is that the world that we see is not the world that is supposed to be. We need to recover a correct view of the world, and this comes often through a sense of displacement.

A famous image to define fairy-story was Chesterton's "Mooreeffoc," the unfamiliar that gives a new life, a new view, of reality. In fact, recovery of a clear view is "exactly what Chesterton's art aims at."[1] Tolkien also famously said that this "Chestertonian" fantasy was not enough. Hence recovering the unfamiliar means recovering a world that has long disappeared. Tolkien does not comment further on this unfamiliarity of recovery, but the theological nature of this observation should not be dismissed. Notice that Tolkien never said that Chesterton's perspective was wrong, but that it was *not enough*. Even in Tolkien's Faërie, there is a sense of unfamiliarity, of displacement. We enter the Perilous Realm, and we step into a strange land.

In this strange land, we recover a clear view of the world. But what sort of "view"? One possible answer is that, entering Faërie, we see like new the moral structure of the world. This could be, and in a way it is. However, some scholars have found Tolkien's defense of recovery strangely inconsistent with his own work. For example, Roger King remarks that, while Tolkien implies that Faërie provides a means for recovering essential moral virtues, *The Lord of the Rings* does not provide the reader with a clear moral standpoint.[2] However, this is mistaken on two counts. First, it is hard to see how Tolkien's *Lord of the Rings* does not provide moral qualities. Virtues of peace, long-suffering, perseverance, are all key to the developing plot of *The Lord of the Rings* and of the character evolution, in particular, of the hobbits. Qualities of love, forgiveness, and friendship, permeate Tolkien's work, and not only his masterpiece. Thus, other Tolkien scholars have stressed the virtues evident in Tolkien's works. Second, by focusing on the recovering of morality, King remains largely unaware of the deeper theological implications of Tolkien's notion of recovery. For the object of recovery is not first or foremost that of morality but that of "things lost," including our familiarity with the world—whether moral, aesthetic, or theological. For example, recovery, not limited to moral

---

1. Milbank, *Chesterton and Tolkien as Theologians*, xiii.
2. King, "Recovery, Escape, Consolation," 44–45.

values, is at the heart of Gandalf's farewell speech to Aragorn announcing that this new reign would mark the beginning of the Age of Men.[3]

Recovery has been fulfilled through victory over Sauron—over evil itself. As a consequence, everything seems to be included in the recovery process about to begin, a process that will reach as far as the Shire. It would be a complete misrepresentation to take Gandalf's proclamation of recovery to include only the moral or sociopolitical dimensions. It encompasses everything in Middle-earth, and as such, recovery is truly holistic.

This, however, does not say much about the means of recovery. On a superficial level, we see that Faërie is, of course, the means of recovery. That is all well and good, but not nearly specific enough. More specifically, to Tolkien, fairy-stories are not the only, not even the primary, means of recovering a clear view. To him, "fairy-stories are not the only means of recovery, or prophylactic against loss. Humility is enough. And there is (especially for the humble) *Mooreeffoc*, or Chestertonian Fantasy."[4] Humility is enough because it relies on the quality of the observer, the quality of the reader, the wanderer in the Perilous Realm. In Faërie, one does not let his human view of the world direct all his knowledge and actions. Humility is the main means of recovery because it provides the humble with a vision from above. And thus, we can say that Faërie is by nature the land of the humble. "Mythopoeia" verbalizes this very conclusion by the repetition of the exhortation "blessed are the timid hearts." By this devotional repetition, Tolkien establishes a relation between the blessedness of those of simple heart in the Sermon on the Mount and the "joy and sorrow" of those walking in Faërie.

This is what Tolkien expressed in "Mythopoeia," though with the very distinct tone, reminiscent of the Beatitudes, as already noted: "Blessed are the timid hearts that evil hate / that quail in its shadow, and yet shut the gate."[5] These two lines are probably deliberately ambiguous regarding the object of the recovery, the object that is clearly *seen*. These lines have a double meaning, and either the object is nature itself, that is creation, or it is human nature. Even in the context of "Mythopoeia," it is difficult to decide. In either sense, however, it is clear enough that recovery means the restoration of the original nature of creation, a recovery of the nature of how things were before the fall. It is the recovery

3. LoTR, III.6.v, 269.

4. OFS, 68.

5. Tolkien, "Mythopoeia," lines 81–82, in *Tree and Leaf*, 88.

of God's creation. In *The Ball and the Cross*, Chesterton says that the fall, the breaking of the communion with God, is the demonstration of the unique paradoxical nature of humankind. We must realize, proclaims Chesterton, that man is a "contradiction in terms"; on earth, always between blessing and curse.[6]

This "contradiction" that is man is seen in estrangement, a recurrent theme in Tolkien's works. One can think, of course, of the partial estrangement between the Elves, more particularly the Noldor, and the Valar after the events leading to the exile of the sons of Fëanor and most of the Noldor from Valinor. This loss, sung by the Elves, is largely shared by most of the peoples of Middle-earth. Michael Tomko reminds us that every single community of Middle-earth is "marked by a sense of loss or failing off, a dim awareness, either strongly or weakly felt, of the fragility of this borrowed time, and a sense of fatigue to face or change its fate."[7] This sense of fate often encountered and experienced by the characters, and thus by the reader, is embodied in the desire of Men to recover what they believe to be their lost share: immortality. This is demonstrated in one of the most fascinating parts of Tolkien's unpublished papers, the "Athrabeth Finrod ah Andreth" ("The Debate of Finrod and Andreth"), in which an elf and a woman debate death, this ultimate human predicament.[8] We will not discuss further the complexities of this debate, but simply point out that Andreth, the woman, strongly believes that, at one point in the history of Middle-earth, Men had lost their initial gift, one similar to the one given to the Elves by Ilúvatar.

We understand now how fairy-stories can convey this power of recovery. Recovery is possible because Faërie itself is a fruit of the imaginative power, and imagination provides the possibility of sub-creation. However, Tolkien also affirms that Chestertonian fantasy has limited power because recovery is its only mark.[9] To view the fantastic in the familiar is but a first step towards true fairy-story. While limited, this type of Fantasy can still have a valid function. In fact, "Tolkien said that recovery is possible in part by rediscovering tradition through fantasy."[10] This Recovery of tradition and mythology is essential to the power of fairy-stories and to Tolkienian Faërie.

6. See Chesterton, *The Ball and the Cross*, 10–11.

7. Tomko, "'An Age Comes On,'" 215.

8. MR, 303–66.

9. OFS, 68.

10. Smith, "Tolkien's Catholic Imagination," 83.

Escape and Faërie

In chapter 12, we have explained Tolkien's use of Escape as a key element to define Faërie. We had concluded that, in Tolkien's view, there can be no myth without Faërie, like there can be no language without myth. The Escape we find through language and myth is a door to Faërie. While we have to distinguish the manner in which Escape is a function of language and myth, this distinction is partly artificial—though necessary. We have seen *Smith of Wootton Major* as an example of the deep relationship between Escape and myth. But we cannot stop here, because Smith does enter Faery. That is essential to the story. In fact, Shippey argues that, in "Wootton Major," Tolkien "defends the real-world utility of fantasy; insists that fantasy and faith are in harmony as visions of a higher world; hopes for a revival of both in a future in which the Nokeses of the world (the materialists and misologists) will have less power."[11] Discovering Faery also leads Smith to touch deathlessness, even though he himself will not participate in the nature of Faery. This ultimate Escape, as Tolkien calls it, is the essence of Faery's embodied story.

Escape, the second function of fairy-stories, serves to distinguish between permanent and fleeting things. Escape, allied to true vision, recovery, provides the means to see truly what is permanent and what is not. Escape living out of imagination (Faërie) serves to identify things "supposed to stay," but soon to be replaced. To explain the contrast between permanent and impermanent things, Tolkien mentions the example of allegedly permanent electric lamps—reminiscent of Chesterton's example in his play *Magic*.[12] They are merely "insignificant and transient." While they certainly represent the march of Science, the 'electric street-lamp" do not represent something impermanent. They are subject to the evolution of science, and subject to the whims of society. Tolkien's comment on the "electric street-lamps" pursues further: "These lamps may be excluded from the tale simply because they are bad lamps; and it is possible that one of the lessons to be learnt from the story is the realization of this fact."[13] The connection with Chesterton is highlighted by Tolkien himself: "Long ago Chesterton truly remarked that, as soon as he heard that anything 'had come to stay,' he knew that it would be very soon

---

11. Shippey, *J. R. R. Tolkien*, 303.

12. See Chesterton, *Magic*, 17.

13. OFS, 70.

replaced—indeed regarded as pitiably obsolete and shabby."[14] Escape is escape from the ugliness, the rawness, the inferiority of the "Robot Age," into the world, real as it should be. In doing so, escape prevents us from being slaves to ever-changing passions.[15]

The opposition between truly permanent things and those apparently permanent is necessary only to the critics. They rely on this opposition to pretend the apparent things are the truly permanent ones. But for Tolkien this is not necessarily the case: the things seen might well be the impermanent ones. What we need is a way to "escape" the impermanence of things which are seen. Thus, the function of escape, a very positive one indeed, is also a proof of humility, as it is for recovery. For Tolkien, true escapism functions as a safeguard against an idolatrous and fateful view of the world. Not everything within the world is inexorable; not all that is found in the world was meant to be. The true escapist lives the permanence of things in a constantly moving world, because he has first recovered a correct view of the world. He has seen the essence of things. The true escapist stands on firm ground because he stands on truly permanent and unmovable ground, and not on his own passing "fashion."

Tolkien further affirms that the function of escape is connected to another desire "as ancient as the Fall," that of conversing with other beings (beasts, etc.), to be in communion with God's creation. Here, Tolkien's theory of fairy-story takes another theological turn, and reaches back to a pre-lapsarian state when we were not at war with the rest of creation.[16] Fairy-stories would provide the means for recovering a unity of relationships. Elves and Dwarves will be reconciled, Hobbits and Elves will depart for Tol Eressëa, and severed kingdoms like Arnor and Gondor will be reunited.

This Escape towards restoration extends beyond the kingdoms of the Free races. Faërie's Escape leads us to, Tolkien writes, the last escape, "the Great Escape: the Escape from Death."[17] This, Tolkien says, is the genuine escape or "fugitive" spirit. It is the final escape from "hunger, thirst, poverty, pain, sorrow, injustice, death."[18] This final meaning of Escape is also deeply theological. In fact, this Great Escape has intense value for Tolkien

14. OFS, 70.

15. OFS, 70.

16. OFS, 70nG, 83.

17. OFS, 74. See also the influence of George MacDonald, for whom death is the most present theme in fairy-stories. See also OFS, 75.

18. OFS, 73.

only because the world is not as it should be. It really is a world of sorrow and suffering, and the final Escape from such a world, towards Consolation, is no desertion. That is an essential part of Tolkien's fairy-story.

This sounds clear enough; however, the question remains whether escape from death is positive or negative. In fact, it could be both, for death can either be seen as an escape out of this world of sin and suffering, or it can be seen as the final escape toward man's true home. The answer might be both, and it is unclear where Tolkien would find the ultimate answer. On the one hand, death is certainly an end and a beginning: the end of a life of sorrow and pain and the beginning of a life of pure bliss. On the other hand, escape is also escape from ultimate death; it is the redemption from death, the hope of eternal life.[19] In defining the role of Escape in this way, Tolkien begins leading his readers towards the great theological ending of his essay.

Escape is thus a holistic view of the world. It transforms language, myth, and Faërie. It allows creatures to fully exercise their sub-creative abilities and fully participate in God-given imagination. We thus "make still by the law in which we're made," concludes Tolkien in the poem "Mythopoeia." Escape, is the entrance door into the world of Faërie, a world that is the true home. And, at last opening the door of a long forgotten home, Escape finds Consolation, the third function of fairy-stories, waiting.

Consolation and Faërie

We have already explained that the eucatastrophe does not deny *dyscatastrophe*, sorrow and failure, but transforms it. True fairy-stories do not overlook the existence and power of sorrow and failure, rather, they presuppose them. In fact, only in the face of true sorrow, and even true, but not ultimate, failure, can eucatastrophe take its full meaning. If there is denial in eucatastrophe, it is the denial of "universal final defeat and in so far is *evangelium*, giving a fleeting glimpse of Joy, Joy beyond the walls of the world, poignant as grief."[20] The finale of *The Lord of the Rings* testifies to this melancholic ending, and Frodo's concluding remarks echo

19. See the *Athrabeth Finrod ah Andreth*, "The Debate of Finrod and Andreth." In this debate Finrod, an Elf-lord, and Andreth, a human, debate the contrasting fate of deathless Elves and Men, bound to die. HoME, X:301–66.

20. OFS, 75.

Tolkien: the Shire has not been saved *for himself*. For Frodo, the Shire has been lost, but it is recovered in Sam, who is Frodo's heir.[21] The Fairy-story will continue, through Frodo's heir, but sub-created consolation still awaits completion.

Despite the continuing sufferings, consolation reaches beyond the grip of sorrow to encompass the final hope for the restoration of Arda. This hope is characteristic of the "Athrabeth Finrod ah Andreth" debate already mentioned. Towards the end of the debate, Finrod clearly states that his true consolation comes from knowing that Arda will be transformed. It is not merely a return to its innocent state. It will be "a third thing and a greater, and yet the same."[22] In the midst of the sufferings of Arda, there is hope, Estel, which is not wishful thinking but is guided by Eru himself. Indeed, as the Athrabeth debate makes very clear, Estel is dependent upon Eru's action of restoration. Estel is thus dependent upon Oienkarmë Eruo (The One's perpetual Production) "which might be rendered by 'God's Management of the Drama.'"[23] Hope lies in Eru's Music and Vision to which he and only he, gives existence. If Elves, Men, and even the Ainur cannot produce hope, it is because they live in the perspective of limited knowledge and being, different from Eru: "Or again, since Eru is for ever free, maybe he made no Music and showed no Vision beyond a certain point. Beyond that point we cannot see or know, until by our own roads we come there, Valar or Eldar or Men."[24] True consolation, then, comes from knowing that mere healing is not the final word. That would entail the possibility of the world being marred again, as it was constantly so when Melkor was "undoing" the sub-creation of the Valar. True consolation comes from knowing that beyond "healing" lies "recreation." Healing is provisional. Restoration is definitive.

In a little-known piece, "Laws and Customs," Manwë makes a very similar declaration regarding Arda's consoling hope: "For Arda unmarred hath two aspects or senses. The first is the Unmarred that they [the Eldar] discern in the Marred . . . : This is the ground upon which Hope is built. The second is the Unmarred that shall be: that is, to speak according to Time in which they have their being, the Arda Healed, which shall be greater and more fair than the first, because of the Marring: this is the

21. LoTR, III.6.ix, 1006.
22. MR, 318.
23. MR, 329.
24. MR, 319.

Hope that sustaineth."[25] This is the Elvish hope, a telling embodiment of Tolkien's notion of consolation as a mark of Faërie. In fact, one of the distinctive of Christian hope and consolation is that what has been one day "marred" will eventually be "restored." As the great neo-Thomist scholar Etienne Gilson remarked: "The true Catholic position consists in maintaining that nature was created good, that it has been wounded, but that it can be at least partially healed by grace if God so wishes."[26] This grand finale of the Drama of Arda is by no means despair and destruction, contrary to the Elvish idea of a catastrophic ending.[27]

Tolkien closes this discussion of consolation with the fairy tale "The Black Bull of Norroway," reprinted in Andrew Lang's *Blue Fairy Book*, a good example of a "joyous and sudden turn." In quoting only the last part of the fairy-tale—"He heard and turned to her,"[28] that stands as the "turn" of the tale—Tolkien indirectly refers to the joyous ending: "And they were married, and he and she are living happily till this day, for aught I ken."[29] Tolkien's call is for fairy-stories to resonate with the *evangelium*. His call to mythopoeic writers is to make primary and secondary worlds sound forth in unison the anthem of the *evangelium*. In true fairy-stories we hear the blast of the trumpet, the triumphant trumpet-call announcing the returning king, the birth and resurrection of the "once and future king."[30] Consolation, joy, is the mark of true fairy-stories, it is their seal. The reader, or the mythopoeic writer, who breaks open the magic seal of fairy-stories lets joy fly out and fill the earth. Fairy-story is Pandora's Joy.

The Recovery dimension of true fairy-stories was put into rhyme by Tolkien in the famous poem "Mythopoeia." Concerned primarily with myth, as we have already seen, the poem nevertheless defines the nature of fairy-stories. Of important significance in "Mythopoeia" is the repetition of the expression "timid hearts," which obviously refers us back to the Sermon on the Mount, and to Jesus' description of the coming kingdom and the vision of the redeemed. This triple blessing carries connotations of beatific vision, the *visio beatifica*, which the Christian is to acquire when restored to complete fellowship with God. In the primary

25. MR, 245.

26. Gilson, *Christianity and Philosophy*, 21.

27. MR, 342.

28. OFS, 76. From Jacobs, *More English Fairy Tales*, 25.

29. Lang, *The Blue Fairy Book*, 398.

30. To borrow the title of White's *The Once and Future King*.

world, only the *theologia viatorum* is available to the human mind. However, the secondary world with its quality of recovery and escape can serve as a provisional window into the beatific vision. Fantasy can thus, in a way, convey an analogical beatific vision through its spiritual nature. First, Faërie is the expression of imagination's freedom from the primary world resulting in the coming to life of a secondary world in which the kingdom can already be seen and enjoyed. Second, Faërie is the spiritual demonstration that the "hallowing" of human nature also affects the imaginative process.

Theological Faërie

Recovery, Escape, and Consolation. These are, for Tolkien, the three functions of fairy-stories. With these three words, we discover the true nature of fairy-stories. But we also discover more clearly the nature and beauty of Faërie. The Perilous Land is the land of real Vision, a Perilous Escape which can only lead us to true Consolation. This led Tolkien to the great theological conclusion of the essay "On Fairy-Stories." Fairy-stories can only be nourished and formed through the greatest fairy-stories of all: the Eucatastrophe of human history, the incarnation of Christ. This can only be so because, to go back to Tolkien's threefold functions of fairy-stories, this ultimate coming of God is the supreme embodiment of Recovery, Escape and Consolation.

First, in the incarnation Man finds the supreme recovery of vision. The original loss is abrogated, but not the legends, not the stories. In the archetypal fairy-story of Christ, legends are "hallowed," metaphysically recovered.[31] Tolkien embodied this "hallowing" of legends in his mythological corpus, most notably in the figure of Elbereth. Tolkien's three-tier definition of Faërie is crystalized in the poem "Snow-white! Snow-white! O Lady clear!," an elven hymn to Elbereth very similar to the aerlinn poem "A Elbereth Gilthoniel."[32]

The poem celebrates Elbereth Varda Elentári the "Starkindler" Queen of the Valar, unseen in *The Lord of the Rings*, but called upon in dark times. The figure of Elbereth is so central because she stands as a symbol of the struggle against Melkor's darkness. She was after all the first to see Melkor's mind, for she knew his mind and rejected what she

---

31. OFS, 78.

32. LoTR, I.i.3, 88–89.

saw.[33] As such, she represents the hope for consolation. In fact, she might stand as the only figure of eschatological consolation—taken in a theological sense. The invocation of Elbereth is, as Richard Purtill puts it, "the clearest statement that Tolkien has given about religion in *The Lord of the Rings* trilogy, and characteristically it is an oblique reference in a series of remarks on Elvish philology."[34] Being a theological statement, it is fitting that the reference to Elbereth would also serve as an example of Tolkien's theological Faërie.

Second, through the Evangelium, God has provided the ultimate Escape from death. In the coming plenitude of the Evangelium, there will be no condescension to the small hobbits by the Big folks. In fact, "in God's kingdom," adds Tolkien, "the presence of the greatest does not depress the small."[35] *Third*, the "Birth of Christ is the eucatastrophe of Man's history."[36] It is the final consolation because in him is restored all that was originally given to Man. Through his thomist sub-creation, Tolkien shows us that in our stories, the human desire for Recovery, Escape and Consolation is embodied. That is the reason for the aesthetic persistence of the longing for fairy-stories. With Tolkien's discussion of the three marks of a true fairy-story we finally reach his true theological vision. If Tolkien's Thomist fantasy was somewhat invisible in our investigation of language, it became clearer in our exploration of the nature of myth and the function of imagination. With the nature of fairy-stories, it has fully blossomed.

Conclusion

Our thesis in this study has been that Tolkien's anthropological, philological, and mythological perspectives come together as one theory of Faërie. This is manifest when the latter is endowed by Tolkien with essential theological virtues. Tolkien best expresses this line of thought in his epilogue to the essay "On Fairy-Stories," in which he emphatically stresses the Christian nature of fairy-stories. He does so in the initial statement that "the peculiar quality of the 'joy' in successful Fantasy can thus be explained as a sudden glimpse of the underlying reality or truth,"

33. S, 26.
34. Purtill, *Lord of the Elves and Eldils*, 111.
35. OFS, 78.
36. OFS, 78.

defending again the close connection between fairy-stories, reality, and truth. In this context, reality and truth must be understood as referring to the essential reality and truth of the Christian story, that is, the Incarnation. Because true fairy-stories answer questions about truth and the nature of reality, and because they bring new wholeness into what is seen in and of the world, they function as a vehicle for the gospel of God's revelation in our created order. This explains why joy, this natural characteristic of fairy-stories, is *par excellence* the joy of the Gospels and the joy of stories. There is an analogical relationship between the joy of the fairy-stories and that of the Christian gospel. They both take root in the same primary truth.[37] Tolkien concludes: "The Birth of Christ is the eucatastrophe of Man's history. The Resurrection is the eucatastrophe of the story of the Incarnation. This story begins and ends in joy."[38] This essential Christian nature of true fairy-stories is further highlighted by Tolkien's conclusion that fairy-stories testify to God's entering history to "hallow" fairy-stories. The Incarnation is the framework of true fairy-stories because it is the divine embodiment of fairy-story.

This further explains Tolkien's general conclusion that the Christian gospel includes within itself the very essence of any true fairy-story. Therefore, all stories disclose this essential quality of true fairy-stories, that is, the *evangelium* itself. In the primary world, the secondary world lives on. As Tolkien said, "Art has been verified. God is the Lord, of angels, and of men—and of elves. Legend and History have met and fused."[39] Faërie, fairy-stories, the secondary world, live out of the renewal of the true fairy-story, and move in the depth of Christ's redeeming work. Renewed in mind and spirit, the myth-maker sub-creates a true fairy-story; and the true fairy-story is nourished by its maker's Christian faith, not because of a "proselytizing" motivation, but simply because of a natural and essential quality of fairy-stories. The secondary world of Faërie is also a world of *evangelium*. Fairy-stories hymn the *Gloria* in God's kingdom.

37. OFS, 78.
38. OFS, 78.
39. OFS, 78.

Conclusion

But from the top of that tower
the man had been able
to look out upon the sea.

—J. R. R. TOLKIEN, *The Monsters and the Critics*

HAVE WE REACHED THE highest peak in Tolkien's realm? Does Tolkien's overarching Thomism provide a unifying view of his achievements? This wanderer believes so. But the best stories are those whose endings still leave room for the reader's imagination. And the best arguments are those that leave room for other, and hopefully better, arguments. As Tolkien wrote at the end of *Roverandom*: "I haven't told you all their arguments, of course; it was long and complicated, as it often is when both sides are right."[1] This book does not pretend to have looked at, or taken account of, all the works written on Tolkien. Nor does it pretend to have covered all aspects of Tolkien's life and works. In fact, the best books do not present all the arguments but leave some space open for readers to explore further on their own. Such is also the case here: many studies quoted in this work have presented good and solid arguments though we have not

1. Tolkien, *Roverandom*, 89.

been concerned with evaluating all of them. The reader can continue his or her own adventure. The objective of this present study has been to look for a uniting element to Tolkien's theory of Faërie.

At the outset of our adventure, we set out for the point from which we could gain an all-encompassing look at Tolkien's theory of fairy-story. The first chapter provided a description of the social, academic, literary, and religious atmosphere in which Tolkien grew up and had his literary being, with a specific interest in his Roman Catholic and Thomist connection. His taste as a writer, literary critic, and as a Roman Catholic believer, is informed by his loves, the books he breathed, and the faith with which he was nourished.

Throughout the three stages of our journey—language, myth, and Faërie—we have encountered the same signposts leading to our destination: our work discloses something about the Creator-God and about our own human nature. This basic line of thought is thoroughly Thomist and provides the theological framework through which Tolkien's overall theory of Faërie should be presented. This theological framework takes its inspiration from the crucial observation that in all the abilities that make us human, our imaginative creativity, our gift for language, and our aesthetic sensibility, there is always present the one that is "never absent and never named,"[2] the "Writer of the Story."[3] The divine origin of our human capacities in no way negates, for Tolkien's Thomism, the place and role of human agency, or of Tolkien's diverse and numerous influences. Myths remain a human endeavor; stories remain dependent on the writing abilities and imagination of the writer. But Tolkien, a Thomist fantasist, was convinced that the truth that could be conveyed in Faërie was the ultimate consequence of God's creative act.[4]

The theological nature of Faërie thus appears clearly and is rooted in a sacramental Catholic view of the world. If everything takes its source from God, then Faërie itself—as a "perilous realm" and a human imaginative sub-creative ability—is rooted in God. Thus we can conclude that Tolkien stood squarely with the other Inklings, and most of the Catholic tradition to which he belonged, in affirming that "Christianity does not abolish *mythopoeia* or poetic knowledge, but makes possible a new era of 'baptized mythology,' mythology that is no longer religion but 'fairy

2. L, 253.

3. L, 252.

4. Tolkien spoke of the "Finger of God, as the one wholly free Will and Agent." L, 204.

tale,' an indispensable poetic evocation of a great mystery that is still unfolding within the world."[5] This unfolding mystery is for Tolkien best embodied in Faërie, which displays the essential qualities of God's revelation, namely, "recovery," "escape," and "consolation." But Faërie, or fairy-tales, does not only represent an attempt to embody these three functions. It represents the imaginative literary embodiment of the onto-logical essence of history: Christ's incarnation. Tolkien's theory of Faërie now appears to be constructed with care and complexity. The complexity involves several layers of interwoven influences and interests. As a first layer, Tolkien's Faërie involves personal interests: among them, Anglo-Saxon and Nordic mythologies, language invention (see *A Secret Vice*), and fantasy literature. This superficial "layer" is the most obvious one, the easiest to investigate, and has led to many fascinating studies. But it would be a mistake to stop our investigation here.

That is why, as a second layer, Tolkien's Faërie has been studied in conversation with the academic, social, and philosophical debates of his day. These conversational elements include mythological and linguistic debates regarding the origin, meaning, and interrelation of, particularly, language and myth. On this level, Tolkien studies have provided fascinat-ing and deeply researched works. As such, they have achieved great ma-turity in their richness and diversity. These studies also demonstrate the difficulty of finding a center of Tolkien's theory, the one dimension that would bring together the three main dimensions of his theory of Faërie. If particular aspects such as language, mythology, and the powers of the imagination have at times each found a central place in Tolkien, none of these seems to be finally a uniting dimension.

At this point, a third, foundational layer of influences can be dis-cerned. This final foundation is a fundamentally theological one. Again, this does not entail that Tolkien was a theologian. However, it does mean that Tolkien's thought was informed by a particular theology, piety, and Christian tradition: English Roman Catholicism nourished by a Thomist, and specifically Newmanian, theology. This is even more important when we consider that this theological tradition had much to say on is-sues regarding language, myth (and truth), and imagination. Thus we reach an important conclusion: Tolkien's theory of fantasy is essentially a theological one. As a Roman Catholic influenced by the teaching of St. Thomas, Tolkien presents us with a very distinctive theory of fantasy—a

---

5. Caldecott, *The Power of the Ring*, 110.

theory in which the central theme is the relation between the Creator and the human artist. The very centrality of the nature of the God-man relationship in Tolkien gives Faërie its essential perilous, hopeful, and wonder-full qualities.

This vision, Tolkien crystalized in a theory of Faërie deeply informed by his theology. As Tolkien wrote in his famous essay on fairy-stories, man is directed towards the redeeming of all he is, including in his imagination.[6] As Newman puts it, Christ "came into the world to regenerate it in Himself, to make a new beginning, to be the beginning of the creation of God, to gather together in one, and recapitulate all things in Himself."[7] Because the Author of the Drama lives both inside and outside our world, Faërie can be the living witness to his presence. Because Tolkien's God is Lord of Elves, Dwarves and Men, of Hobbits and Ents, he can infuse the world with the joyous aesthetic sense of the eucatastrophe. Such was Tolkien's deepest conviction, which led him to embody his personal view into a fantasy corpus that ranks as one of the most influential in history.

Our adventure ends here. There is, of course, still before us the journey home downwards from the summit of Tolkien's Thomist Faërie. This, however, is a journey each of us needs to take alone. For a little while more, we can look over Tolkien's realm. And then go back to our Primary World. In his unpublished preface to George MacDonald's *The Golden Key*, Tolkien wrote: "I think it would be better just to leave you and George MacDonald alone for a while for a walk or a talk together and let you find first what you could do for yourselves with your own eyes and ears."[8] It is time to do the same and let Tolkien's works speak for themselves. Reader, contemplate Faërie.

6. OFS, 79.

7. Newman, *Sermons*, 61.

8. "Tolkien's Draft Introduction to "The Golden Key," in Tolkien, *Smith of Wootton Major*, 72.

Bibliography

Works by Tolkien

Tolkien, J. R. R. *The Adventures of Tom Bombadil*. London: George Allen & Unwin, 1962.

———. *Ancrene Wisse: The English Text of the Ancrene Riwle*. London: Oxford University Press, 1962.

———. *The Annotated Hobbit*. Edited by Douglas A. Anderson. Boston: Houghton Mifflin, 1996.

———. "Appendix 1: The Name Nodens." In *Report on the Excavation of the Prehistoric, Roman, and Post-Roman Site in Lydney Park, Gloucestershire*, 132–37. Oxford: University Press for the Society of Antiquaries, 1932.

———. *Beowulf and the Critics*. Edited by Michael Drout. Tempe: Arizona Center for Medieval and Renaissance Studies, 2002.

———. *Beowulf: A Translation and Commentary, together with Sellic Spell*. Edited by Christopher Tolkien. Boston: Houghton Mifflin, 2014.

———. *The Book of Lost Tales*. Edited by Christopher Tolkien. The History of Middle Earth 1. Boston: Houghton Mifflin, 1983.

———. *The Book of Lost Tales*. Edited by Christopher Tolkien. The History of Middle Earth 2. Boston: Houghton Mifflin, 1984.

———. "Chaucer as a Philologist: *The Reeve's Tale*." *Transactions of the Philological Society* 33 (1934) 1–70.

———. *The Children of Húrin*. Edited by Christopher Tolkien. Boston: Houghton Mifflin, 2007.

———. "The Devil's Coach-Horses." *The Review of English Studies* 1 (1925) 331–36.

———. "On Fairy-Stories." In *Essays Presented to Charles Williams*, edited by C. S. Lewis, 38–89. London: Oxford University Press, 1947.

———. *The Fall of Arthur*. Edited by Christopher Tolkien. London: HarperCollins, 2013.

———. *The Fellowship of the Ring: Being the First Part of The Lord of the Rings*. London: HarperCollins, 1997.

———. *Finn and Hengest: The Fragment and the Episode*. Edited by Alan Bliss. Boston: Houghton Mifflin, 1983.

———. "Goblin Feet." In *Oxford Poetry 1915*, edited by G. D. H. Cole and T. W. Earp, 64–65. Oxford: Blackwell, 1915.

———. *The History of Middle Earth Index*. Edited by Christopher Tolkien. London: HarperCollins, 2002.

———. *The Hobbit: There and Back Again*. New York: Ballantine, 1982.

———. "Holy Maidenhood." *The Times Literary Supplement* 110 (1923) 281.

———. "The Homecoming of Beorhtnoth Beorhthelm's Son." *Essays and Studies* 6 (1953) 1–18.

———. "The Lay of Aotrou and Itroun." *The Welsh Review* 4 (1945) 254–66.

———. *The Lays of Beleriand*. Edited by Christopher Tolkien. The History of Middle Earth 3. Boston: Houghton Mifflin, 1985.

———. *The Legend of Sigurd and Gudrún*. Edited by Christopher Tolkien. Boston: Houghton Mifflin Harcourt, 2009.

———. *The Letters of J. R. R. Tolkien*. Edited by Humphrey Carpenter and Christopher Tolkien. Boston: Houghton Mifflin, 2000.

———. *The Lost Road and Other Writings*. Edited by Christopher Tolkien. The History of Middle Earth 5. Boston: Houghton Mifflin, 1987.

———. *Middle English "Losenger": Sketch of an Etymological and Semantic Enquiry*. Paris: Les Belles Lettres, 1953.

———. "A Middle English Vocabulary." In *Fourteenth Century Verse and Prose*, by Kenneth Sisam. Oxford: Clarendon, 1962.

———. *The Monsters and the Critics, and Other Essays*. London: HarperCollins, 1997.

———. *Morgoth's Ring: Being the First Part of the Later Silmarillion*. Edited by Christopher Tolkien. The History of Middle Earth 10. Boston: Houghton Mifflin, 1993.

———. *Mr. Bliss*. Boston: Houghton Mifflin, 1983.

———. *The Nature of Middle-earth*. Edited by Carl F. Hostetter. Boston: Houghton Mifflin Harcourt, 2021.

———. *The Old English Exodus, Text, Translation, and Commentary*. Edited by Joan Turville-Petre. Oxford: Clarendon, 1981.

———. *On Fairy Stories: Expanded Edition with Commentary and Notes*. Edited by Verlyn Flieger and Douglas Anderson. London: HarperCollins, 2008.

———. "The Oxford English School." *The Oxford Magazine* 48 (1930) 778–82.

———. *The Peoples of Middle Earth*. Edited by Christopher Tolkien. The History of Middle Earth 12. Boston: Houghton Mifflin, 1996.

———. "Philology: General Works." *The Year's Work in English Studies* 4 (1925) 20–37.

———. "Philology: General Works." *The Year's Work in English Studies* 5 (1926) 26–65.

———. "Philology: General Works." *The Year's Work in English Studies* 6 (1927) 32–66.

———. Preface to *The Ancrene Riwle (the Corpus Ms.: Ancrene Wisse)*. London: Burns & Oates, 1955.

———. "Research v. Literature." *The Sunday Times*, April 14, 1946.

———. *The Return of the King: Being the Third Part of the Lord of the Rings*. London: HarperCollins, 1997.

———. *The Return of the Shadow: Being the First Part of the History of the Lord of the Rings*. Edited by Christopher Tolkien. The History of Middle Earth 6. Boston: Houghton Mifflin, 1988.

————. *Roverandom.* Boston: Houghton Mifflin, 1998.

————. *Sauron Defeated: Being the Fourth Part of the History of the Lord of the Rings.* Edited by Christopher Tolkien. The History of Middle Earth 9. Boston: Houghton Mifflin, 1992.

————. *The Shaping of Middle Earth.* Edited by Christopher Tolkien. The History of Middle Earth 4. Boston: Houghton Mifflin, 1986.

————. "Sigelwara Land, Part 1." *Medium Aevum* 1 (1932) 183–96.

————. "Sigelwara Land, Part 2." *Medium Aevum* 3 (1934) 95–111.

————. *The Silmarillion.* Edited by Christopher Tolkien. Boston: Houghton Mifflin, 2004.

————. *Sir Gawain and the Green Knight.* Edited by E. V. Gordon and Norman Davis. 2nd ed. Oxford: Clarendon, 1967.

————. *Sir Orfeo.* Oxford: Academic Copying Office, 1944.

————. *Smith of Wootton Major.* Edited by Verlyn Flieger. London: HarperCollins, 2005.

————. "Some Contributions to Middle-English Lexicography." *The Review of English Studies* 1 (1925) 210–15.

————. *Tales from the Perilous Realm.* London: HarperCollins, 1998.

————. *The Treason of Isengard: Being the Second Part of the History of The Lord of the Rings.* Edited by Christopher Tolkien. The History of Middle Earth 7. Boston: Houghton Mifflin, 1989.

————. *Tree and Leaf.* London: HarperCollins, 2001.

————. *The Two Towers, Being the Second Part of the Lord of the Rings.* London: HarperCollins, 1997.

————. *Unfinished Tales of Númenor and Middle-earth.* Edited by Christopher Tolkien. 3 vols. Boston: Houghton Mifflin, 1980.

————. *The War of the Jewels: Being the Second Part of the Later Silmarillion.* Edited by Christopher Tolkien. The History of Middle Earth 11. Boston: Houghton Mifflin, 1994.

————. *The War of the Ring: Being the Third Part of the History of The Lord of the Rings.* Edited by Christopher Tolkien. The History of Middle Earth 8. Boston: Houghton Mifflin, 1990.

————. "'Words of Joy': Five Catholic Prayers in Quenya (Part Two)." *Vinyar Tengwar* 44 (2002) 5–20.

Works on Tolkien

Anderson, Douglas A., ed. *The Annotated Hobbit: Revised and Expanded Edition.* Boston: Houghton Mifflin, 2002.

Auden, W. H. "At the End of the Quest, Victory." *The New York Times,* January 22, 1956. https://archive.nytimes.com/www.nytimes.com/books/01/02/11/specials/tolkien-return.html.

————. "The Hero Is a Hobbit." *The New York Times,* October 31, 1954. https://archive.nytimes.com/www.nytimes.com/books/01/02/11/specials/tolkien-fellowship.html.

————. "The Quest Hero." In *Understanding "The Lord of the Rings": The Best of Tolkien Criticism,* edited by Rose A. Zimbardo and Neil D. Isaacs, 40–61. Boston: Houghton Mifflin Harcourt, 2005.

Barber, Dorothy K. "The Meaning of *The Lord of the Rings.*" In *Tolkien and the Critics*, edited by Neil Isaacs and Rose A. Zimbardo, 38–50. Notre Dame, IN: University of Notre Dame Press, 1968.

Birzer, Bradley J. *J. R. R. Tolkien's Sanctifying Myth: Understanding Middle Earth.* Wilmington: ISI, 2002.

Bradley, Marion Zimmer. *Men, Halflings, & Hero Worship.* Baltimore: T-K Graphics, 1966.

Caldecott, Stratford. *The Power of the Ring: The Spiritual Vision behind "The Lord of the Rings."* New York: Crossroad, 2005.

Caldecott, Stratford, et al. *Tolkien, Faërie et Christianisme.* Geneva: Ad Solem, 2002.

Candler, Peter. "Tolkien or Nietzsche, Philology and Nihilism." In *Tolkien among the Moderns*, edited by Ralph C. Wood, 95–130. Notre Dame, IN: University of Notre Dame Press, 2015.

Carpenter, Humphrey. *The Inklings: J. R. R. Tolkien, C. S. Lewis, Charles Williams, and Their Friends.* New York: Ballantine, 1981.

———. *J. R. R. Tolkien: A Biography.* London: HarperCollins, 1995.

Carter, Lin. *Tolkien: A Look behind "The Lord of the Rings."* New York: Ballantine, 1969.

Chance, Jane. *The Lord of the Rings: A Mythology for England.* Lexington: University Press of Kentucky, 2001.

———. *The Lord of the Rings: The Mythology of Power.* Lexington: University Press of Kentucky, 2001.

———, ed. *Tolkien and the Invention of Myth: A Reader.* Lexington: University Press of Kentucky, 2004.

Connolly, Sean. *Inklings of Heaven: C. S. Lewis and Eschatology.* Leominster: Gracewing, 2007.

Cox, John. "Tolkien's Platonic Fantasy." *Seven* 5 (1984) 53–69.

Davis, Howard. "*Ainulindale*: The Music of Creation." *Mythlore* 9 (1982) 6–10.

Doughan, David. "An Ethnically Cleansed Faërie? Tolkien and the Matter of Britain." *Mallorn* 32 (1995) 21–24.

Drout, Michael C., ed. *Beowulf and the Critics.* Tempe: Arizona Center for Medieval and Renaissance Studies, 2002.

———. "A Mythology for Anglo-Saxon England." In *J. R. R. Tolkien and the Invention of Myth*, edited by Jane Chance, 229–47. Lexington: University Press of Kentucky, 2004.

Eden, Bradford Lee. "The 'Music of the Spheres': Relationships between Tolkien's *The Silmarillion* and Medieval Cosmological and Religious Theory." In *Tolkien the Medievalist*, edited by Jane Chance, 183–93. New York: Routledge, 2003.

Fisher, Jason. Review of *Inside Language: Linguistic and Aesthetic Theory in Tolkien*, by Ross Smith. *Mythlore* 27 (2008) 172–76.

———, ed. *Tolkien and the Study of His Sources: Critical Essays.* Jefferson, NC: McFarland, 2011.

Fisher, Matthew. "Working at the Crossroads: Tolkien, St. Augustine, and the Beowulf-Poet." In *The Lord of the Rings, 1954–2004: Scholarship in Honor of Richard E. Blackwelder*, edited by Wayne G. Hammond and Christina Scull, 217–30. Milwaukee: Marquette University Press, 2006.

Flieger, Verlyn. *Interrupted Music: The Making of Tolkien's Mythology.* Kent, OH: Kent State University, 2005.

———. "J. R. R. Tolkien and the Matter of Britain." *Mythlore* 23 (2000) 47–59.

———. "Naming the Unnamable: The Neoplatonic 'One' in Tolkien's *Silmarillion*." In *Diakonia: Studies in Honor of Robert T. Meyer*, edited by Thomas Halton and Joseph P. Williman, 127–33. Washington, DC: Catholic University of America Press, 1986.

———. "Owen Barfield." In *The J. R. R. Tolkien Encyclopedia: Scholarship and Critical Assessment*, edited by Michael C. Drout, 50–51. New York: Routledge, 2007.

———. *A Question of Time: J. R. R. Tolkien's Road to Faërie*. Kent, OH: Kent State University, 1997.

———. *Splintered Light: Logos and Language in Tolkien's World*. Grand Rapids: Eerdmans, 2002.

Flieger, Verlyn, and Carl Hostetter, eds. *Tolkien's Legendarium*. Westport, CT: Greenwood, 2000.

Garth, John. *Tolkien, Exeter College, and the Great War*. Oxford: Exeter College, 2014.

———. *Tolkien and the Great War: The Threshold of Middle-earth*. Boston: Houghton Mifflin, 2003.

Giddings, Robert, ed. *J. R. R. Tolkien: This Far Land*. London: Vision, 1983.

Gilson, Christopher. "His Breath Was Taken Away: Tolkien, Barfield, and Elvish Diction." *Tolkien Studies* 14 (2017) 33–51.

Hammond, Wayne G., and Christina Scull, eds. *J. R. R. Tolkien: Artist & Illustrator*. Boston: Houghton Mifflin, 1995.

Hanks, D. Thomas, Jr. "Tolkien's 'Leaf by Niggle': A Blossom on the Tree of Tales." *Journal of Inklings Studies* 2 (2012) 23–48.

Hart, Trevor, and Ivan Khovacs, eds. *Tree of Tales: Tolkien, Literature, and Theology*. Waco, TX: Baylor University Press, 2007.

Harvey, David. *The Song of Middle-earth: J. R. R. Tolkien's Themes, Symbols, and Myths*. London: Allen & Unwin, 1985.

Helms, Randel. *Tolkien and the Silmarils*. Boston: Houghton Mifflin, 1981.

Higgins, Sørina, ed. *The Inklings and King Arthur: J. R. R. Tolkien, Charles Williams, C. S. Lewis, and Owen Barfield on the Matter of Britain*. Berkeley: Apocryphille, 2017.

Himes, Jonathan. "What J. R. R. Tolkien Really Did with the Sampo." *Mythlore* 22 (2000) 69–85.

Hostetter, Carl. "Languages Invented by Tolkien." In *J. R. R. Tolkien Encyclopedia: Scholarship and Critical Assessment,* edited by Michael D. C. Drout, 332–44. New York: Routledge, 2007.

Hutton, Ronald E. "The Pagan Tolkien." In *The Ring and the Cross: Christianity and the Lord of the Rings*, edited by Paul E. Kerry, 57–70. Madison, NJ: Fairleigh Dickinson University Press, 2011.

Isaacs, Neil D., and Rose A. Zimbardo, eds. *Tolkien and the Critics: Essays on J. R. R. Tolkien's "The Lord of the Rings."* Notre Dame, IN: University of Notre Dame Press, 1968.

Johnson, Kirstin. "Tolkien's Mythopoesis." In *Tree of Tales: Tolkien, Literature, and Theology*, edited by Trevor Hart and Ivan Khovacs, 25–38. Waco, TX: Baylor University Press, 2007.

Joosten, Michael. "Poetry in the Transmission Conceit of *The Silmarillion*." In *Tolkien's Poetry*, edited by Julian Eilman and Allan Turner, 153–62. Zurich: Walking Tree, 2013.

Kerry, Paul E. *The Ring and the Cross: Christianity and the Writings of J. R. R. Tolkien*. Madison, NJ: Fairleigh Dickinson University Press, 2000.

Kerry, Paul E., and Sandra Miesel, eds. *Light beyond All Shadow: Religious Experience in Tolkien's Work*. Madison, NJ: Fairleigh Dickinson University Press, 2011.

Kilby, Clyde. *Tolkien and "The Silmarillion."* Wheaton: Shaw, 1976.

King, Roger. "Recovery, Escape, Consolation: Middle-earth and the English Fairy Tale." In *J. R. R. Tolkien: This Far Land*, edited by Robert Giddings, 42–55. London: Vision, 1983.

Kocher, Paul. *Master of Middle-earth: The Fiction of J. R. R. Tolkien*. Boston: Houghton Mifflin, 1972.

Kotowski, Nathalie. "About Russian Translations of Tolkien's Works (Part Two)." *Vinyar Tengwar* 12 (1990) 18–20.

Lobdell, Jared, ed. *A Tolkien Compass*. LaSalle, IL: Open Court, 1975.

———. *The World of the Rings: Language, Religion, and Adventure in Tolkien*. Chicago: Open Court, 2004.

Madsen, Catherine. "'Light from an Invisible Lamp': Natural Religion in *The Lord of the Rings*." In *Tolkien and the Invention of Myth: A Reader*, edited by Jane Chance, 35–47. Lexington: University Press of Kentucky, 2004.

Martinez, Michael. "What Is the Munby Letter?" *Middle-earth Blog*, December 8, 2011. http://middle-earth.xenite.org/2011/12/08/what-is-the-munby-letter.

McIntosh, Jonathan. *The Flame Imperishable: Tolkien, St. Thomas, and the Metaphysics of Faerie*. Kettering, OH: Angelico, 2017.

Oser, Lee. *The Return of Christian Humanism: Chesterton, Eliot, Tolkien, and the Romance of History*. Columbia: University of Missouri Press, 2007.

Pearce, Joseph. *J. R. R. Tolkien: Man and Myth*. San Francisco: Ignatius, 1998.

———, ed. *Tolkien, a Celebration: Collected Writings on a Literary Legacy*. San Francisco: Ignatius, 1999.

Petty, Anne C. "Identifying England's Lönnrot." *Tolkien Studies* 1 (2004) 69–84.

Purtill, Richard L. *Lord of the Elves and Eldils*. San Francisco: Ignatius, 2006.

Rateliff, John D. *The History of "The Hobbit."* 2 vols. Boston: Houghton Mifflin, 2007.

Rutledge, Amelia A. "'Justice Is Not Healing': J. R. R. Tolkien's Pauline Construct in 'Finwë and Míriel.'" *Tolkien Studies* 9 (2012) 59–73.

Scull, Christina, and Wayne G. Hammond. *The J. R. R. Tolkien Companion and Guide*. 2 vols. Boston: Houghton Mifflin, 2006.

Shippey, Tom A. "Grimm, Grundtvig, Tolkien: Nationalisms and the Invention of Mythologies." In *The Ways of Creative Mythologies: Imagined Worlds and Their Makers*, edited by Maria Kuteeva, 7–17. Manchester: Manchester University Press, 1997.

———. "Heroes and Heroism: Tolkien's Problems, Tolkien's Solutions." *Lembas Extra* (1991) 267–83.

———. *J. R. R. Tolkien: Author of the Century*. Boston: Houghton Mifflin, 2002.

———. "A Missing Army, Some Doubts about the Alfredian Chronicle." *Geardagum* 4 (1982) 41–55.

———. "Orcs, Wraiths, Wights: Tolkien's Images of Evil." In *J. R. R. Tolkien and His Literary Resonance: Views of Middle-earth*, edited by George Clark and Daniel Timmons, 183–98. Westport, CT: Greenwood, 2000.

———. "Rewriting the Core: Transformations of the Fairy Tale in Contemporary Writing." In *A Companion to the Fairy Tale*, edited by Hilda Ellis Davidson and Anna Chaudhri, 253–74. Cambridge: Brewer, 2003.

———. *The Road to Middle-earth*. Boston: Houghton Mifflin, 2003.

———. *Roots and Branches: Selected Papers on Tolkien*. Zurich: Walking Tree, 2007.

————. "'The Undeveloped Image: Anglo-Saxon in Popular Consciousness from Turner to Tolkien." In *Literary Appropriations of the Anglo-Saxons from the Thirteenth to the Twentieth Century*, edited by Donald Scragg and Carole Weinberg, 215–36. Cambridge: Cambridge University Press, 2000.

Smith, Arden R. "Transitions in Translations." *Vinyar Tengwar* 11 (1990) 16–20.

Smith, Mark Eddy. *Tolkien's Ordinary Virtues: Exploring the Spiritual Themes of "The Lord of the Rings."* Downers Grove, IL: InterVarsity, 2002.

Smith, Ross. "Fitting Sense to Sound: Linguistic Aesthetics and Phonosemantics in the Work of J. R. R. Tolkien." *Tolkien Studies* 3 (2006) 1–20.

————. *Inside Language: Linguistic and Aesthetic Theory in Tolkien.* Zollikofen: Walking Tree, 2007.

Smith, Thomas W. "Tolkien's Catholic Imagination: Mediation and Tradition." *Religion & Literature* 38 (2006) 73–100.

Tolley, Clive. "Tolkien's 'Essay on Man': A Look at 'Mythopoeia.'" *The Chesterton Review* 28 (February/May 2002) 79–95.

Tomko, Michael. "'An Age Comes On': J. R. R. Tolkien and the English Sense of History." In *The Ring and the Cross: Christianity in the Writings of J. R. R. Tolkien*, edited by Paul E. Kerry, 205–23. Madison, NJ: Fairleigh Dickinson University Press, 2011.

Wood, Ralph C. "Conflict and Convergence on Fundamental Matters in C. S. Lewis and J. R. R. Tolkien." *Renascence* 55 (2003) 315–38.

Wright, Marjorie Evelyn. "The Cosmic Kingdom of Myth: A Study in the Myth-Philosophy of Charles Williams, C. S. Lewis, and J. R. R. Tolkien." PhD diss., University of Illinois, 1960.

Zimbardo, Rose A, and Neil D. Isaacs, eds. *Understanding "The Lord of the Rings": The Best of Tolkien Criticism.* Boston: Houghton Mifflin, 2004.

General Bibliography

Allchin, A. M. *N. F. S. Grundtvig: An Introduction to His Life.* Aarhus: Aarhus University Press, 1998.

Allitt, Patrick. *Catholic Converts: British and American Intellectuals Turn to Rome.* Ithaca, NY: Cornell University Press, 1997.

Altick, Richard D. *Victorian People and Ideas: A Companion for the Modern Reader of Victorian Literature.* New York: Norton, 1973.

Aquinas, Thomas. *The Division and Methods of the Sciences: Questions V and VI of His Commentary on the De Trinitate of Boethius.* Translated by Armand Maurer. 4th ed. Toronto: Pontifical Institute of Mediaeval Studies, 1986.

————. *On Creation: Quaestiones disputatae de potentia Dei, Q. 3.* Washington, DC: Catholic University of America Press, 2011.

————. *On the Power of God.* Translated by Lawrence Shapcote. London: Burns, Oates, & Washbourne, 1932.

————. *Summa Contra Gentiles.* Vol. 1. Translated by A. C. Pegis. Notre Dame, IN: University of Notre Dame Press, 1975.

————. *Summa Contra Gentiles.* Vol. 2. Translated by J. F. Anderson. Notre Dame, IN: University of Notre Dame Press, 1975.

————. *Summa Contra Gentiles.* Vol. 3. Translated by V. J. Bourke. Notre Dame, IN: University of Notre Dame Press, 1975.

———. *Summa Theologiae: Latin Text and English Translation, Introductions, Notes, Appendices, and Glossaries.* 61 vols. Andover: Blackfriars in conjunction with Eyre & Spottiswoode, 1964.

———. *Truth.* 3 vols. Translated by Robert W. Mulligan. Chicago: Regnery, 1952–54.

Auden, W. H. Foreword to *History in English Words,* by Owen Barfield, 7–12. London: Linisfarne, 2002.

Barfield, Owen. "Enlightenment." In *A Barfield Sampler,* edited by Jeanne Clayton Hunter and Thomas Kranidas, 46–48. Albany: State University of New York Press, 1993.

———. *History in English Words.* London: Lindisfarne, 2000.

———. *History, Guilt, and Habit.* Middletown, CT: Wesleyan University Press, 1979.

———. "Introducing Rudolph Steiner." http://www.sab.org.br/antrop/Barfield_on_Steiner.htm.

———. *Orpheus: A Poetic Drama.* London: Steiner, 1983.

———. "Philology and the Incarnation." http://rsarchive.org/RelAuthors/BarfieldOwen/philology_and_the_incarnation.php.

———. *Poetic Diction: A Study in Meaning.* Middletown, CT: Wesleyan University Press, 1984.

———. *The Rediscovery of Meaning and Other Essays.* Middletown, CT: Wesleyan University Press, 1977.

———. *Romanticism Comes of Age.* Middletown, CT: Wesleyan University Press, 1967.

———. *Saving the Appearances: A Study in Idolatry.* New York: Harcourt, Brace & World, 1965.

———. *This Ever Diverse Pair.* Edinburgh: Floris Classics, 1985.

———. *Unancestral Voice.* Middletown, CT: Wesleyan University Press, 1965.

———. *What Coleridge Thought.* Middletown, CT: Wesleyan University Press, 1971.

Beckerlegge, Gwilym. "Professor Friedrich Max Müller and the Missionary Cause." In *Religion in Victorian Britain.* Vol. 5, *Culture and Empire,* edited by John Wolffe, 177–220. Manchester: Manchester University Press, 1997.

Bednar, Gerald J. *Faith as Imagination: The Contribution of William F. Lynch.* Kansas City: Sheed & Ward, 1996.

Birzer, Bradley J. *Sanctifying the World: The Augustinian Life and Mind of Christopher Dawson.* Front Royal, VA: Christendom, 2003.

Blumenfeld-Kosinski, Renate. *Reading Myth: Classical Mythology and Its Interpretations in Medieval French Literature.* Stanford: Stanford University Press, 1997.

Boland, Vivian. *Ideas in God according to Saint Thomas Aquinas: Sources and Synthesis.* Leiden: Brill, 1996.

Bosch, Lourens van den. *Friedrich Max Müller: A Life Devoted to Humanities.* Leiden: Brill, 2002.

Bradley, Patrick. "Victorian Lessons: Education and Utilitarianism in Bentham, Mills, and Dickens." *The Concord Review* 10 (1999) 69–86.

Bradley, S. A. J. *N. F. S. Grundtvig: A Life Recalled: An Anthology of Biographical Source-Texts.* Aarhus: Aarhus University Press, 2008.

Branch, Michael. "Finnish Oral Poetry, *Kalevala,* and *Kanteletar.*" In *A History of Finland's Literature,* edited by George C. Schoolfield, 4–33. Lincoln: University of Nebraska Press, 1998.

Briggs, Asa. *Victorian Cities.* Berkeley: University of California Press, 1993.

Burstein, Janet Handler. "Journey beyond Myth: The Progress of the Intellect in Victorian Mythograhy and Three Nineteenth-Century Novels." PhD diss., Drew University, 1975.

Calvert, Alexander. *The Catholic Literary Revival: Three Phases in Its Development from 1845 to the Present.* Milwaukee: Bruce, 1935.

Challoner, Richard. *The Garden of the Soul, or, A Manual of Spiritual Exercises and Instructions for Christians.* London: Burnes & Oates, 1884.

Chase, Richard. *Quest for Myth.* New York: Greenwood, 1976.

Chen, Fanfan. "A New Periodization of Fantastic Literature according to Owen Barfield's Evolution of Human Consciousness and Language." *Arcadia* 42 (2006) 397–414.

Chesterton, G. K. *All Things Considered.* New York: Lane, 1910.

———. *The Autobiography of G. K. Chesterton.* New York: Sheed & Ward, 1936.

———. *The Ball and the Cross.* New York: Lane, 1909.

———. *Charles Dickens.* New York: Dodd, Mead, and Co., 1911.

———. *The Collected Works of G. K. Chesterton.* Edited by G. J. Marlin et al. Vol. 1. San Francisco: Ignatius, 1986.

———. *The Collected Works of G. K. Chesterton.* Edited by G. J. Marlin et al. Vol. 4. San Francisco: Ignatius, 1987.

———. *The Collected Works of G. K. Chesterton.* Edited by G. J. Marlin et al. Vol. 34. San Francisco: Ignatius, 1986.

———. *The Complete Father Brown.* 2 vols. West Valley City, UT: Waking Lion, 2006.

———. *The Defendant.* London: Johnson, 1902.

———. *The Everlasting Man.* Westport, CT: Greenwood, 1974.

———. *Greybeards at Play: Literature and Art for Old Gentlemen.* London: Johnson, 1900.

———. Introduction to *Aesop's Fables*, translated by V. S. Vernon Jones. https://www.gutenberg.org/files/11339/11339-h/11339-h.htm.

———. *Magic.* New York: Knickerbocker, 1913.

———. *The Man Who Was Thursday: A Nightmare.* New York: Sheed & Ward, 1975.

———. *The Paradoxes of Mr. Pond.* New York: Dodd, Mead & Co., 1937.

———. *A Short History of England.* New York: Lane, 1917.

———. *St. Thomas Aquinas.* London: Hodder & Stoughton, 1933.

Clement of Alexandria. *Stromata.* In vol. 2 of *The Ante-Nicene Fathers: Translations of the Writings of the Fathers Down to A.D. 325*, edited by Alexander Roberts and James Donaldson, 299–568. Grand Rapids: Eerdmans, 1978.

Clodd, Edward. *Myths and Dreams.* Whitefish, MT: Kessinger, 2004.

Clute, John, and John Grant, eds. *The Encyclopedia of Fantasy.* New York: St. Martin's Press, 1997.

Coleridge, Samuel Taylor. *Biographia Literaria.* In vol. 7.1 of *The Collected Works of Coleridge*, edited by James Engell and W. Jackson Bate. Princeton: Princeton University Press, 1983.

———. *The Friend.* In vol. 4 of *The Collected Works of Coleridge*, edited by Barbara E. Rooke. Princeton: Princeton University Press, 1969.

———. *Shakespeare, Ben Jonson, Beaumont and Fletcher, Notes and Lectures.* Liverpool: Howell, 1881.

Coulson, John. *Newman and the Common Tradition: A Study in the Language of Church and Society.* Oxford: Clarendon, 1970.

————. *Religion and Imagination: "In Aid of a Grammar of Assent."* Oxford: Clarendon, 1981.

Cyprian. *Treatises.* Translated and edited by Roy J. Deferrari. Washington, DC: Catholic University of America Press, 1958.

Darwin, Charles. *The Descent of Man and Selection in Relation to Sex.* New York: Appleton, 1909.

Dasent, Sir George Webbe. *Popular Tales from the Norse.* Edinburgh: Edmonston and Douglas, 1859.

Dawson, Christopher. *Christianity and European Culture: Selections from the Work of Christopher Dawson.* Washington, DC: Catholic University of America Press, 1998.

————. *The Crisis of Western Education.* Washington, DC: Catholic University of America Press, 2010.

————. *Dynamics of World History.* Edited by John J. Mulloy. New York: Sheed & Ward, 1956.

————. *Enquiries into Religion and Culture.* Washington, DC: Catholic University of America Press, 2009.

————. *The Formation of Christendom.* New York: Sheed & Ward, 1967.

————. *Historic Reality of Christian Culture: A Way to the Renewal of Human Life.* New York: Harper, 1960.

————. *The Judgment of Nations.* New York: Sheed & Ward, 1942.

————. *The Making of Europe: An Introduction to the History of European Unity.* Washington, DC: Catholic University of America Press, 2002.

————. *Progress and Religion: An Historical Enquiry.* London: Sheed & Ward, 1937.

————. *Religion and the Rise of Western Culture.* London: Sheed & Ward, 1950.

————. *Understanding Europe.* Washington, DC: Catholic University of America Press, 2009.

Dickens, Charles. *Hard Times.* Edited by George Ford and Sylvere Monod. New York: Norton, 1966.

Dorson, Richard Mercer. *Peasant Customs and Savage Myths, Part 1.* The History of British Folklore 2. London: Routledge, 1999.

The Douay-Rheims Holy Bible. Fitzwilliam, NH: Loreto, 2004.

Echeverria, Donna Rose. "Christopher Dawson Revisited." *Fides et Historia* 29 (1997) 24–37.

Engell, James. *The Creative Imagination: Enlightenment to Romanticism.* Cambridge: Harvard University Press, 1981.

Feinendegen, Norbert, and Arend Smilde, eds. *The 'Great War' of Owen Barfield and C. S. Lewis: Philosophical Writings, 1927–1930.* Coll. Inklings Studies Supplements 1. Oxford: Oxford C. S. Lewis Society, 2015.

Ffinch, Michael. *G. K. Chesterton.* San Francisco: Harper & Row, 1986.

Foster, Kenelm. "Mr. Dawson and Christendom." *Blackfriars* 31 (1950) 421–27.

Gilbert, John, ed. *The Poetical Works of Henry Wadsworth Longfellow.* London: Routledge, Warne, and Routledge, 1860.

Gill, W. A. "The Origin and Interpretation of Myths." *MacMillan's Magazine* 332 (1886) 121–29.

Gilson, Etienne. *Christianity and Philosophy.* Translated by Ralph MacDonald. New York: Sheed & Ward, 1939.

————. *The Philosophy of St. Thomas Aquinas.* Translated by Edward Bullough and edited by G. A. Elrington. 2nd ed. Salem, NH: Ayer, 1989.

Godfrey, Kevin M. "The Imagination in the Religious Epistemology of John Henry Newman: A Basis for His Phenomenology of Belief." PhD diss., Saint Louis University, 1996.

Griffith-Boscawen, A. S. T. *Fourteen Years in Parliament*. London: Murray, 1907.

Grimm, Jakob. *Deutsche Grammatik*. Berlin: Haartwitz und Gossmann, 1878.

Grimm, Jakob, and Wilhelm Grimm. *German Household Tales*. Boston: Houghton Mifflin, 1897.

Grimm, Wilhelm. *Old Danish Ballads from Grimm's Collection*. London: Hope and Co., 1856.

Harrold, Charles Frederick. *John Henry Newman: An Expository and Critical Study of His Mind, Thought, and Art*. London: Longmans, Green, and Co., 1945.

Hartland, Edwin Sidney. *The Science of Fairy Tales: An Inquiry into Fairy Mythology*. London: Scott, 1916.

Heimann, Mary. *Catholic Devotion in Victorian England*. Oxford: Clarendon, 1995.

Hitchcock, James. "Christopher Dawson: A Reappraisal." *The American Scholar* 62 (1993) 111–18.

Hodges, Horace Jeffrey. "Praeparatio evangelium: Beowulf as Antetype of Christ." http://anthony.sogang.ac.kr/mesak/mes122/Hodges.htm.

Honko, Lauri, ed. *Religion, Myth, and Folklore in the World's Epics: The Kalevala and Its Predecessors*. Berlin: de Gruyter, 1990.

Hunter, Jeanne Clayton, and Thomas Kranidas, eds. *A Barfield Sampler*. Albany: State University of New York Press, 1993.

Hunter, Lynette. *G. K. Chesterton: Explorations in Allegory*. New York: St. Martin's Press, 1979.

Jacobs, Joseph. *More English Fairy Tales*. London: Nutt, 1894.

Justin Martyr. *The First Apology; The Second Apology; Dialogue with Trypho; Exhortation to the Greeks; Discourse to the Greeks; The Monarchy, or, The Rule of God*. Translated by Thomas B. Falls. Washington, DC: Catholic University of America Press, 1948.

Kenny, Anthony. *Aquinas on Mind*. London: Routledge, 1993.

Kingsley, Charles. *What, then, Does Dr. Newman Mean? A Reply to a Pamphlet Lately Published by Dr. Newman*. London: Macmillan, 1864.

Klubertanz, George Peter. *St. Thomas Aquinas on Analogy*. Chicago: Loyola University Press, 1960.

Kretzmann, Norman. *The Metaphysics of Creation: Aquinas's Natural Theology in Summa Contra Gentiles II*. Oxford: Clarendon, 1999.

Kretzmann, Norman, and Eleonore Stump, eds. *The Cambridge Companion to Aquinas*. Cambridge: Cambridge University Press, 1993.

Kvideland, Reimund, and Henning K. Sehmsdorf. *Nordic Folklore: Recent Studies*. Bloomington: Indiana University Press, 1989.

Ladd, Tony. *Muscular Christianity: Evangelical Protestants and the Development of American Sport*. Grand Rapids: BridgePoint 1999.

Lang, Andrew. *Ballades and Verses Vain*. New York: Scribner's Sons, 1884.

———. *The Blue Fairy Book*. New York: Dover, 1966.

———. *The Book of Dreams and Ghosts*. London: Longmans, Green, and Co., 1897.

———. *The Brown Fairy Book*. New York: Dover, 1965.

———. *Custom and Myth*. London: Longmans, Green, and Co., 1893.

———. *The Green Fairy Book*. New York: Dover, 1966.

———. *Letters on Literature*. London: Longmans, Green, and Co., 1889.

———. *Magic and Religion*. New York: AMS, 1901.

——. *The Making of Religion*. New York: AMS, 1968. https://www.gutenberg.org/cache/epub/12353/pg12353.html.

——. *Modern Mythology*. New York: AMS, 1968.

——. *Myth, Ritual, and Religion*. 2 vols. London: Longmans, Green, and Co., 1913.

——. *New Collected Rhymes*. New York: Longmans, Green, and Co., 1905.

——. *The Orange Fairy Book*. New York: Dover, 1968.

——. *Sir Walter Scott*. New York: Scribner's Sons, 1906.

Lewis, C. S. *The Allegory of Love*. Oxford: Clarendon, 1936.

——. *The Collected Letters of C. S. Lewis*. Edited by Walter Hooper. 3 vols. San Francisco: HarperSanFrancisco, 2004–7.

——. *God in the Dock: Essays on Theology and Ethics*. Grand Rapids: Eerdmans, 1970.

——. "Historicism." *The Month*, October, 1950.

——. *Surprised by Joy: The Shape of My Early Life*. New York: Harcourt, Brace & World, 1955.

——. *Till We Have Faces: A Myth Retold*. New York: Harcourt & Brace, 1956.

Lewis, Clyde J. "Disintegration of the Tory-Anglican Alliance in the Struggle for Catholic Emancipation." *Church History* 29 (1960) 25–43.

Liddell, Henry G., and Robert Scott, eds. *A Greek-English Lexicon*. Vol. 2. Oxford: Clarendon, 1940.

Lönnrot, Elias, ed. *The Kalevala*. Oxford: Oxford University Press, 1999.

Lyttkens, Hampus. *The Analogy between God and the World: An Investigation of Its Background and Interpretation of Its Use by Thomas of Aquino*. Uppsala: Lundequistska bokhandeln, 1953.

Mallory, J. P., and Douglas Q. Adams, eds. *Encyclopedia of Indo-European Culture*. London: Taylor & Francis, 1997.

Maritain, Jacques. *Art and Scholasticism: With Other Essays*. Minneapolis: Filiquarian, 2007.

Martin, C. F. J. *Thomas Aquinas: God and Explanations*. Edinburgh: Edinburgh University Press, 1997.

McCabe, Herbert. *On Aquinas*. London: Continuum, 2008.

McGlathery, James M., ed. *The Brothers Grimm and Folktale*. Urbana: University of Illinois, 1988.

McGrath, Francis. "John Henry Newman and the Dispensation of Paganism." *International Journal for the Study of the Christian Church* 1 (2001) 26–42.

McInerny, Ralph M. *Rhyme and Reason: St. Thomas and Modes of Discourse*. Milwaukee: Marquette University Press, 1981.

McIntire, C. T. "Mid Victorian Anti-Catholicism, English Diplomacy, and Odo Russell in Rome." *Fides et Historia* 13 (1980) 23–33.

Meiners, R. K. Review of *What Coleridge Thought*, by Owen Barfield. *Criticism* 15 (1973) 174–82.

Milbank, Alison. *Chesterton and Tolkien as Theologians: The Fantasy of the Real*. London: T. & T. Clark, 2007.

Milbank, John. "Scholasticism, Modernism, and Modernity." *Modern Theology* 22 (2006) 651–71.

Muirhead, John H. *Coleridge as Philosopher*. London: Allen & Unwin, 1930.

Müller, F. Max. *Auld Lang Syne*. Vol. 1. New York: Scribner's Sons, 1899.

——. *Chips from a German Workshop*. Vol. 4, *Essays Chiefly on the Science of Language*. London: Longmans, Green, and Co., 1875.